Lara Connell

STOLEN TRUTHS

MIGUEL ÁNGEL FUENTES

STOLEN TRUTHS

IVE Press

Chillum — 2016

Cover Design
   © IVE Press

Cover Art
   © IVE Press

Text
   © IVE Press, Chillum
   Institute of the Incarnate Word, Inc.
   All rights reserved.

IVE Press, Chillum, MD

www.ivepress.org

ISBN-10: 1-939018-65-X
ISBN-13: 978-1-939018-65-6

Printed in the United States of America

To all youth
who sincerely desire
to know the Truth

CONTENTS

TRANSLATOR'S NOTE

This book was originally written and published in Spanish, and many of its sources come from Spanish or Italian. You will find that many citations from the original sources have been translated since they do not exist in English. Nevertheless, you are encouraged to further your knowledge on these topics by reading the original sources or similar books on the same. We hope that you do not dwell on the technical terms, but truly seek the truths that are portrayed therein.

INTRODUCTION

Throughout my years as a priest, I have met many Catholic youth who seemed full of potential to become good men and women for the Church and for our country, to become future professionals sure of the values for which they should work and fight, willing to challenge the temptations of the world and to forge not only exemplary families, but also a country based on the truth, the common good and the faith. Unfortunately, many of them did not fulfill the expectations that had been stirred up. Some faltered in their moral principles, settling for what the world had to offer, sometimes selling their consciences for political positions or to secure their distinct professions. Others lost their faith, holding onto the faint vapor of skepticism or to an almost complete disbelief. Others maintained their faith and moral principles, but simply became discouraged in the fight seeing many of their old friends falling into the previously mentioned hazards. Nonetheless, many have persevered and have become excellent Christians on a personal level; but—like many fellow citizens—they could be called the "wasted snipers" of Catholic culture (*Woe to the lonely!* says Scripture). In other words, each one does what he can and his good works disappear like ripples from a small rock falling into the sea; they lacked the resolve to fight united.

One of the crucial moments when the intellect or will of a great many of these youth entered into crisis occurred during their time in university. University studies, on a world-wide level are fraught with frightful gaps. The principal one is the lack of cultivation of the spirit (and among the spiritual disciplines, principally the vision of the transcendent, that is to say, openness to the supernatural world and metaphysical thought). In other words, notwithstanding a few honorable exceptions, the universities of our time form materialists of the most blatant sort; they mold men and women who go out from their lecture halls already defeated in spiritual battles. The cause is not simply the inability to teach the most important matters that every intelligent being should consider (such as the philosophy and theology taught in many English speaking universities, which of course, have other problems) but rather is the certain destruction—sinisterly planned—of every religious, spiritual and philosophical ideal that may exist in the mind of the young people who innocently (or not so innocently) fall into the hands of those professional deformers. Over the past few decades this phenomenon can also be observed in intermediate education.

And so many of the convictions or the serene vision that common sense, family tradition, or rudimentary religious formation have given to many Catholic youth of our time, crumble before the powerful sophisms of false scientific arguments; unproven (and sometimes improvable) arguments, exaggerated data, etc. These common fallacious arguments call into question the fundamental truths on which natural law is based, testing the primitive knowledge of the truth and of the faith itself. All this is presented with the adornment of a false halo upon the science of our times. The only result is that the youth who start out with some solid convictions—if they even had any—end up with *stolen truths*. This is the reason for our title. They emerge as materialistic doctors, positivist psychologists, preying lawyers, unscrupulous economists, or simply uncivilized professionals lacking moral values or any interests that are not economic… in short, poor salesmen.

The result is a legion of pseudo-skeptics and pseudo-atheists.[1] I say *pseudo* ("false") because many are not skeptics or atheists. What happened to some French university students who got on the same train as a priest may well happen to them. (What I will tell you happened many years ago.) Upon seeing the priest they began to make fun of the faith, the Church, and God. When the priest was able to start a conversation with them, he asked them what they believed.

"Us? Some of us are atheists," responded one of them, "And others skeptics."

"How interesting!" remarked the priest, and he began to ask them, "Which work of Aristotle have you liked most?"

"I haven't read any," he responded.

"And Plato?"

"Not him either; well, only some pages that were in one of our class readings."

"And you haven't read the works of St. Augustine, nor St. Thomas, or the speeches of Lacordaire, nor the documents of the Popes..." Then he enumerated to them the principle authors who had touched in one manner or another upon the theme of God or one of the fundamental themes of life; and to all of these they went on responding that they had read nothing or practically nothing. Finally, the priest said to them, "Well then, young men, you are not skeptics or atheists."

"And what are we then?"

"Simply ignorant," he responded.

---

[1] One of the greatest dramas of our times is the incapability to understand the meaning of common terms. Recalling the numerous questions I have received asking about the skeptics, atheists, agnostics, etc., I have included a list of vocabulary words at the end of the book to aid you with some terms.

In the following pages you will find no more than an "introduction" to the biggest problems of life: God, the soul, science, religion, truth, etc. It is already a benefit that these ideas are a "problem" for man. As long as they retain this character, the intelligence will be required to think about them, and that is precisely why we have our mind. We trust fully in the power of human reason to reach the truth. Therefore, it is not those who question the big things who end up thinking wrongly, but those who refuse to think or to discuss them at all. Regarding the Truth, we could say something similar to what Jesus said about heaven: it is only given to those who fight for it.[2]

---

[2] "The kingdom of heaven has suffered violence, and men of violence take it by force." (Mt 11:12)

1.

THE STOLEN
TRUTH ABOUT
"THE TRUTH"

Is everything relative? Is there no truth?

Can we come to know the truth? Or is everything relative? In short, can each one of us have *his own truth*? Probably one of the first things that will make your intellectual edifice or your faith waver is relativism: the conception that refuses to admit absolute principles into the field of knowing and acting. Normally a young person begins his studies with a series of principles or truths that he accepts as absolutes, whether they be convictions of natural or supernatural order (the truths of faith) or truths of popular certainty. The value of these truths is precisely where an adverse educational institution will begin its attack. The first truth that they will steal from you is the conviction that there is truth and that you can come to know the truth.

With relativism each person has *his* own truth. Everyone comprehends things with his own personal vision based on his likes, his education or his interests. Not only is it difficult for those who think along these lines to come to an adequate understanding of what others think, but this also makes it impossible to come to any agreement, given that such an agreement would not, properly speaking, be a truth that is valid, objective and obligatory for all. Thus, they begin to overthrow religious principles, the moral criteria by which we are governed. The victim of this crushing attack drowns in an authentic "intellectual depression."

Relativism is the fatal cancer that corrodes contemporary culture. Nevertheless, it is also the biggest fallacy that can pass through the human mind and cannot be accepted unless it deceives us by subtle sophisms. Relativism, within the limits of knowledge, denies the possibility of attaining universal and objective truths. Within the moral realm, it denies us the ability to arrive at knowledge of objective values and goods and so act accordingly. It does not allow for the affirmation that one type of behavior is evil for everyone or that another is always good. In daily life, those who fall into this error are all those who do not accept absolute truths. They are those who claim that "everyone has his own truth," and who apply the label of "fundamentalism" to anyone who firmly upholds the truth of the faith. In our times, one of its most notable consequences is that the path has been paved for New Age ideas, the religion of relativism. "The ground [for the acceptance of New Age ideas] was well prepared by the growth and spread of relativism."[3]

Relativism adopts various forms:[4]

1) *Individualistic relativism* teaches that each individual determines the truth of any assertion. Therefore, there will be (or there could be) as many truths as there are people. Something could be true for John and not for Joe, and both are valid truths: "their truth." In an important Argentinean newspaper, I read the following assertion about a soccer game: "The game ended in a fair tie even though it also would have been fair if either team had won." (May 2004) Three just cases in three contradictory situations! It was not the author of this unfortunate article who invented this tricky phrase, but Protagoras, whose thesis was "man is the measure of all things."[5] Plato described him saying, "as Protagoras tells us [...] man is 'the measure of all things,' and that things are to

---

[3] PONTIFICAL COUNCIL FOR CULTURE AND PONTIFICAL COUNCIL FOR INTERRELIGIOUS DIALOGUE, "Jesus Christ the Bearer of the Water of Life: A Christian reflection on the 'New Age,'" 2003, §1.3, cf. §2.3.1, *www.vatican.va/roman_curia/pontifical_councils/interelg/documents/rc_pc_interelg_doc_20 030203_new-age_en.html* (accessed May 17, 2014).

[4] Cf. J. BARRIO GUTIÉRREZ, "Relativismo: I. Filosofía," in *Gran Enciclopedia Rialp* (Madrid: Ediciones Rialp, 1991), editorial translation.

[5] PROTAGORAS, quoted in SEXTUS EMPIRICUS, *Outlines of Pyrrhonism*, trans. R. G. Bury (Cambridge: Harvard University Press, 1933), 131, book I, ch. xxxii, no. 216.

me as they appear to me, and are to you as they appear to you."[6] From this idea it follows that there is not one truth but infinite truths, as many as there are people in the world. It is easy to realize that this is very widespread in our society. We hear it under the title of "point of view;" everyone has his own "points" of view. Thus, *opinion* has more value than truth. And not only does everyone have *his truth*, but everyone has the right to form his truth, even on issues of which he is almost entirely ignorant. This is why an athlete is asked his opinion not only about his sport but also about moral questions, about the pope, philosophy and history. The value of what he says is *relative*; it will be valuable only for him. From this point of view, which may be the most widespread, relativism is the greatest source of isolation among human beings: the ostracism of intelligences which remain exiled within the isolated confines of their master. With the acceptance of relativistic philosophy, there would be no room for teachers; there remains only an orienteer of opinion, or better, only those who would offer their opinion just in case another would like to make it his own. Curiously, this works for everything... except for those who teach relativism. Their assertions that everything is relative and that there are no objective truths is the most objective and universal affirmation they could make! Let those who doubt this, or timidly suggest the opposite, or who are of the opinion that there just might be an absolute, be warned! They immediately denounce him as the most dangerous fanatic, the fanatic who thinks there is such as thing as truth and who would die for it. "There is no objective truth"—this is the most objective of truths—says the relativist. In spite of the absurdity you will perceive at reading these lines, it will be

---

[6] PLATO, *Cratylus* in *Plato: Complete Works,* ed. John M. Cooper (Indianapolis: Hackett Publishing Company, 1997), 103, no. 385.

even more surprising for you to know that this is held, not by an honest yet rural baker, but by a philosopher honored as the father of relativism, Auguste Comte. By the age of nineteen he had written: "Everything is relative; this is the only absolute principle."[7] Poor Comte, even in his old age he continued to say the same nonsense!

2) *Cultural relativism* rests upon the truth of historical culture. This was defended by Oswald Spengler in his well-known work *The Decline of the West*. Each culture—Chinese, Hindu, Egyptian, Babylonian, Greco-Roman, Arabic, American, Western—makes its own appraisal of what is real and has its own manner of understanding the cosmos, different from other cultures and non-exchangeable with any of them. No culture can hope that their appraisal be absolute or universally valid. It does not differ much from individual relativism; only in that it is less radical. In place of the individual, each culture or town is the fount of truth-opinion.

3) *Sociological relativism* was created and defended by Émile Durkheim; it makes what determines the truth of judgment dependent upon social groups. According to Durkheim, the social group pressures its members in an irresistible and unconscious way, imposing on them modes of conduct and criteria for judgment. This coercion is not felt when the individual accepts and fulfills the social norms, and therefore falls into the illusion of believing that it is he himself who spontaneously and voluntarily imposes them. The force of social pressure only exposes itself when such norms are broken. The individual receives his entire mental world from society. The ideological world would be a reflection of the society in which he lives; true and false, good and bad,

---

[7] GERTRUD LENZER, ed., *Auguste Comte and Positivism: The Essential Writings* (Piscataway, New Jersey: Transaction Publishers, 2009), 4.

beautiful and ugly—the whole axiological gamut—would be determined as such by the social group and the individual would limit himself to passively receiving them. They consider society as prior to man and to the person.[8] The foundation is the same; the factor that determines the truth changes.

4) *Racial relativism* rests upon the truths of race. This form of relativism was defended in general by Nazism and in a particular manner by its theorist Alfred Rosenberg. All cultural manifestation would be determined by race, which should not be confused with the social group, given that one society itself can be made up of many different races. Philosophy, science, religion, art would be the expressions of a race, which molds its vital force in them. Race would be the creating principle and the conditioning element of all cultural production, which would have to be valued positively, if it deals with a superior race, or negatively, in the case of inferior races. Thus, there would be no single truth, since there is not only one race; there would be one Aryan truth, another Slav, another Jewish, etc.[9]

5) *Political relativism* is one of the most widespread forms of relativism in our society. This relativism, as its name suggests, makes the truth depend on political commitments, be it on the majority vote or agreements between political parties or on other ways of achieving agreement (consensus). This is why if we are all in agreement that abortion is legal; abortion will actually be legal and therefore 'good.' If we are all in agreement about permitting prostitution, it will no longer be an offense or even a sin. If the majority has voted to teach error, it will cease being an error and become a truth.

---

[8] Cf. GUTIÉRREZ, "Relativismo: I. Filosofía," editorial translation.

[9] Cf. Ibid.

This relativism, steeped into the core of our culture, produces grave harm, beginning by threatening human liberty. John Paul II wrote: "This view of freedom leads to a serious distortion of life in society. If the promotion of the self is understood in terms of absolute autonomy, people inevitably reach the point of rejecting one another. Everyone else is considered an enemy from whom one has to defend oneself. Thus society becomes a mass of individuals placed side by side, but without any mutual bonds. Everyone wishes to assert himself independently of others and intends to make his own interests prevail. Still, in the face of other people's analogous interests, some kind of compromise must be found, if one wants a society in which the maximum possible freedom is guaranteed to each individual. In this way, any reference to common values and to a truth absolutely binding on everyone is lost, and social life ventures on to the shifting sands of complete relativism. At that point, everything is negotiable, everything is open to bargaining: even the first of the fundamental rights, the right to life. This is what is happening also at political and governmental levels: the original and inalienable right to life is questioned or denied on the basis of a parliamentary vote or the will of one part of the people—even if it is the majority. This is the sinister result of a relativism which reigns unopposed: the 'right' ceases to be such, because it is no longer firmly founded on the inviolable dignity of the person, but is made subject to the will of the stronger part. In this way democracy, contradicting its own principles, effectively moves towards a form of totalitarianism. The State is no longer the 'common home' where all can live together on the basis of principles of fundamental equality, but is transformed into a tyrant State, arrogates to itself the right to dispose of the life of the weakest and most defenseless members, from the unborn child to the elderly, in the name of a public interest which is really nothing but the interest of one part."[10]

What is the fundamental criticism of relativism? Or better yet, formulating it in a more interesting way: is it true that there is no truth? I am not formulating it incorrectly; we do not have to ask ourselves if there is "objective truth," given that truth and objective truth are really equivalent concepts. Truth is the conformity of our mind to things; for either there is objective truth (conformed to reality) and therefore valid for all intelligent beings or there is simply no truth but opinions that are diverse valuations about things. Is there, then, objective truth? We have already said that "the most essential criticism that can be formulated against relativism, in addition to those of an extrinsic character, like the demonstration from universal evidence of an absolute, is that all relativism implies *an intrinsic contradiction.* In maintaining that no judgment enjoys the property of being true in an absolute sense and that all truth is relative, an unavoidable consequence arises: the judgment, *'all truth is relative,'* cannot have the character of absolute validity, which destroys relativism with its own weapons. If, given certain factors or conditions, we admit as true that every truth is relative, then with a different given factor we will have to admit as true that every truth is absolute, which is a contradiction with the fundamental thesis of relativism. Besides this general inconsistency of relativism, the criticism of relativism would be similar to the one of skepticism and subjectivism."[11]

Moreover, the existence of the truth (truth as something objective and universal, invariable and superior to any human

---

[10] ST. JOHN PAUL II, *Evangelium Vitae* (Boston: Pauline Books & Media, 1995), no. 20.

[11] Cf. GUTIÉRREZ, "Relativismo: I. Filosofía," editorial translation.

opinion) is guaranteed by common sense. Common sense is such that—basing ourselves in objective truths—we get married, sow seeds, board a boat or a plane, buy and sell, and let ourselves get killed defending our country and people we love. Because there is no doubt that there is objective truth, we repeat sayings which contain objective truths cultivated by popular philosophy: "he who does not look forward, falls behind;" "looks are deceiving;" "don't count your chickens before the eggs are hatched;" "the early bird gets the worm;" "like father, like son;" etc. Would it not seem that we believe in the objective value of things and of the truths that they express? Who would marry if fidelity meant one thing *for me* and another *for you*? Who would get on a boat if he were not sure of the principle that the boat can float? Or who would board a plane based only on the *opinion* of the pilot that his plane is capable of staying in the air?

We not only have popular certainty about the existence and objective value of truth, but scientific certainty about those things. The truth exists and that cannot be denied. Among others, St. Thomas Aquinas says that he who denies the existence of truth implicitly affirms that truth exists, since if the truth did not exist it would be true that it would not exist; and if something is true, it is necessary that truth exists.[12] It seems to be a tongue twister, but it is a syllogism… a perfect one. Our intelligence is capable of reasoning and of comprehending the being of things or reality. We know about the being of things, we learn it through sound philosophy and recognize it through experience, in spite of professing ourselves to be the most stubborn subjective philosophers. The most blatant denier of our ability to know the absolute

---

[12] Taught, among other places, in ST. THOMAS AQUINAS, *Summa Theologica* (Westminster, Maryland: Christian Classics, 1981), I, Q. 2, Art. 1, ad. 3.

of things is capable of moving heaven and earth in order to receive his salary. (How does he know that something is his? And what if the boss thinks he does not have to pay him?) Tread carefully, opinions will not matter nor will each one have his own truth with regards to touching a man's wife or his goods. Furthermore, if a thief says he has his truth and that he likes my car more than his and therefore decides to take it for himself, how will I respond as the miserable relativist? "Sir, if this is the way you see thing, here are the keys. I'm sorry for having thought badly about you."

A relativist can teach relativism for his whole life fully convinced of its truth (which would be contrary to relativism). But what if he were to go to a "relativist" restaurant and when he ordered chicken they brought him cat, because the owner of a restaurant, from *his point of view,* thought that cat was the same as chicken. Not only could he see his whole system overturned in a few seconds, but also spend the rest of his "relative" life in prison for trying to kill the owner of a restaurant. Every relativist is necessarily inconsequential in real life.

It is difficult to make a relativist understand his error (not to demonstrate his error but to make him accept it). This is because relativism is a form of *foolishness,* and this foolishness is not only a sin but also the punishment which falls on those who do not love the truth. It can only be done, however, by teaching him in the one way he will understand: by asking for my money back. If he tells me that what he teaches is only valuable for him, and it is very likely that I have another opinion, which he will neither share nor contradict, then it would be better for him to return my money and have me go home. I can learn my opinion by myself!

For Further Reading

- Balmes, James. *Criterion.* New York: P. O'Shea, 1875.
- Chesterton, G. K. *Orthodoxy.* San Francisco: Ignatius, 1995.
- Maritain, Jacques. *Introduction to Philosophy.* Lanham, Maryland: Rowman & Littlefield Publishers, 2005.
- Pieper, Josef. *In Defense of Philosophy: Classical wisdom stands up to modern challenges.* San Francisco: Ignatius Press, 1992.
- ———. *Leisure: The Basis of Culture.* San Francisco: Ignatius Press, 2000.
- ———. *Living the Truth: The Truth of All Things and Reality and the Good.* San Francisco: Ignatius Press, 1989.

Available in Other Languages

- Aliotta, Antonio. "Relativismo." In vol. V of *Enciclopedia Filosófica*, 2nd ed. Florence: Sansoni, 1967.
- Garrigou-Lagrange, Reginald. *El Sentido Común.* Madrid: Palabra, 1980.
- Gutiérrez, J. Barrio. "Relativismo: I. Filosofía." In *Gran Enciclopedia Rialp.* Madrid: Ediciones Rialp, 1991.
- Orozco-Delclós, Antonio. *La Libertad en el Pensamiento*, Madrid: Rialp, 1977.
- Velazco, Miguel Ángel. *Los Derechos de la Verdad.* Madrid: MC, 1994.

28

2.

THE STOLEN TRUTH ABOUT GOD

The Existence of a Personal God

Does God exist? Is His existence a religious or scientific question? Can one be a professional and believe in God? For many, their contact with the scientific world (or more accurately, falsely scientific) is the door they use to enter the atheist or at least agnostic world. Many times I have heard the phrase, "I declare myself agnostic," from the mouths of famous people; probably ignorant of the fact that this declaration is equivalent to declaring oneself lame or blind or impotent in the intellectual plane. The knowledge of God is certainly a religious question, if what is intended by "religious question" is a problem of faith. But it is *also* a scientific question, since philosophy is a science, and our intelligence, by philosophizing, arrives at this great truth.

In order to understand the scope of this subject, we must review the teachings the Church gives us about God. The teaching about God the Church gives us is a theological teaching, that is to say, composed of truths about God that the Church holds to be revealed (either because they are contained in Sacred Scripture or revealed in tradition and have been defined as such by the Magisterium of the Church). This teaching also contains truths which our intelligence can reach through our natural efforts. We know not only of God's existence but also his attributes or qualities, his intimate essence (He is one God in three distinct persons, that is to say *Trinity*), and we know his plan of salvation for men (revealed in Sacred Scripture, particularly in the New Testament).

Some of these truths are not accessible scientifically since they surpass the capacity of our intellect. These truths superior to our natural power are called "intrinsically supernatural mysteries," and as such can only be known by God and by those to whom God wants to manifest them (reveal them or *unveil* them). This is the case of the mystery of the Trinity, of original sin, of the Incarnation of God (Jesus Christ) and his saving work. Science cannot reach these truths with its proper method, since this method starts with natural things and rises to the knowledge of causes by natural methods and by the abilities of natural human reason alone. But strictly speaking, science can *neither* refute *nor* contradict them; precisely, by definition, they elude its area of study. A blind man cannot see colors, but neither can he say that there are no colors, nor that what I see as white is green, since he does not have the capacity to capture them; they elude his faculty. A deaf man cannot hear sounds, but neither can he say that an orchestra is out of tune, since the world of sounds is unknown to him. Science, therefore, stops being science if it enters into a field that is not its own. In this manner, a scientist has no authority to speak of what is not within his field. Being a mathematician or biologist doesn't authorize someone to speak of what his mathematical or biological science has not taught him or about those topics for which it did not qualify him. Likewise, a deaf astronomer cannot give his opinion about symphonies even if he is the best astronomer. I believe this should be made clear in order to determine who is competent, because many of the problems raised against the faith are put forward by people who do not have faith, and, what's worse, from disciplines that have nothing to do with faith (that is to say, with the plane of supernatural mystery).

Anyway, we will not speak here about this intrinsically supernatural world, but only about the natural order and that which is within our intellectual reach. What was said in the previous paragraph equally applies: the problem of the existence of God is a natural truth, but a metaphysical or philosophical one; which means that there continues to be an unwarranted invasion of field when objections (or denials) against a philosophical truth no longer come from philosophy but from purely experimental science (that is, science that does not reach the philosophical level). A doctor can speak with authority about sicknesses or object to this or that therapeutic treatment, but he cannot, insofar as he is a doctor, argue about the essence of things, since medicine leaves him blind, deaf and mute in that metaphysical world. The same can be said about the mathematician, the astronomer, the biologist and other scientists (to embark on these topics they will have to also be philosophers). Unfortunately, the majority of the opposition to strictly philosophical truths comes from below and outside the philosophical fields. And we make room for them!

Cornelio Fabro, one of the most eminent philosophers of the twentieth century, wrote: "The problem of God is the first and last question of man, because he looks for the First Principle of being and of not being; due to its centrality it can be said that it is *the essential problem of the essential man* and due to its universality it is *the problem of common man.*"[13]

The problem of God (whether God exists or not) is the most universal problem, to the point that all men think about it, regardless of whether they are old or young, poet, soldier, artisan, peasant, or philosopher, whether man or woman. No matter what they believe, whether they are atheist, agnostic or believer. The atheist is he who, facing such thoughts, has lost his way even as far as to deny God; the agnostic has abandoned the path and the believer has arrived to port. It is not an easy trip, according to what philosophers and theologians say. St. Thomas himself says that some have not been able to dedicate themselves to this study because of

---

[13] CORNELIO FABRO, *Le Prove dell'Esistenza di Dio* (Brescia: Editrice La Scuola, 1990), 7, editorial translation.

defects in their temperament, others because they have demanding familial obligations and others, in the end, because of laziness. And even those who do dedicate themselves to philosophy reach the heights of the knowledge of God only with effort, particularly when they are blinded by their passions. From here the great mercy of God facilitates our knowledge by means of his own revelation.[14] But in spite of all these difficulties, this is the most exciting adventure that we could embark on.

The philosophers of every age have tried to prove the existence of God. Many different proofs come from their work. Father Cornelio Fabro, in his work, *"Le Prove dell'Esistenza di Dio"* (Proofs of the Existence of God), analyzes the proofs given by the ancient philosophers, such as Socrates, Plato, Aristotle, Cleanthes, Philo, Plotinus, Proclus, etc.; the first Christian thinkers like Origen, Gregory of Nyssa, Augustine, Boethius, John Damascene, etc.; Arabic and Jewish philosophers like Al-Farabi, Avicebron, Avicenna, Algazel, Averroes, Maimonides; medieval philosophers and theologians such as Bonaventure, Thomas Aquinas, John Duns Scotus, William of Ockham, Dante Alighieri, Nicholas of Cusa; modern thinkers such as Descartes, Pascal, Locke, Leibniz, Vico, Wolff, Kant, Hegel, Rosmini, Newman, Kierkegaard, etc. We can see that this is a topic of interest to many, and many have come to God from the most diverse fields, from more or less serious proofs, some more convincing than others. In some cases they reach this conclusion even by arguments that started with false principles, and could have ended in the opposite, the denial of God.

---

[14] Cf. ST. THOMAS AQUINAS, *Summa Contra Gentiles* (London: University of Notre Dame Press, 1975), book I, ch. 4.

We can divide the proofs (or *vías*, as they are called by philosophical tradition) in two categories: the five Thomistic vías or ways and "everything else." In regard to scientific rigor, the truly provable vías are the five vías used by St. Thomas. The others can give us an approximation of the truth of the existence of God, but are insufficient by themselves.

1. THE "OTHER" PROOFS (SECONDARY ARGUMENTS)

There are proofs that, by placing us on the "trail of discovery", begin to indicate the existence of God. Strictly speaking they do not fully demonstrate the truth, but they open our intelligence and put it on the path towards this great truth.

a) By the existence of man, who is intelligent and free.

The existence of man, who is intelligent and free, can demonstrate the existence of God because there is no effect without a cause capable of producing it.

A being that thinks, reflects, reasons and desires cannot originate without an intelligent and creative cause. As this intelligent and creating cause is God, it follows that the existence of man proves the existence of God.

It is an indubitable fact that I have not always existed, that the years and days of my life can be counted. If I began to exist at a given moment, who gave me life?

1. It was not me. Before existing, I was nothing, I did not have being; and that which does not exist does not produce anything.

2. It was not just my parents. The true author of a work can repair his work when it deteriorates and remake that same work when it is destroyed. My parents cannot heal me when I am sick with a grave illness, nor resurrect me after my death. If my parents alone were the authors of my life, why did they not make me perfect? What father and mother would not try to make their children perfect? Furthermore, my soul is simple and spiritual. It cannot come from my parents: neither from their body, because then it would be material; nor from their soul, because the soul is indivisible; nor from their creating power, because no created being can create.

3. I cannot owe my existence to any visible being in creation. Insofar as I am endowed with understanding and will, I am superior to all irrational beings.

If I am not the product of myself, my parents, or any other created being, then only a creator Spirit who is Uncreated explains my existence; somebody who was able to bring something, my soul, out of nothing, which is to say, to create it. And since a being that has all these qualities (spirit, un-created and creator) is what everybody calls God, therefore my existence and my nature necessitate the existence of God.

b) By the existence of moral law[15]

The existence of a moral law would also prove the existence of God. There exists, in effect, an immutable, absolute and universal moral law: it commands doing good, prohibits doing evil and rules the consciences of all men (I will speak specifically of this law in a later chapter). He who

---

[15] The following comes from ANTONIO ROYO MARÍN, *Dios y su Obra* (Madrid: BAC, 1963), 34.

obeys this law feels the satisfaction of completing his duty and he who disobeys is the victim of remorse.

Just as there is no effect without a cause, there is no law without a legislator. This moral law requires the existence of an author, who is God. Then, by the existence of moral law we come to the conclusion of the existence of God.

He is the Supreme Legislator who imposes on us the unavoidable duty of doing good and avoiding evil. He is the witness of all our actions and the unmovable judge who rewards or punishes with peace or remorse of conscience, respectively.

Our conscience teaches us: (1) that an essential difference exists between good and evil; (2) that we should do good and avoid evil; (3) that every evil act deserves punishment and every good act is worthy of reward.

This is why our conscience is pleased and approves itself when it behaves well and reproves and condemns itself when it behaves badly. Therefore, a moral law exists in us, imprinted and engraved on our conscience.

What is the origin of this law? Evidently, it has to be a legislator who declares the law, as there is no effect without a cause. This moral law is immutable in its principles, independent from our will, obligatory for all men and cannot have any author other than a supreme and sovereign being, who is none other than God.

In addition to all that has been said, it must be kept in mind that without a legislator the moral law cannot have any sanctions; it could be broken with impunity. There are two options: either God is the author of this law and therefore He exists; or moral law is an illusion and in this case the difference between good and evil, virtue and vice, justice and iniquity would not exist and society would be impossible.

This *intimate feeling* manifests to all men the existence of God. By natural instinct, principally in moments of anxiety or danger, the shout "My God!" escapes from us. It is the shout of nature. "It is that God is here below the most popular of all beings," said Lacordaire, "The poor call upon him, the dying invoke his name, the wicked fear him, the good bless him, […] there is neither place, nor time, nor circumstance, nor sentiment, in which God does not appear and is not named. […] Anger feels that it has not reached its last expression until it has cursed that adorable name; and even blasphemy is the homage of faith that reveals itself in its own forgetfulness."[16] No one blasphemes that which does not exist; the rage of the impious, like the blessings of the good, gives testimony to the existence of God.

c) By the universal belief of the human race[17]

We can also arrive at the existence of God by examining the acknowledgement of this point by all nations. The argument can be explained thus: all nations, civilized or uncivilized, in all the regions of the world and in all times, have accepted the existence of a Supreme Being. It is impossible that all of them would have been mistaken about such transcendent truth, especially one so contrary to the passions. We must admit with all humanity that God exists.

When we speak of "all nations," we should understand a "moral" totality. Materially, exceptions can be found, individuals and sometimes even tribes of atheists or semi-atheists. (At least we can hypothesize; in the chapter

---

[16] HENRI LACORDAIRE, *God: Conferences* (London: William Clowes and Sons, 1870), 13-14.

[17] The following comes from ROYO MARÍN, *Dios y su Obra*, 31-32.

dedicated to religious phenomena we will see that many scholars deny that there are *entire atheistic nations*.) But when these exceptions are just that— *exceptions*—certain moral unanimity can be spoken of.

It is indubitable that these peoples have been mistaken about the nature of God. Some have adored rock gods, others animals in place of God, and many the stars (especially the sun and the moon). Many have attributed good and evil qualities to their idols, etc. But all have recognized the existence of a divinity, to which they have given worship. This is shown in the temples, the altars and the sacrifices, whose traces are found everywhere, as much among the ancient peoples as among the modern. In antiquity, the historian Plutarch wrote: "And if you will take the pains to travel through the world, you may find towns and cities without walls, without letters, without kings, without houses, without wealth, without money, [...] but there was never seen nor shall be seen by man any city without temples and Gods, or without making use of prayers, oaths, divinations, and sacrifices."[18] With reason an author has said: "I have searched for atheism or the lack of belief in God among the human races, from the lowest to the highest. Atheism does not exist anywhere, and all the peoples of the earth, the savages of America like the blacks of Africa, believe in the existence of God."[19]

That all men unanimously acknowledge such an important point is necessarily the expression of the truth. Such a concurrence cannot be explained by any other cause. It was

---

18 PLUTARCH, quoted in WILLIAM GOODWIN, ed., vol. V of *Plutarch's Morals* (Boston: Little, Brown, and Company, 1874), 379-380.

19 QUATREFAGES, quoted in ALBERT HILLAIRE, *La Religión Demostrada* (Barcelona: Luis Gili, 1955), editorial translation.

not the (pagan) priests who convinced men of the existence of God, moreover it must be said that all priesthood takes its origin from a prior belief in the existence of a God to whom worship is due. Human passions cannot explain it, since the passions tend to erase the idea of God, which is both contrary to them and condemns them. Prejudices cannot explain it, since one prejudice does not extend through all time, all peoples, all men. Sooner or later, science and common sense will make a prejudice vanish. Ignorance cannot explain it, because there have always been fervent believers in God among the greatest of wise men. Fear cannot explain it (as some ethnological theory has claimed), since no one fears what does not exist: the fear of God proves his existence. It cannot be attributed to the political agenda of rulers, since no ruler has decreed the existence of God. On the contrary, the majority of rulers have wanted divine authority to confirm their laws; this is proof that divine authority was admitted by their subjects.

Therefore, the belief of all nations can only have its origin in God Himself, who has made Himself known from the beginning of the world to our first parents and has been known through his creatures.[20]

---

[20] "At a rather well attended meeting, an unbeliever spoke against the existence of God; and seeing that everybody kept silent, added, 'Never would I have believed that I am the only one who does not believe in God, among such intelligent people.' To which the master of the house replied, 'You are wrong, sir; you are not the only one. My horses, my dog, and my cat share this honor with you; only they are smart enough not to boast about it.'" (HILLAIRE, *La Religión Demostrada,* editorial translation.)

d) By the natural desire for perfect happiness[21]

This argument can be explained in the following manner: it is clear to us that every human being has a natural and innate desire to achieve full happiness. It is also clear to us that this desire cannot be useless or ineffective. Finally, it is clear to us that we cannot reach happiness except in an infinite Good, which cannot be any other than God.

1. It is clear to us, with total certainty, that the human heart craves full and perfect happiness with an innate and natural desire.

This proposition is evident to every reflective spirit. It shows precisely that all men in the world aspire to be happy in the highest possible degree. No one in his right mind can put a stop or any limit on the happiness he wants to reach— the more, the better. The absence of an indispensable minimum of happiness can throw us into the arms of despair; it will not root out the desire for happiness in us but only increase it still more. Pascal said that someone who commits suicide searches for his own happiness in hanging himself, given that he believes—although grievously wrong—that in death he will find the end of his pains and distress. It is, then, an indisputable fact that all men aspire, with a strong, natural, spontaneous and innate desire, to the maximum happiness possible. This is a desire that springs forth from the depths of human nature itself.

2. It is also clear to us, in all certainty, that a properly natural and innate desire cannot be in vain; that is, it cannot be

---

[21] The following comes from ROYO MARÍN, *Dios y su Obra*, 32-33.

resolved into an non-existent or unachievable objective or end.

This is because of the fact that nature does nothing in vain; everything has its purpose and explanation. On the contrary, this natural and innate desire, a reality in the human race, would not have sufficient reason for being, and it is known that "nothing exists nor can exist without sufficient reason for its existence."

3. It is clear, finally, that the human heart cannot find its perfect happiness in anything other than the possession of an Infinite Good. Therefore, the Infinite Good exists, which we call God.

Man can find his full happiness neither in any of the created goods in particular nor in the entire and simultaneous possession of all of them because he cannot possess them all nor would they be sufficient even if all of them could be attained. (Universal experience plainly teaches us that no one can possess nor has ever possessed all the external goods—riches, honors, fame, glory, power—and all the goods of the body—health, pleasures- and all the goods of the soul—science, virtue—at the same time. Many of them are incompatible and can never come together in one individual alone). None of them bring together any of the essential conditions for objectively perfect happiness, since they are created goods (and therefore finite and imperfect). They do not exclude all the evils (since the greatest evil is to lack the Infinite Good, even with the possession of everything else). They do not fully satisfy the heart of man (as our own and others' experience clearly shows). Finally, they are fleeting and perishable; they are easily lost and will disappear totally with death. Then, it is impossible that man can find his true and full happiness in them.

Only an Infinite Good can completely fulfill the immense aspirations of the human heart, fully satisfying their natural and innate appetite for happiness. Therefore, it has to be concluded that this Infinite Good really exists—that is if we do not want to fall into the absurdity of declaring a natural and innate appetite experienced by absolutely the entire human race as meaningless.

2. THE VÍAS OR WAYS OF ST. THOMAS AQUINAS (TRULY DEMONSTRATIVE ARGUMENTS)[22]

We will now look at the arguments that are truly demonstrative, laid out in their entirety with great clarity by Thomas Aquinas. They are called "vías," being itineraries for the mind to arrive at the existence of God.

---

[22] For this point, I will use the explanation of FR. ANTONIO ROYO MARÍN, in *Dios y su Obra*, 11-31. I will summarize only some paragraphs, skip others, and add some information taken from other books or more current sources. I do not quote the text because of its length, but I assure that almost all that follows is from this Spanish Dominican.

a) The first vía: the vía of movement

The first vía to demonstrate the existence of God can be formulated in the following manner: *The movement of the universe requires a First Unmoved Mover, which precisely is God.*

St. Thomas Aquinas says: "It is certain, and evident to our senses, that in the world some things are in motion. Now whatever is in motion is put in motion by another, for nothing can be in motion except it is in *potentiality* to that towards which it is in motion; whereas a thing moves inasmuch as it is in act. For motion is nothing else than the reduction of something from potentiality to actuality. But nothing can be reduced from potentiality to actuality, except by something in a state of actuality. Thus that which is actually hot, as fire, makes wood, which is potentially hot, to be actually hot, and thereby moves and changes it. Now it is not possible that the same thing should be at once in actuality and potentiality in the same respect, but only in different respects. For what is actually hot cannot simultaneously be potentially hot; but it is simultaneously potentially cold. It is therefore impossible that in the same respect and in the same way a thing should be both mover and moved, i.e. that it should move itself. Therefore, whatever is in motion must be put in motion by another. If that by which it is put in motion be itself put in motion, then this also must needs be put in motion by another, and that by another again. But this cannot go on to infinity, because then there would be no first mover, and, consequently, no other mover; seeing that subsequent movers move only inasmuch as they are put in motion by the first mover; as the staff moves only because it is put in motion by the hand. Therefore it is necessary to arrive at a first mover, put in motion by no other; and this everyone understands to be God."[23]

This argument is of an incontrovertible demonstrative force to any reflective spirit accustomed to the highest philosophical speculation. But we are going to display this in a clearer, simpler way so that readers who are not used to the highest philosophical reasoning can understand.

In the world around us there are an infinite number of things that move. It is a fact that does not need any demonstration: it is enough to open our eyes and contemplate the movement which can be observed everywhere.

And now: leaving aside the movement of the living beings which, precisely because of their life itself, have an *immanent* movement which allows them to grow or move from one place to another without any *apparent* influence other than their own nature or will; it is certainly clear and indisputable that *inanimate* beings (those belonging to the mineral world) cannot move by themselves, but need someone to move them. If nobody moves a stone, it will remain still and inert for all eternity, since it cannot move itself. It has *no life* and, therefore, it lacks any immanent movement.

So, let us apply this clear and evident principle to the cosmos and ask ourselves who has put and continues to put into movement the colossal machine of the universe, *which does not have within itself the cause of its own movement, since it is made up of inanimate beings from the mineral world.* And as much as we would like to multiply the intermediate movers, there is no other way than to arrive at a First Unmoved Mover incomparably more powerful than the universe itself, since it

---

[23] AQUINAS, *Summa Theologica,* I, Q. 2, Art. 3.

dominates with sovereign power and it rules with infinite wisdom. Truly to demonstrate the existence of God, it is enough to contemplate the wonderful show of a starry night, knowing that those luminous little dots, like brilliant dust amid all the immensity of space are gigantic suns moving at fantastic speeds even though they seem motionless.

Jesús Simón explains this argument in a beautiful and provocative manner: "We know by experience, and it is a certain principle of mechanics, that matter is *inert*, that is, in itself indifferent to movement or rest. Matter does not move nor can it move by itself: to do so, it needs an extrinsic force that impels it. If we see an airplane flying through the air, we think instantly about the motor that puts it in movement; if we see a locomotive advancing majestically on the rails, we think about the expansive force of the steam it carries within. Moreover: if we see a rock coursing through the air, we think instantly about the hand or catapult that has hurled it.

Behold, then, our case.

The stars are immense agglomerations of matter, monstrous globes that weigh thousands of quadrillions of tons, like the Sun, and hundreds of thousands, like Betelgeuse and Antares. Then they also are inert in and of themselves. To put them in movement would have necessitated a force that is *infinite, extra-cosmic, and coming from the exterior*, an *omnipotent* hand that had hurled them like projectiles through space . . .

Whose hand is this? Where does the incomparable strength capable of such colossal marvels proceed from? The force that subdued the worlds?

There can only be one reply: the hand, the omnipotence of God."[24]

Hillaire, in his work *La Religión Demostrada [The Demonstrated Religion]*, expounds the same argument in the following way: "It is a principle admitted by the *physical and mechanical sciences* that matter cannot move itself: a statue cannot abandon its pedestal; a machine cannot move without the force of a motor; a body at rest cannot put itself in motion; this is called the *principle of inertia*. So, it is necessary to have a motor in order to produce movement.

Then, the earth, the sun, the moon, the stars travel in immense orbits without ever crashing into each other. The earth is a colossal ball with a circumference of 40,000 kilometers (25,000 miles), which according to the astronomers make one complete rotation in the space of a day, moving the points located around the Equator with a velocity of 28 kilometers (17.5 miles) per second. In one year it makes one complete trip around the sun and goes some 30 kilometers (18.75 miles) per second. And also on the earth, the winds, the rivers, the tides, the germination of plants, everything proclaims the existence of movement.

All movement supposes a mover. Also, as it cannot suppose an *infinite* series of movers that communicate movement among themselves—since an *infinite number is as impossible as a stick without ends*—it is necessary to come to a first being that communicates movement without having received it. Thus, it is necessary to come to a *first unmoved mover*. Now, this first being, this first cause of movement, is God, who justly receives the name of *First Mover* of the universe.

---

[24] JESÚS SIMÓN, *A Dios por la Ciencia* (Barcelona: Editorial Lumen, 1947), 28, editorial translation.

We admire the genius of Newton, that discovered the laws of the movement of the stars; but, what an intelligence was necessary to establish them, and what a power to be able to launch into space and move with such speed and regularity these innumerable worlds that constitute the universe! On the rock of St. Helena, Napoleon said to General Bertrand: 'My victories have made you believe in my genius: the Universe makes me believe in God... What is the most beautiful military handiwork in comparison to the movement of the stars...?'"[25]

This argument, entirely demonstrative in itself, reaches its maximum certainty and manifestation if it is combined with the admirable order that reigns in the rapid movement of the stars spinning around their axes, which cross among themselves without ever crashing or colliding in anyway while traveling in their orbits at fantastic speeds. This proves that these movements do not obey a blind force of nature itself—that would produce confusion and chaos—but that they are directed by a sovereign power and an infinite intelligence, as we will see below in explaining the *fifth vía* of St. Thomas.

It is known that the movement of the universe requires a First Mover that impels or moves all the other beings that move. Given its sovereign perfection, this First Mover, by necessity, has to be *unmovable*. In other words, it cannot have been moved by any other mover, but it has to possess in itself and by itself the infinite force that gives impulse to the movement of all other beings that move. This infinitely perfect unmoved First Mover receives the adorable name of God.

---

[25] NAPOLEON, quoted in HILLAIRE, *La Religión Demostrada*, 6-7, editorial translation.

b) The second via: the via of efficient causality

The second way to demonstrate the existence of God can be synthesized in the following manner: *the efficient second causes necessarily demand the existence of an efficient First Cause, which we call God.*

In philosophy *efficient cause* is understood to be that which, in acting, produces an effect distinct from itself. Thus, the sculptor is the efficient cause of the statue he sculpts; the father is the efficient cause of his son.

The *efficient second cause* is understood to be that which has been made by another previous efficient cause. Thus, the father is the efficient cause of his son, but at the same is the result of his own father who brought him to existence as an anterior efficient cause. Therefore, *all the causes of the universe* are second causes, except the uncaused First Cause, whose existence we are about to investigate.

St. Thomas Aquinas explains: "In the world of sense we find there is an order of efficient causes. There is no case known (neither is it, indeed, possible) in which a thing is found to be the efficient cause of itself, for so it would be prior to itself, which is impossible. Now in efficient causes it is not possible to go on to infinity, because in all efficient causes following in order, the first is the cause of the intermediate cause, and the intermediate is the cause of the ultimate cause, whether the intermediate cause be several, or only one. Now to take away the cause is to take away the effect. Therefore, if there be no first cause among efficient causes, there will be no ultimate, nor any intermediate cause. But if in efficient causes it is possible to go on to infinity, there will be no first efficient cause, neither will there be an ultimate effect, nor any intermediate efficient causes; all of which is plainly false. Therefore it is necessary to admit a first efficient cause, to which everyone gives the name of God."[26]

As we have seen, the argument of the second via is also completely and totally evident and demonstrative. But in order to bring this closer into the reach of those uninitiated into philosophy, we are going to give an example that is very clear to everyone: the origin of life of the universe. It is an indisputable fact that in the world there are living beings that have not always existed but that have begun to exist, for example, every single human person. All of them received life from their parents, who had received it from theirs and so on. It is impossible to infinitely continue the list of our great-grandparents. It will necessarily arrive at the first living being who was the first and the origin of all the others. Eliminating the first one will automatically abolish the second and the third and all the others. From this it would have to be concluded that actual living beings do not really exist and this is ridiculous and absurd. Therefore, a First Living Being, who is the cause and origin of all the others, exists.

Now, this First Living Being unites, along with many others, the following characteristics:

1. It does not have father or mother, because if it did it would not be the first living being but the third and this is absurd and contradictory, given that this refers to the first living being in absolute.

2. It has never been born, because if it had it would have begun to exist and someone would have had to give it life since nothing can come out of absolutely nothing, since nothing does not exist and what does not exist cannot

---

produce anything. So, this first living being had life because of itself, without having received it from anyone.

3. This means that it is eternal and has always existed, without ever having begun to exist.

4. Therefore, all other living beings necessarily proceed from him, because it is absurd and contradictory to admit two or more first living beings: the first in any order of things is identified with absolute unity.

5. From it springs, as from their originating cause and creator, all living beings in the visible universe: men, animals and plants, and all those of the invisible universe: the angels about whom the Scriptures speak.

6. Consequently, it is superior to and infinitely above all the living beings of the universe, to which it communicated existence and life.

We necessarily conclude then, that the First Living Being, which brings together these characteristics, has an adorable name: it is, simply, God.

Hillaire explains the same saying, "The *physical and natural* sciences teach us that there was a time in which no living being existed on earth. From where, then, has all the life, the life of plants, the life of animals, and life of man, that now exists on it come?

Reason tells us that not even the *vegetative life* of a plant and even less the *sensitive life* of the animals, and much less the *intellective life* of man, has been able to be brought forth from matter. Why? Because nobody gives what he does not have; and as matter lacks life, it cannot give it.

Atheists find themselves in a corner with the dilemma: either life has been *spontaneously born* on the world, a product of the matter by *spontaneous generation*, or a *distinct cause of the world* has to be admitted, one that fertilizes the matter and makes life spring forth. Now then: after the conclusive experiments of Pasteur, there are no longer truly learned men who dare to defend the *hypothesis of spontaneous generation*. True science establishes that a living being is *never born without the vital germ, seed, egg or sprout*, which comes from another living being of the same species.

But what is the origin of the first living being of every species? Go back as far as you like, from generation to generation: it will always have to come to a first creator, who is God, the *first cause of all things*. This is the old argument of the *chicken and the egg*; even though it is old it has not stopped being an annoyance to atheists."[27]

This argument about the origin of life is a simple particular case in the general argument about the necessity of an efficient First Cause and can be applied to all the other beings existing in the universe. Each one of the beings, living or not, which populate the immensity of the universe, establishes a conclusive proof for the existence of God; because all these beings are necessarily *the effect of a cause that has produced them*, the work of a creating God. Of course, those thinkers who deny the validity of the "principle of causality" (which says there is no effect without a cause) will not accept this reasoning. For example, the recently re-acclaimed William James, who affirmed in one of his main works that "Causation is indeed too obscure a principle to bear the weight of the whole structure of theology."[28] What James affirms can be easily written on paper and it is even easier to make everybody believe it from a university chair, especially

---

[27] HILLAIRE, *La Religión Demostrada*, 8-9, editorial translation.

[28] WILLIAM JAMES, *The Varieties of Religious Experience: A Study in Human Nature* (New York: Longmans, Green, and Co., 1902), 437, cited in FULTON SHEEN, *Religion Without God* (New York: Longman's Green, 1928).

when they have an appreciative respect and not a critical spirit towards him... but it is not possible to live it. It is probable that James himself, having a stomachache, would have thought, "It must have been the unripe peaches that I ate yesterday," or "This is happening because I am a glutton." To put even more simply, he must have had to stop one of his children from putting his finger in the electric outlet, or from getting too close to the lions in the New York Zoo. He is carried by his *vital conviction* that there is a relationship among these events of cause and effect, the principle of causality, and although he may *intellectually* deny those relationships, they nonetheless appear *vitally* evident to him. This shows that foolish philosophers, when lounging around their houses in pajamas, tend to be guided by common sense, which they abandon along with their pajamas, when they leave to teach class. The day that they stop doing so, they end up sleeping in a drain like Diogenes or in the asylum like Nietzsche.

Now we will see this same thing from a different point of view.

c) The third via: the contingency of beings

The fundamental argument of the third via to prove the existence of God can be synthesized in the following manner: *the contingence of all the things in the world brings us with all certainty to the knowledge of the existence of a Necessary Being which exists by himself and which we call God.*

We will clarify some concepts:

- *a contingent being* is that which exists, but could also not exist; or in other words, that began to exist and will stop existing one day; the corruptible beings of the universe are such beings.

- *a necessary being* is that which exists and cannot stop existing; or in other words, that which, having existence from himself and by himself, has always existed and will never stop existing.

St. Thomas explains the argument: "The third way is taken from possibility and necessity, and runs thus. We find in nature things that are possible to be and not to be, since they are found to be generated, and to corrupt, and consequently, they are possible to be and not to be.

"But it is impossible for these always to exist, for that which is possible not to be at some time is not. Therefore, if everything is possible not to be, then at one time there could have been nothing in existence. Now if this were true, even now there would be nothing in existence, because that which does not exist only begins to exist by something already existing. Therefore, if at one time nothing was in existence, it would have been impossible for anything to have begun to exist; and thus even now nothing would be in existence — which is absurd.

"Therefore, not all beings are merely possible, but there must exist something the existence of which is necessary. But every necessary thing either has its necessity caused by another, or not. Now it is impossible to go on to infinity in necessary things which have their necessity caused by another, as has been already proved in regard to efficient causes. Therefore we cannot but postulate the existence of some being having *of itself* its own necessity, and not receiving it from another, but rather causing in others their necessity. This all men speak of as God."[29]

---

[29] AQUINAS, *Summa Theologica,* I, Q. 2, Art. 3.

It is an absolutely demonstrative reasoning in the scientific sense of the word, and the existence of God appears so effectively that it is as convincing as a geometric theorem. It is not possible to avoid the evidence nor is there any danger that scientific progress will someday find a way to discredit it, because these metaphysical principles transcend sensible experience and are above and beyond the scientific progress.

It is clear and evident that the necessary being is identified with God, keeping in mind some of the characteristics that simple natural reason can discover with certainty in him. Here are the principles:

1. The necessary being is infinitely perfect. This is clear by the mere act of existence in virtue of its own essence or nature, which supposes the entirety of all possible perfections in their highest degree. Because it possesses the *plenitude of being* and the being contains all perfections: it is, therefore, infinitely perfect

2. There is not more than one necessary being. The necessary Being is infinite and two infinites cannot exist at the same time. If they are distinct, they are neither infinite nor perfect, because neither of the two possesses what pertains to the other. If they are not distinct they do not form more than one being.

3. The necessary being is eternal. If it had not always existed or if it had to stop existing, it clearly would not exist by virtue of its own nature. Given that it exists by itself, it cannot have a beginning, an end, or succession.

4. The necessary being is absolutely immutable. To change is to acquire or lose something. But the necessary Being cannot acquire anything, because it possesses all perfections; and it cannot lose anything because the simple possibility of losing something is incompatible with its supreme perfection. Therefore it is immutable.

5. The necessary being is absolutely independent, because it does not need anyone. It is perfectly sufficient in itself since it is the Being that exists by itself: infinite, eternal, the most perfect. 6. The necessary being is a spirit. A spirit is an intelligent being, capable of thinking, understanding and loving. It is a being that cannot be seen nor touched with the corporeal senses; thus it is different from material beings, which have opposing characteristics. The necessary Being must, most certainly, be spirit, without body or matter. Because if it were *corporeal* it would be limited in its being, as all bodies are. If it were material it would be divisible and would not be infinite. Neither would it be *infinitely perfect*, because the material cannot be the beginning of intelligence and life, which are a thousand times higher than matter. Therefore, the necessary Being is a spiritual being, infinitely perfect and transcendent.

So, these and other qualities of the necessary being, which natural reason is able to discover effortlessly and with all certainty, absolutely coincide with the divine attribute.

Therefore, the necessary being is God. Consequently, the existence of God is beyond a doubt, in light of mere natural reason.

d) The fourth via: the different degrees of perfection

The fourth via arrives at the existence of God by considering the different degrees of perfection found in created beings. It is, maybe, the most profound from the metaphysical point of view; but, for this same reason, it is the most difficult for those uninitiated in higher philosophical speculations to grasp.

St. Thomas explains: "The fourth way is taken from the gradation to be found in things. Among beings there are some more and some less good, true, noble and the like. But 'more' and 'less' are predicated of different things, according as they resemble in their different ways something which is the maximum, as a thing is said to be hotter according as it more nearly resembles that which is hottest;[30] so that there is something which is truest, something best, something noblest and, consequently, something which is uttermost being; for those things that are greatest in truth are greatest in being, as it is written in Metaph. ii. Now the maximum in any genus is the cause of all in that genus; as fire, which is the maximum heat, is the cause of all hot things. Therefore there must also be something which is to all beings the cause of their being, goodness, and every other perfection; and this we call God."[31]

The argument of this fourth way is similar to the previous ones. Beginning with a completely true and evident experimental fact—the existence of various degrees of perfection in beings—natural reason conceives the necessity of a perfect being that possesses perfection in the highest degree and that possesses *it by its own essence and nature, without having received it from anyone.* And that is, therefore, the cause or source of all the various degrees of perfections that we find in all other beings. This perfect being, then, origin and fount of all perfection, is precisely who we call God.[32]

---

[30] It does not matter that in fact other things much hotter than ordinary fire exist; this example of Thomas Aquinas' is one example taken from ordinary language.

[31] AQUINAS, *Summa Theologica*, I, Q. 2, Art. 3.

[32] Anyone who desires to broaden his knowledge of this argument can do so by reading works like those of Fabro cited in the bibliography.

e) The fifth via: the order and end of the universe

St. Thomas explains, "The fifth way is taken from the governance of the world. We see that things which lack intelligence, such as natural bodies, act *for* an *end*, and this is evident from their acting always, or nearly always, in the same way, so as to obtain the best result. Hence it is plain that not fortuitously, but designedly, do they achieve their end. Now whatever lacks intelligence cannot move towards an end, unless it be directed by some being endowed with knowledge and intelligence, as the arrow is shot to its mark by the archer. Therefore some intelligent being exists by whom all natural things are directed to their end; and this being we call God."[33]

This proof of the existence of God, in addition to being totally valid (even Kant himself was favorably disposed with respect to it), is the clearest and most understandable. This is why it has been extensively developed by writers and orators who find it the easiest and simplest way to make the existence of God understandable, even to the less educated. For this reason, I will give some examples, taken from the order of the universe. In the book by Fr. Royo Marín various examples can be found beginning with the order of the cosmos, with the world of physical-chemical forces, with vegetative and animal life, with the sensible realm, and others taken from the work of Ricardo Viejo-Felíu, *El Creador y su Creación* (*The Creator and His Creation*).[34] Departing from Royo Marín's book momentarily, I will support my argument with

---

[33] AQUINAS, *Summa Theologica*, I, Q. 2, Art. 3.

[34] A truly valuable work: FR. RICARDO VIEJO-FELÍU, S.J., *El Creador y su Creación* (Puerto Rico: Ponce, 1952).

You can also see the work by FR. JESÚS SIMÓN, S.J., *A Dios por la Ciencia*. (There is a more current edition from Ed. Sol de Fatima, Madrid.)

what Fr. George Loring says about the order of the universe in his well-known book, *To Save You*:[35]

"Look at the sky. Can you count the stars? The Atlas of the Heavens, which they have begun to publish, will consist of twenty volumes, in which there will be 500,000,000 stars. The total number of stars in the Universe is calculated to be some 200,000 trillion stars, a number with 24 digits! The sun has ten planets: Mercury, Venus, Earth, Mars, Jupiter, Saturn, Uranus, Neptune and Pluto. The nine known and the tenth just discovered: Planet X, located by the Pioneer probe in 1987; we have known of its existence for 20 years. Our galaxy, the Milky Way, has 100,000 million suns.[36] And there are about 100,000 million galaxies such as ours. The Andromeda's Nebulosa consists of 200,000,000 stars. Well, if some holes in the sand could not have been made by themselves, would the millions of stars in the heavens make themselves? Someone has made the stars. That being, the Primary Cause of the whole Universe, we call God.

"The moon is 238,6464 miles from Earth. The Sun is 93,150,00 miles away. Pluto is 3,726,000,000 miles distant. Beyond our Solar System, Sirius is 8 light years away, and Arthur is 36 light years distant. Light which travels at a speed of 300,000 kilometers [186,300 miles] per second, in one year covers a distance equivalent to 200,000,000 times around the

---

[35] I cite almost textually, leaving out only some paragraphs and slightly modifying others. The text of GEORGE LORING, *To Save You* (Los Angeles: St. Paul's Publishing Co., 2005), 6-11 has many footnotes laying a foundation for each affirmation; for reasons of space, I will include only some citations I consider fundamental. The rest can be seen in his work.

[36] MANUEL CARREIRA, *Antropocentrismo Científico y Religioso* (Madrid: Ed. A.D.U.E., 1983).

earth. Measured in kilometers, it is about 10 billion of them.[37] In order to have an idea of what a billion is, let us consider that a billion seconds are equal to almost 32 years. The speed of light according to the laws of physics cannot be surpassed. The speed of light is the maximum speed which can be attained as demonstrated by Einstein's equation of $E=mc^2$, speed at which mass would become infinite.[38] Outside our galaxy, the nearest galaxy, the Andromeda's Nebulosa, is 2 million light years away.[39] The Coma of Virgo is 200 million light years away and the Cumulus of Hydra is 2,000 million light years distant.[40]

"This is the limit for optical telescopes. Radio telescopes can probe deeper. The farthest away a star has been detected is Quasar PKS 2,000-330 which is 15,000 million light years distant. Quasars are radio stars which emit Hertz waves. They were first detected in 1960.

"There are millions of stars much larger than Earth in the heavens. Earth is a ball with a circumference (meridian) of 24,840 miles. The sun is 1,300,000 times bigger than Earth. The star, Antares, from the Scorpio constellation is so large that its size is the equivalent of 115 million suns. Alfa of Hercules, which is 1,200 light years away and is the largest of all known stars, is eight thousand billion times larger than the sun. In order to understand the enormity of these celestial bodies, we can say that the orbit of the moon around the

---

[37] MANUEL CARREIRA, *El Creyente Ante la Ciencia* (Madrid: Cuadernos BAC, 1982), II, 3, no. 57.

[38] STEPHEN HAWKING, *A Brief History of Time* (New York: Bantam Books, 1988).

[39] STEPHEN WEINBERG, *The First Three Minutes: A Modern View of the Origin of the Universe* (New York: Basic Books, 1993).

[40] FRED HOYLE, *The Intelligent Universe* (London: Michael Joseph Limited, 1983).

Earth fits in the sun, and that the radius of Antares is the equal to the diameter of the Earth's orbit, that is about 300,000,000 kilometers [186,300,000 miles], and that the diameter of the orbit of Pluto, which is 12,000 million kilometers [7,452 million miles], is a tenth of the radius of Alfa of Hercules. All of the data mentioned above was calculated for me by an astronomer. The largest known radio star is DA-240, which has a diameter of 6,000,000 light years. The diameter of this radio-star is 60 times greater than the diameter of our galaxy, the Milky Way, which is only about 100,000 light years.

"These gigantesque balls travel at great speeds. The Earth travels at 62,100 miles per hour, which is about 18.6 miles per second. The sun is traveling towards the Constellation of Hercules at a rate of 186 miles per second. The Constellation of Virgo is moving away from us at a speed of 621 miles per second. The Cumulus of Boyero is leaving us at a speed of 62,100 miles per second. Because of the speedy motion towards the red ray spectrum we can calculate that there are stars that are moving at a rate of 171,396 miles per second, or about 92% the speed of light.

"The movement of the stars is so exact that one can make an almanac years in advance. An almanac lists the rising and the setting of the sun every day, the eclipses which will occur during the year, the day they will take place, the hour, minute and second, how long they will last, what part of the Sun or Moon will be hidden, from what point on the Earth they will be visible, etc. On June 30, 1972, all of Spain was engrossed in the partial eclipse of the Sun which the press had been talking about for several days. On October 2, 1959, a total eclipse of the sun was visible from the Canary Islands. This occurred at noon, just as had been predicted eons before. Because of this they installed an observation post where scientists from all over the world gathered on Punta de Jandia in Fuerteventura. The previous eclipse of the Sun which was seen from the Canary Islands occurred on August 30, 1905 and it is known that we will have to wait until the twenty-second century has passed before we see another total eclipse of the Sun from within our borders [Loring is speaking of Spain]. In 2005, we will be able to see a ring-shape eclipse from Cadiz.[41] Halley's comet (so named in honor of the astronomer, Edmund Halley, a friend and contemporary of Isaac Newton) as had been foreseen in the nineteenth century, passed close to us in 1910. It again passed near Earth (302,000,000 miles) in March of 1986 as had been predicted. All news media in the world spoke of the comet. Halley (1646-1742), who observed the comet in 1662, calculated its orbit and predicted that it would appear every 76 years, and it has happened. It will be seen again in the year 2062. When it passed close to the Earth in 1986, it was photographed by the European probe named Giotto which approached the nucleus of the comet at a distance of 310 miles. The length of the comet's tail is 31,000,000 miles and is formed by rarefied gases [...] The nucleus of the comet is formed by solid gases at a temperature of 100°C below zero. It dimensions are 7.5 by 8.5 by 18 kilometers. The Chinese already knew about the comet a thousand years before Christ. It has gone around the sun thousands of times, and it will finally consume itself, as each time it approaches the sun, it loses weight when heated by the sun, and part of the nucleus's solid gases evaporate. The comet's tail does not go backwards, as the wake of a jet plane, but because it confronts the solar wind, it appears to be going towards the sun,

---

[41] *Editor's Note*: Loring's work was first published in 1998.

somewhat like an old fashioned locomotive, whose smoke went sideways when encountering a strong side wind.

"All of this would be impossible to know if the order of the movement of the stars were not mathematically calculable. For this reason James Jeans, illustrious mathematician, President of the Royal Astronomical Society of England and Professor of the University of Oxford, as well as one of the greatest contemporary astronomers, in his book, *The Mysterious Universe*, affirms that the Creator of the Universe had to be a great mathematician,[42] and Einstein says, 'Nature is the realization of the mathematical ideas of God.'[43] Paul Dirac, Professor of Theoretical Physics at the University of Cambridge and one of the outstanding scientists of our generation, said in the *Scientific American* journal: 'God is a mathematician of a very high order'.[44]

"All this marvelous order requires a great intelligence to direct it. What would happen in a square where there is a great deal of traffic—if the drivers suddenly became paralyzed and the vehicles, without intelligence, were abandoned to their own motion? Why mayhem would occur!

"The more complicated and perfect an order is, the greater the organizing mind must be. It is assumed that you require more intelligence to build a clock than to build a wheelbarrow. If you are shipwrecked on the high seas and grasp onto a floating object, and arrive at a deserted island, even though you find no trace of man, not a shoe, not a piece

---

[42] JAMES JEANS, *The Mysterious Universe* (Whitefish, Montana: Kessinger Publishing, 2009).

[43] DESIDERIO PAPP, *Einstein,* 3rd ed. (Madrid: Ed. Espasa Calpe, 1979), XIII, 7.

[44] PAUL DIRAC, "The Evolution of the Physicist's Picture of Nature," *Scientific American* 208:5 (May 1963): 53.

MIGUEL ÁNGEL FUENTES

of clothing, nor an empty sardine can, nothing; but if you wander through the island and find a hut, you immediately realize that there was another person present before your arrival. You comprehend that the shelter is evidence of man's intelligence. You realize that the shelter did not happen by itself, that those stakes driven into the ground, and those branches that form the roof and swivel the door are the fruit of human intelligence. If a few branches that form a hut require human intelligence, should not intelligence be required in order to align the millions and millions of stars that float through the heavens with mathematical precision? Isaac Newton (1642-1727) and Johannes Kepler (1571-1630) discovered the mathematical rules which govern the movement of the Universe; but one must remember that they did not establish said rules, as stars had been in existence for many years before Newton and Kepler were born. Therefore, one must surmise that someone authored those rules in the beginning. That is why the astronaut, Borman, said while on the Moon: 'We have arrived here thanks to laws that were not made by man.' And Newton said: 'The universe could not have been born without being projected by an intelligent being.'[45] 'It is sufficient for me,' said Albert Einstein, Physics Nobel Prize winner, 'to reflect on the marvelous structure of the Universe, and to humbly attempt to penetrate in at least an infinitesimal part of the wisdom which is manifested in Nature.'[46] He also said: 'God does not play craps [dice].'[47] The intelligence which puts in order the movement of the stars in

[45] ISAAC NEWTON, "Scholium Generale," in *Philosophiae Naturalis Principia Matematica*, cited in GEORGE LORING, *To Save You*, 11.

[46] ANTONIO DÚE ROJO, *El Cosmos en la Actualidad Científica* (Madrid: Ediciones FAX, 1962), I, 5.

[47] MAX BORN, *Ciencia y Conciencia de la Era Atómica*, 1st ed. (Madrid: Alianza Editorial, 1971), IX.

64

the skies and directs with such great perfection the machine of the Universe is God's intelligence. This is why the Bible says, *The heavens declare the glory of God*' (Ps 19:2). Creatures are the fingers that point me to God. But there are people who just stare at the finger, look no farther and don't see past it."[48]

Here ends Loring's quote. But no less surprising than the order of the cosmos is the order of every being. Just ask a doctor to explain to you the marvelous mechanism of feminine fertility and maternity and you will see an extraordinary order that cannot correspond to anything but to an ordaining intelligence. Accordingly, in the marvelous hormonal mechanism by which every woman is prepared throughout each fertility cycle for ovulation and all that follows ovulation, there is an extraordinary and harmonious interaction of precise orders between many glands to prepare the whole organism for a possible conception. This preparation not only provides for the female body, but also for the embryo's protection in the case that conception takes place. Conception, then, having taken place, the fertilized cell, that is, the human embryo, via a mysterious and mathematical process, begins to develop until its culmination at birth: this development is the same rigorous process that has consistently occurred from the conception to the birth of millions of human beings. The same holds, in a non-depreciative way, when we consider beings of inferior forms and see the same phenomenon of a surprising order; for example, the wisdom of one simple bumblebee.[49] In effect, the bee solves the problem of constructing a honeycomb, in such a way that the least amount of wax allows for the largest

---

[48] GEORGE LORING, *To Save You*, 6-11.

[49] I take this example from ROYO MARÍN, *Dios y su Obra*, 25, no. 22. It can also be read in other books.

amount of honey. Reaumur discovered this two centuries ago by applying algorithms of infinitesimal calculus that had been discovered by Leibnitz. But what was curious was that these learned men, making the calculation for the first time, erred, whereas the bee, without calculating, without studying, did not err. And such efficiency was employed, even before Reaumur, or Leibnitz, or Pythagoras had been born! The discovery went like this. Reaumur, the famous inventor of the Thermometric Scale that carries his name, suspecting what would in effect happen, proposed the following problem to his colleagues: What angles must be given to the basic shapes of the honeycomb's hexagonal cross-section so that it has the maximum capacity with the least surface area? König applied the theory of maximums and minimums of infinitesimal calculus, and found the shape's acute angle of 70° 34'; naturally the obtuse angle would be the complement. Measuring the shape of the honeycomb they found constant angles and the angle was 70° 32'. Apparently the little animal had been wrong in the insignificant calculation of two minute degrees! Not long after, a boat sank off the French coast due to an error in the calculation of longitude. When asked, the captain peacefully presented his calculations, which were correct. Everyone was disoriented. They had to look for the cause elsewhere. They reviewed and studied the operations and they found a typo in the logarithmic table that impacted all of the longitudinal calculation. Once the error was corrected, König returned to the problem proposed by Reaumur, that the acute angle of the shape given was (70° 32'). The mathematicians had erred, but the bee had not erred nor errs now. It thus constructs a honeycomb with the least expense of wax and in the way that admits the greatest amount of honey.

From all this it can be concluded that if an infinitely wise and powerful *Creator* does not exist, then *the dynamic order* that governs the cosmos—from galaxies down to beehives—should be attributed to chance. There is no other solution. It is clear that chance cannot explain this order in any way. Therefore, *that wise and infinitely powerful Creator exists.*

The world, in a word, *is the result of an infinite understanding.* This is why the belief in God pertains to one of the human intelligence's *normal functions.* For this same reason, an atheist is a clinical case just as someone who has lost his mind,[50] because to admit nothing more than a blind clashing of natural forces is to accept *an unintelligence more intelligent than intelligence itself.* Incredulity does not consist in not believing, but in believing what is complex before believing what is simple.

3. SCIENTISTS AND GOD[51]

Due to what we have just finished explaining, it should not surprise us if in our times there were scientists who said they did not believe in God. However, along with these, there are many others, who are actually the majority, many of whom are considered the most prestigious in the scientific world, who have believed in God, not only because of their faith (some have and others have not been Christians), but

---

[50] Cf. TIHAMÉR TÓTH, *Creo en Dios* (Madrid: Sociedad de Educación Atenas, 1939), 127.

[51] Two excellent summaries can be referred to: "Fe y Cientificos del Siglo XX," *arvo.net,* February 5, 2005, *arvo.net/fe-y-ciencias/fe-y-cientificos-del-siglo-xx/gmx-niv90-con10052.htm* (accessed May 10, 2014);

and "Cientificos del Pasado Creen en Dios," *arvo.net,* February 5, 2005, *arvo.net/fe-y-ciencias/cientificos-del-pasado-creen-en-dios/gmx-niv90-con10051.htm* (accessed May 10, 2014).

MIGUEL ÁNGEL FUENTES

also by their science. Neither should it surprise us that true thinkers fall into anti-scientific arguments when they deal with the denial of God. To cite only one example, when William James, to whom we have referred before, taught that the existence of God could not be demonstrated, he did not give any proof other than the *argument of authority* (a fundamental argument in theology that has little value in philosophy and even less in science): "The bare fact that *all* idealists since Kant have felt entitled either to scout or to neglect them shows that they are not solid enough to serve as religion's all-sufficient foundation."[52] This is not an acceptable way for a scientist to proceed! The majority of scientists—if not all of them—were also in agreement that the sun orbited earth when Copernicus (and then Galileo) raised the theory that it was the planets that orbited the sun. Where would we be today if science had been guided by the argument of the majority? With this motive, let us see what some of the most studious and outstanding in the world of science have to say about God:

Copernicus, a Polish astronomer (1473-1543), proved that the earth was round, explained its movements and the rotation of the solar system and defended heliocentricity before Galileo. He said: "If there is one science capable of ennobling the soul of man and raising it above the defilements of earth, it is astronomy [...] for how could anyone observe the mighty order with which our God governs the universe without feeling himself inclined [...] to the beholding of the Creator himself, the source of all goodness."[53]

---

[52] JAMES, *The Varieties of Religious Experience: A Study in Human Nature*, 437.

[53] COPERNICUS, quoted in JACQUES DE BIVORT DE LA SAUDÉE, *God, Man and the Universe* (London: Burns & Oates, 1954), 54.

THE STOLEN TRUTH ABOUT GOD

Galileo Galilei, Italian astronomer and physicist (1564-1642) who many scientists, including atheists, consider a paradigm of the "man of science," died professing his faith in God and in the apostolic Roman Catholic Church.

Kepler, German astronomer (1571-1630), who formulated the laws that bear his name, in spite of living a very unfortunate life, writes: "I give thanks to Thee, O Lord Creator, Who hast delighted me with Thy makings and in the works of Thy hands have I exulted."[54] And elsewhere: "The day will come when we will be able to read God in Nature as we read of Him in Sacred Scriptures."[55] "[...] now, I have completed the work of my profession, having employed as much power of mind as Thou didst give to me; to the men who are going to read those demonstrations I have made manifest the glory of Thy works, as much of its infinity as the narrows of my intellect could apprehend."[56]

Isaac Newton, English physicist, astronomer and mathematician (1642-1727), considered by many scientists as one of the greatest of all time in intelligence and ingenuity, did not have any objection to writing that: "This most beautiful system of the sun, planets and comets, could only proceed from the counsel and dominion of an intelligent and powerful Being. And if every star is the center of a system similar to ours, it is true that since all of them have the seal of the same plan; they all should be submissive to one and the same being. And if the fixed stars are the centers of other like systems, these, being formed by the same wise counsels,

---

[54] JOHANNES KEPLER, *Epitome of Copernican Astronomy & Harmonies of the World* (Amherst, New York: Promethus Books, 1995), 240.

[55] JOHANNES KEPLER, quoted in "Cientificos del Pasado Creen en Dios," editorial translation.

[56] KEPLER, *Epitome of Copernican Astronomy & Harmonies of the World,* 240.

must be all be subject to the dominion of One [...] This Being governs all things, not as the soul of the world, but as Lord over all [...] The Supreme God is a Being eternal, infinite, absolutely perfect."[57]

The Swedish physician and naturalist, Carl von Linné (1707–1778), considered to be the founder of botany and one of the greatest botanists of all time, author of more than fifteen great works, had firm religious convictions. This can be seen in these words of wisdom from his work *Systema Naturae*: "I came out of a dream when God passed by, close to me: I saw him and was filled with wonder... I tracked God's footsteps over creatures and found in each one, even in those I could scarcely make out, an endless wisdom and power, an unreachable perfection."[58]

The Italian physicist Alexander Volta (1745-1827), inventor of the electrophone and the battery that bears his name, testified: "I have studied and reflected much. Now I see God in everything..."[59]

The French astronomer Hervé-Auguste-Etienne-Albans Faye (1814-1902), speaking about atheism said: "In denying God, it is as if from those heights one was allowed to fall heavily to the floor [...] It is false that science has come to the denial of God by itself. It happened in certain periods of conflict with the institutions of the past. Thus some atheistic philosophers are found in the decadence of the ancient Greco-Roman society, at the end of the eighteenth century and surely even today, because it is proper to the fight. Soon

---

[57] ISAAC NEWTON, *The Mathematical Principles of Natural Philosophy,* trans. Andrew Motte (New York: Daniel Adee, 1846), 35.

[58] CARL VON LINNÉ, quoted in "Cientificos del Pasado Creen en Dios," editorial translation.

[59] Ibid.

spirits will return to eternal truths, deeply shocked at having opposed them for so long."[60]

The Czech Gregor Johann Mendel (1822-1869) was an Augustinian friar, father of all genetics and most of modern biology. Without many words about his religious life, he practiced his Christian faith without contradicting his science.

The French chemist and bacteriologist Louis Pasteur (1822-1895), founder of modern asepsis and modern antisepsis, never refrained from praying the rosary while traveling by train, in spite of some vain university students who mocked him without knowing who he was; they thought he was a simple ignorant countryman. Pasteur said, "The more I know, the more nearly is my faith that of the Breton peasant. Could I but know all I would have the faith of a Breton peasant woman"[61] (making reference that his science does not contradict the faith of a simple countryman).

The German-born American-naturalized engineer Wernher von Braun (born in 1912), who placed in orbit the first American satellite Explorer I, was called "the rocket genius." He worked as a manager for NASA on the projects of the Saturn skyrocket and the project Apollo (the rockets taking men to the moon) and he possessed a deep religious sense: "The materialists of the 19th century and their Marxist heirs of the 20th, tried to tell us that, as science gives us more knowledge about the creation, we could live without faith in a Creator. Yet so far, with every new answer, we have discovered new questions. The better we understand the intricacies of the atomic structure, the nature of life, or the master plan for the galaxies, the more reason we have found

---

[60] Ibid.

[61] CHARLES HERBERMANN et al., ed., "Pasteur," in vol. XI of *The Catholic Encyclopedia* (New York: Robert Appleton Company, 1911), 537.

to marvel at the wonder of God's creation. [...] Man needs faith just as he needs food, water or air. [...] we need faith in God".[62]

The French physician Alexis Carrel (1873-1944), an atheist converted by seeing a miracle at Lourdes, said: "I want to believe and I do believe all that the Catholic Church wants us to believe, and in that I experience no difficulty, for I find nothing there at all that contradicts the certain facts of science."[63] "I am neither a philosopher nor a theologian; I speak and write only as a man of science."[64]

Pascual Jordan (b. 1902) was a German physicist, founder of quantum mechanics along with Max Born and Werner Heisenberg. In his book entitled *Der Naturwissenschaftler vor der religiösen Frage* (The Man of Science Before the Religious Problem), he wrote: "It is not without reason that I have titled this book, *Der Naturwissenschaftler vor der religiösen Frage*. The intention was to explain how all the impediments, all the myths that ancient science had brought forth to obstruct the path of access to religion have today disappeared. [...] The determinist claim that God stood back and didn't work within nature, which followed its course regularly, has now lost its foundation. [...] In the innumerable amount of always new and indeterminate results, the action, the will, the authority of God can be seen. [...] We do not claim that the

---

[62] "Why I Believe: Wernher von Braun Talks About Science and God," in vol. 111, part 13 of *Congressional Record: Proceedings and Debates of the 89th Congress First Session* (Washington: United States Government Printing Office, 1965): 18072.

[63] "Novena of preparation for Christmas," *Spiritual Newsletter* of the Abbey of Saint-Joseph de Clairval, December 18, 2012, www.clairval.com/lettres/en/2012/12/18/2191212.htm (accessed March 1, 2014).

[64] ALEXIS CARREL, *Viaje a Lourdes* (Barcelona: Ed. Iberia, 1949), 12, editorial translation.

action of God in nature has been made scientifically visible or demonstrable [...] but that, in what concerns religious faith, new physics has denied that denial: it has proved that those conceptions of ancient science that were furnished as proof against the existence of God are erroneous."[65]

The neurobiologist John Eccles, director of the department of Biochemistry at the University of Cambridge, speaking about the materialism of many scientists, said: "I believe that hypothetical materialism is even the most widespread belief among scientists. But it does not contain more than a promise: that all will be explained, including the most intimate forms of human experience, in terms of nerve cells... This is nothing more than *a type of religious faith*; or better, it is *a superstition that is not founded on evidence worthy of consideration.* As we progress in our understanding of the structure of the human brain, the singularity of the human being with respect to all other things in the material world will become clearer."[66]

Henry Margenau, collaborator with Einstein, Heisenburg and Scheoedinger, physicist at Yale University, founder of three important scientific magazines, eight doctorates *honoris causa*, and president of the American Association of Philosophy and Science, said: "Almost everybody clearly admits that the universe has had a beginning, and although there are some in astronomy, like Carl Sagan, who are actively antireligious, others, like Robert Jastrow, who work in the same field, are not. And Jastrow is more prestigious than Sagan as a scientist and physicist. While Sagan is a publicist,

---

[65] "Fe y Cientificos del Siglo XX," editorial translation.
[66] Ibid.

Jastrow is a physicist who has researched the topic about which he speaks. And Jastrow is a religious man."[67]

John von Neumann, Hungarian mathematician (1903-1957), the son of a rich Jewish banker, was considered by many as the most brilliant mind of the twentieth century comparable only to Albert Einstein. He actively participated in the Manhattan Project, the group of scientists that created the first atomic bomb, participated and directed the production and beginnings of the first computers, and as a scientist was an advisor to the United States Security Counsel in the fifties. He is creator of games theory (thousands of economists currently work in this field and publish hundreds of pages daily). Additionally, the mathematic formulas he described served as the base for the Utility Theory used to resolve problems of General Equilibrium. In 1937, he published *A Model of General Economic Equilibrium,*[68] of which E. Roy Weintraub said in 1938 that it was "the single most important article in mathematical economics."[69] This scientist at the end of his life converted to Catholicism.

And I end with this text from the Italian scientist Enrico Medi: "When I tell a young person: Look, there is a new star, a galaxy, a neutron star 100 million light-years away, yet the protons, electrons, neutrons and mesons which are found there are identical with those which are found in this microphone... Identity excludes probability. That which is identical is not probable... Therefore there is a cause, outside of space, outside of time, the master of being, which made

---

[67] Ibid.

[68] J. V. NEUMANN, "A Model of General Economic Equilibrium," vol. 13, co. 1 of *The Review of Economic Studies* (1945-1946): 1-9.

[69] E. ROY WEINTRAUB, *General Equilibrium Analysis: Studies in Appraisal* (Michigan: University of Michigan Press, 1996), 74.

being to be in this way. And this is God… The being—I am speaking scientifically—which has caused things to be identical at a distance of billions of light-years, exists. And the number of identical particles in the universe is 10 raised to the 85th power… Do we wish then to take in the song of the galaxies? If I were Francis of Assisi I would say: O galaxies of the immense heavens, give praise to my Lord, for he is omnipotent and good. O atoms, O protons, O electrons, O bird-songs, O blowing of the leaves and of the air, in the hands of man as a prayer, sing out the hymn which returns to God!"[70]

Clearly, it cannot be said that science has problems with God; some scientists may… but not because of their science.

* * *

In conclusion, we can say that the truth of the existence of God is such a clear truth that Sacred Scripture harshly treats the pagan wise men who did not perceive a Creator though the beauty and power of their works.

For all men who were ignorant of God were foolish by nature; and they were unable from the good things that are seen to know him who exists, nor did they recognize the craftsman while paying heed to his works; but they supposed that either fire or wind or swift air, or the circle of the stars, or turbulent water, or the luminaries of heaven were the gods that rule the world. If through delight in the beauty of these things men assumed them to be gods, let them know how much better than these is their Lord, for the author of beauty created them. And if men were amazed at their power and working, let them perceive from them how much more powerful is he who formed them. For from the greatness and beauty of created things comes a corresponding perception of their Creator […] for if they had the power to know so much that they could investigate

---

[70] St. John Paul II, "Scientists and God," July 17, 1985, *www.vatican.va/holy_father/john_paul_ii/audiences/alpha/data/aud19850717en.html* (accessed March 1, 2014).

the world, how did they fail to find sooner the Lord of these things? (Wis 13:1-5, 9)

For Further Reading

- Loring, George. *To Save You*. Los Angeles: St. Paul's Publishing Co., 2005.
- Picard, Max. *The Flight from God*. Wichita, Kansas: Eighth Day Press, 2002.
- Sheen, Fulton. *Religion Without God*. New York: Longman's Green, 1928.

Available in Other Languages

- Carreira, Manuel. *El Creyente ante la Ciencia*. Madrid: Cuadernos BAC, 1982.
- Fabro, Cornelio. *Dios: Introducción al Problema Teológico*. Madrid: Rialp, 1961.
- ———. *Drama del Hombre y Misterio de Dios*. Madrid: Rialp, 1974.
- ———. *Le Prove dell'Esistenza di Dio [The proof for the existence of God]*. Brescia: La Scuola, 1990.
  (This is an excellent study with an analysis of the proofs of the existence of God by the first philosophers of history).
- Frankl, Víktor. *La Presencia Ignorada de Dios*. Barcelona: Herder, 1985.
- Garrigou-Lagrange, Reginald. *Dios: I. Su existencia, II. Su naturaleza*. 2 vols. Madrid: Palabra, 1980.
- Hillaire, Albert. *La Religión Demostrada*. Barcelona: Luis Gili, 1955.
- Löw, Reinhard. *Le nuove prove che Dio existe [The new proofs that God exists]*. Casale Monferrato: Piemme, 1996.
  (Löw has been the Director of the Institute of Investigation in Philosophy in Hannover, and is a specialist in the relationship between the natural sciences and philosophy. This is a current demonstration, from the scientist's point of view, of the traditional proofs, and of what the author calls the "new scientific proofs.")
- Royo Marín, Antonio. *Dios y su Obra*. Madrid: BAC, 1963.
- Simón, Jesús. *A Dios por la Ciencia*. Barcelona: Lumen, 1947.
- Venturini, Nello. *I Filosofi e Dio: Dizionario Storico-Critico*. Barzago: Marna, 2003.
- ———. *La Ricerca dell'Assoluto: Dio, c'è? Chi è?*. Rome: Coletti, 1998.
- Viejo-Felíu, Ricardo. *El Creador y su Creación*. Ponce, Puerto Rico: Universidad Católica de Santa María, 1952.

3.

THE STOLEN TRUTH ABOUT YOUR SOUL

We Have a Spiritual and Immortal Soul

May they never steal the truth about your soul...

Man is a rational creature composed of body and soul. Maybe someone will tell you that we do not have a soul and that we are simply a body with more evolved functions than other beings. It is also possible that you will hear that the brain's chemical and electrical functions (neurological functions) explain the reality of our thoughts. Also, in our days, there is more and more talk about a *science* that would deal with these ideas: *neurophilosophy*. This actually brings up a crucial topic, since the most essential things of our life—and the *other* life—depend on whether we have a soul or do not have one (since, if we do not have a spiritual and immortal soul, everything ends with this life).

We say that man is a being composed of body and soul (in which the soul is the *form* of the body). This teaching, known as the hylemorphic theory, taught by Aristotle, is entirely compatible with Biblical and Catholic teachings (theologians, Fathers of the Church, and the Magisterium). The Judeo-Christian tradition affirms that it is God who creates each soul and infuses it into this new human being (this moment is called *animation*).

All other interpretations reduce themselves to *monism* which denies the differences between the body and soul (*monos* means "one" in Greek), or else fall into a *dualism*, making the body and the soul two completely different substances, accidently united. The latter thinks that man is composed of two substances, which accidentally united, are merely related to one another. (We can attribute this position today above all to Descartes but fundamentally to Plato—who taught that the body is to the soul as the ship is to the pilot or the paintbrush is to the artist.)

Within monism different classes can be distinguished. There is a *spiritualist* monism that reduces man to his soul while his body is nothing more than something purely apparent. The Docetists taught this in the past and currently it has been revived by some New Age Gnostics (although they shouldn't really be believed when they speak about *spirit* or *spiritualism*, since many of them believe that the *spirit* is a species of matter, more subtle than the rest of matter, and therefore they are essentially base materialists). *Materialistic* monism (Gassendi, Hobbes), on the other hand, reduces all intellectual activity to sensible operations; we only know what we perceive through the senses. In our times this is spread by some scientists who deny the soul and reduce man to his body and his intellectual and volitive activity to brain functions. *Neutro* monism (Bertrand Russell, Spinoza) claims that human beings are neither spiritual nor material, but a third thing, a substance undifferentiated in itself and from which the spirit and the body are partial or relative aspects—phenomenon.

Let us see what we can demonstrate about the reality of the soul.

1. THE EXISTENCE OF THE SOUL

Deep down no serious thinker denies that we have a "soul;" the argument, in every case, revolves around the "nature" of the soul. I say that no serious thinker denies the existence of the soul if we understand the soul to be "a vital principle." In effect, our experience brings us to this affirmation: all of us are living beings, as is every plant and every animal. Vital principle means a "principle" which unites this one and entire reality[71] and from which its unity, vitality and, above all, its finality emanate. I am not going to go into this difficult point; I do not think anyone will argue against it. Basically all philosophers, whatever school they belong to, will accept that we are not just a conglomeration of organs, tissues and functions accidentally juxtaposed (like potatoes in a bag), but rather that our organs are perfectly connected among themselves; and this is the *central argument*, that they are perfectly united under the *direction* of the entire being that is "Me." (A group of men running after a ball does not form a team, in spite of being a group of intelligent human beings, unless there is a mastermind—their coach—who organizes and coordinates them so that they can play *as a team*. Even less can a group of organs, tissues, functions, etc. be expected to work for the perfection of the whole—for example in the first stages of embryonic development, so well-studied in our time,—*if there is no coordinating or unifying principle,* which philosophy calls the *soul*).

Up to this point, I would say that we agree. The term *soul* is used in a very general manner, and thus it can be said that plants and animals also have a soul or a vital principle that gives them life and permits them to act. Animals, plants, and minerals do not have a spiritual soul, but they do have a sensitive or vegetative or mineral soul. To prevent confusion, philosophy generally speaks of *substantial form*, avoiding the use of the word soul. The soul of non-human beings should not be confused with the "soul" attributed to them by some erroneous doctrines of the past and revived today by New Age.

---

[71] *Editor's Note:* "this one and entire reality" refers to the individual living being.

So, we live, feel, think, play, reason, love, choose, etc. All these operations spring from our being, therefore from a principle that gives our being life, the capacity to feel, to love and reason, to choose freely. This same principle gives us the capacity to grow, evolve, and perfect ourselves. All of the actions of our being are coordinated and ordered among themselves, and some sacrifice for the good of the whole, which is "Me". There is then, a vital principle that explains this being's perfect unity with well-defined ends; *I myself am this being.* This is my soul.

2. THE NATURE OF THE SOUL

I said that up to this point, all basically reasonable thinkers will agree. (Of course there are many that are not reasonable, even though they pride themselves of being such.) The problem begins to seriously arise when they try to define the *nature* of this principle. Is it something physical or corporal, something vegetative, or something spiritual?

Throughout the history of philosophy there have been many diverse theories about the soul, as we mentioned previously. Plato held that souls pre-existed before the *apparition* of our bodies and they are sent to us like prisoners in a jail,[72] but he also defended the immortality of the soul. Aristotle, on the other hand, contended that the soul is the substantial form of the body, and therefore its substantial unity. Plotinus maintained that it is an emanation from the One (the third, after Understanding and before the World); he identified the soul with a conscience. For the stoics, man's

---

[72] Cf. PLATO, quoted in ROGER VERNEAUX, *Textos de los Grandes Filósofos: Edad Antigua* (Barcelona: Herder, 1982), 46-48, editorial translation.

soul was part of the universal wind or fire that made up the soul of the world.

With all this said, one must wait until William of Ockham (1280-1349) who put into doubt for the first time the very reality of the soul and said that it is impossible to prove its existence, much less, its immortality. For Ockham this knowledge is only found in the realm of faith, not reason. Later, Descartes (1596-1650) goes back to dualism of body and soul; as G. Ryle baptized it as "the ghost in the machine."[73] This dualism becomes more radical: Descartes speaks of the substance that is thought and the substance that is extension. Beginning with him, a large part of the history of philosophy will accommodate variations of the theme of the Cartesian *cogito* and the ways to solve the mind-body relationship. For Englishman Hume, the pretended substantial reality of the soul is merely a fictitious construction. Kant, who was very influenced by Hume, held that "the self" cannot be thought of as an immortal "substantial soul"; in the best of cases it is a regulating idea of reason in the realm of unifying psychological activity and a postulate of practical reason (of morality). The current age will inherit this profound distrust for the subject, epitomized by *Psychology without a Soul* as Lange (1828-1875) entitled one of his most celebrated works.

What can we say? Even with the risk of opposing many of these "sacred cows" of philosophy, we can say that our reason brings us to understand that we not only have a soul but that it is also simple, spiritual and immortal. Now, demonstrating this is another story, which we will attempt to do.

---

[73] GILBERT RYLE, *The Concept of the Mind* (Chicago: University of Chicago Press, 2002).

a) *The soul is simple*

In its essence the soul is simple and indivisible, unlike material things that are composed and divisible. We can demonstrate this by analyzing the operations of the soul.[74]

Perception proves the simplicity of the soul. We have an *undivided perception* of material things and this cannot be explained by anything but the simplicity of the soul. If the soul were composed of parts, each one of these parts would perceive either the whole object or only one part of it. In the first case there would be as many complete perceptions as parts of the soul, and in the second case as many partial perceptions as parts of the soul, but never one undivided perception of the object.

Reflection proves the simplicity of the soul. The soul can return or "withdraw" from itself so as to know itself in its acts. But *that which is made of parts cannot know itself as a whole*, because the component parts are necessarily external one from the other. Supposing that one part could know itself, the others would be entirely extraneous. Only a simple substance is capable of retreat or return to itself, that is to say, to be lead back to itself through reflection.

Simplicity equals immateriality, and a simple and immaterial being can encompass various potencies or faculties (intellect and will), and produce multiple and diverse acts.

---

[74] Cf. REGIS JOLIVET, *Tratado de Filosofía: Psicología* (Buenos Aires: Carlos Lohlé, 1956), 586-587, editorial translation.

b) *The soul is spiritual*

We are corporeal beings; this is undeniable and it would be a waste of time detaining ourselves to prove it (even though some modern currents of thought speak of astral or ethereal bodies, in the end no one knows what they mean by it). Our senses prove corporeality. We are influenced by other bodies and their actions: we endure the heat of fire and the cold of ice, our wounds hurt us, we feel pleasure and displeasure according to the impressions foods, situations, and activities bear on our senses.

But there is something more important than corporeal experience: all this is lived by me as something which I am in reality. I am not only a body, but *I know that I am* and with this we begin to transcend the corporeal. "This knowledge that I possess of my own corporeal being is an intellectual fact, not sensible knowledge. The senses are not enough for the subject who experiences them to conceive of something universal—something beyond the individual—such as the fact of being a body. Man does need the senses to acquire this notion; and not only this notion, but also for all others, but the faculty that grasps them is not the senses but rather the understanding."[75] The same happens with our desiring (called "volition"): even when we want corporeal things, we do not only want things whose usefulness attracts us, but also goods that are of no use to us but are *good things in themselves and worthy of our love.* The animal loves and defends his territory and fights intruders; this forms part of his proper survival instinct (it needs this territory for its preservation and that of its species). However, it can neither conceive of the idea of a *homeland* nor, consequently, *love it.* The animal has an

---

[75] ANTONIO MILLÁN-PUELLES, *Léxico Filosófico* (Madrid: Rialp, 1984), 359, editorial translation.

instinctive love connected to its individual or specific *interest*; it does not love because of any idealism, tradition, or spiritual values. An animal will kill and allow himself to be killed to defend a few acres of jungle or desert, but it could never do that for the flag that represents it or for its anthem or for its poetry. The first love, which man also shares with animals, is material; the second, which is exclusive to man, is spiritual.

A trained parrot can repeat a line or a verse, and can enjoy the sound or the musicality of his sounds; but it cannot understand the concepts nor fall in love with the infinite worlds that they evoke. A rooster can be physically aroused in front of a female of his kind, but the leaves of an olive tree would never nostalgically remind him of the green earthy eyes of his hen, nor would a ravine next to his hen house evoke the memory of the deep, intense gaze of his hen. It is simply that neither the olive tree nor the ravine give off hormones by which the whole process of sexual arousal ordered towards the conservation of the species begins. The animal does not transcend these actions and reactions.

We are, therefore, body and spirit in substantial unity: the soul is the form of the body. From this it follows that the human soul is spirit. "Spiritual" describes every being that does not depend on the material, neither for its existence nor for its operations. That the soul is spiritual we can verify by its acts, just as the existence of God is proved by his works. It is an evident principle that a being's operations are always in conformity with his nature: a laborer is known by his work. Our soul produces acts that transcend the material (that is to say, they are spiritual), like thoughts, judgments and choices; therefore, our soul is spiritual.

We can see this by three classes of acts, eminently superior to any other act done by man: the acts of thinking (formulating ideas), of reasoning (inventing, advancing) and of freely desiring. These acts transcend the purely sensible, as we can see when comparing them to analogous acts of animals.

1. Man thinks, abstracts, and draws universal, general and absolute ideas from the material images supplied through the senses. He conceives intellectual and eternal truths. He knows things unperceived by the senses, purely spiritual objects like truth, goodness, beauty, justice and injustice. He knows how to distinguish causes and their effects, the substances and the accidents, etc. The animal sees, hears and knows how to find his way, recognizes his master, remembers the thing that hurt him, etc. But the animal does not have general ideas; he only knows that which his senses encounter; the concrete, the particular, and the material. He knows, for example, this tree or that flower, but he cannot elevate himself to the general idea of a tree or a flower. Therefore, the dog warms himself with pleasure by the fire, but he will not have the idea to light the fire or even to add a combustible object so it won't go out.

Furthermore, man knows moral good and evil: he enjoys doing good and feels guilty doing evil. The animal does not know any more than pleasurable good and sensible pain; it does not feel remorse. Both truth and moral good and evil can be known only by the intellect.

2. Man reasons, invents, progresses and speaks. Man analyzes, compares, judges his ideas, and from the principles and axioms that he knows, deduces consequences. He calculates; he is aware of things; he knows what he does, and why he does it. He discovers the laws and hidden forces of nature and knows how to use them for wonderful inventions. With his rational faculty, he discovers the sciences, the arts, the industries, and every day he discovers something admirable. An animal does not reason, calculate, nor is he

conscious of his actions; he is guided only by instinct. He will never learn writing, math, history, geography, science, art, not even the alphabet. He never invents nor makes any progress; birds construct their nests today as they did the day after being created.

Only man speaks: man possesses spoken and written words. Only man has the explicit and formal intention of communicating what he thinks. He captures the thoughts of others and says things that have happened in other times and that have no relation with his nature. An animal only shouts to show, sometimes in spite of himself, the pleasure or pain that he feels, but he will never have language because he does not think. The best taught parrot is no more than a repetitious machine; while, even the most ignorant savage can always express what he thinks.

3. Only man acts freely. He is free to choose between the different things that present themselves. When he does something, he says: "I could very well not do it." An animal is not free; blind instinct guides him and does not permit him to deliberate or choose. This is why he is not responsible for his actions; and, if punished after having done something improper, he will not repeat it because he remembers the pain caused by the punishment.

We call this faculty of freely acting the will. The will tends towards goods inaccessible to the senses and their appetites. It wants an infinite good, moral good, virtue, order, honor, science. Sometimes to attain these goods it will even come to sacrificing sensible goods, which are the only ones that would move the will if it were an organic faculty. So the will, enamored with spiritual goods and despising material objects, is a spiritual faculty that can only be found in a spirit.

The will is the absolute master of its operations; it determines whether it acts or not. The will is free. My conscience tells me when my body looks for pleasure, I can resist it. When my stomach feels hunger, I can choose not to satisfy it; furthermore, I can inflict upon my body punishments and austerities, in spite of the suffering of the senses. How can we have dominion and free will over our instinctive tendencies? If the intellect and the will had no proper acts, independent of the body, if our soul were not a spirit, this would be impossible.

Finally, man has a sense of the divine; he elevates himself toward God, his Creator, and adores him. He has the hope of a future life, and since this religious sentiment is exclusively his, the pagans defined man as a religious animal.

This is why, man, in spite of his physical inferiority, has dominion over the animals, tames them, domesticates them, makes them serve his need and pleasures, and orders them around as master, as he orders the entire creation. A child can drive a herd of oxen, each one, taken separately, a hundred times stronger than him. Where does this dominion come from? It is certainly not from his body, it comes from his intelligent soul, because it is spiritual, created in the image of God.

Man is the only being of creation that brings together in himself a corporeal and a spiritual nature, communicating with the material world through his senses and the spiritual world through his intelligence.

By all this one can understand why the renowned British scientist and neurologist Sir Francis Walshe (1885-1973, member of the Royal College of Physicians, pioneer in the description and analysis of the human reflections in physiological terms, editor of the journal *Brain*, scholar and lecturer about the function of the cerebral cortex in relation with movements and about the neural physiology in relation to the consciousness of pain, president of the Association of

Neurologists and of the Royal Society of Medicine, specialist of the philosophical problems of the mind-brain relationship), said: "I believe that we must return to the old concept of the spiritual soul: this integral part of the nature of man which is something immaterial, incorporeal, without which one is not a human person."[76]

It is so important to understand well this relationship between the body and soul that we should say that it is not our soul that behaves in a passive manner with respect to the body (in other words, that the body moves it, uses it because it needs it, and is served by it as an instrument), but rather that it is our body that has a certain passive attitude with respect to our soul. Consequently, it does not have to be united to our body for anything more than carrying out the particular operations of vegetative and sensitive life, which are not proper to the human spirit, even though they depend on it. It is moreover our body that needs our spirit in order to be able to live with the unique ways and manners of life that can exist in a body. The transcendence of the spiritual in human activity is so clear that man should not be spoken of as only a being composed of body and soul, but more properly spoken of as *a soul and its body*.[77]

c) The soul cannot be reduced nor explained by man's brain material alone.

One of the most popular myths spread by the press these days is that what believers call the soul can, in reality, be explained by brain activity. It would not be necessary to

---

[76] FRANCIS WALSHE, quoted in LORING, *To Save You*.

[77] This is the title of a valuable book by ABELARDO PITHOD, *El Alma y su Cuerpo* (Buenos Aires: Grupo Editor Latinamericano, 1994).

suppose a spiritual soul since all the activities we say the soul carries out are, in reality, brain activity, and therefore material. There are many scientists who think this and even speak of "neuroscience," "neurophilosophy," and "philosophy of the mind," disciplines followed by many of those who identify the brain with the human *mind* or the soul with the body (because that is the brain: a corporeal organ). What is true in this? Little to nothing.[78] In many cases, we do not even have a "scientific" treatment of the subject by those who are considered "great scientists" in the present world. For example, the Australian philosopher David Chalmers describes the problem in the following way: "The hard problem, in contrast, is the question of how physical processes in the brain give rise to subjective experience."[79] Also, Francis Crick, winner of the Nobel Prize for Physiology and Medicine, asks "how to explain mental events as being caused by the firing of large sets of neurons."[80] In both cases we have a deceptive presentation, because they are not asking what we believe they are asking. They have already answered: they both assume "mental events" or "consciousness," *are*

---

[78] This can be seen with respect to the valuable work of ALEJANDRO SERANI MERLO, "Dificultades en la Neurofilosofía: ¿Dónde Está el Problema en el Problema Mente-Cerebro?," *Persona y Bioética* 3:7-8 (July 1999).

Also: CARLOS MARMELADA, "Sobre el Origen de la Inteligencia Humana," *Grupo Ciencia, Razón y Fe de la Universidad de Navarra,* January 20, 2003, *www.unav.es/cryf/origeninteligencia.html* (accessed September 21, 2014);

MARÍA GUDIN, "Cerebro y Persona," *arvo.net,* October 4, 2009, *arvo.net/cerebro-humano/cerebro-y-persona/gmx-niv884-con17556.htm* (accessed September 21, 2014);

MARÍA GUDIN, "Cerebro y Afectividad," in *Colección Astrolabio Salud* (Pamplona: EUNSA, 2001).

[79] DAVID CHALMERS, "The Puzzle of Conscious Experience," *Scientific American* (December 1995): 81.

[80] FRANCIS CRICK AND CHRISTOF KOCH, "The Problem of Consciousness," *Scientific American* (September 1992): 111.

produced by the brain processes or—what is equivalent—by the discharge of neurons! Is there a place—in such arguments—to ask ourselves if mental phemonena are something spiritual? No one even wants to try proposing that.

Some scientists, although they solve the problem incorrectly, have had the honesty to recognize that there are some problems that appear to escape any materialist explanation. These problems are at least four: consciousness, intentionality, subjectivity, and mental causality.[81] As Serani Merlo explains it: [about *consciousness*] "what is difficult to understand for the current scientific focus would be: how can the shapeless grey and white matter that is in my cranium be conscious? *Intentionality* [...] is that property by which our mental states refer to something: how can relating to something be an intrinsic trait of the world? [...] *Subjectivity* [...] refers to the fact that *I can feel my pains and you cannot* [...] The fourth feature has to do with the popular conviction that our mental states have causal effects over the physical world and the difficulty derived from this fact, of linking these two types of realities. For example, I decide to lift my arm and behold my arm lifts. How can something so insubstantial and ethereal like a conscious mental state, have some impact on a physical object like the human body?"[82]

One could get excited thinking that the scientists who ask these questions will try to answer them. False hope. In most cases, they are limited to presenting the following thesis which belongs to Searle and which is, with certain variations, that of the majority of materialist scientists: "Mental

---

[81] For example: J. SEARLE, *The Rediscovery of the Mind* (Cambridge, Massachusetts: MIT Press, 1992).

[82] SERANI MERLO, "Dificultades en la Neurofilosofía": 231, editorial translation.

phenomena, all mental phenomena whether conscious or unconscious, visual or auditory, pains, tickles, itches, thoughts, indeed, all of our mental life, are caused by processes going on in the brain."[83] Or as he says elsewhere, "Conscious states are caused by neurobiological processes in the brain, and they are realized in the structure of the brain. To say this is analogous to saying that digestive processes are caused by chemical processes in the stomach and the rest of the digestive tract."[84] After saying something as serious as what we just described (so serious that it implies the denial of the spiritual soul), Searle does not consider it pertinent to make any remarks justifying the validity of his thesis; he considers it obvious. Other authors, like Chalmers, an Australian philosopher, admit that the problem is "difficult," but will not lift a finger to solve it. The closest they come to an explanation can be expressed in the words of F. Crick: "most neuroscientists now believe that…"[85], that is to say, using the argument of authority (which is to ask for an act of faith) that has the value as an opinion which has no proof at all ("they think that"). It is a considerable abuse to ask us to make an act of faith in their statement that the soul does not exist and that the brain is what thinks and loves and is conscious… and to not move one finger to prove it. There are many ways a person can lose his soul; but to forfeit the soul by having faith in Crick, Chalmers, Searle, or any other materialist scientist is one of the most stupid reasons. Probably the hell for materialists, those who have denied the

---

[83] JOHN SEARLE, *Minds, Brains, and Science* (Cambridge: Harvard University Press, 2003), 18.

[84] JOHN SEARLE, *Consciousness and Language* (Cambridge: Cambridge University Press, 2002), 48-49.

[85] CRICK and KOCH, "The Problem of Consciousness," 111.

existence of the spirit, has a special place for those fools who get there by believing other fools!

This is why it is important to know, as Serani Merlo says, that "the large part of the scientists and philosophers who assume, consciously or unconsciously, the materialist thesis, suppose that the force of the truth arises from the discoveries of contemporary science.

Then, anyone with a few years of reviewing neuro-scientific literature will be able to recognize that there is not experimental work, or any interpretation of experimental data, published in any serious scientific magazine, that allows one to claim in a clear, rigorous, and unmistakable way, that the electrochemical, biochemical or genetic molecular activity of the cerebral cortex cause the mental phenomenon in a total, proximate and sufficient way. In an analogous fashion mammary glands produce milk and the islets of Langerhans, insulin. For that same reason, no scientific evidence exists that permits assuring in an obvious indubitable, unmistakable, and experimentally verifiable way, that physical-corporeal matter, as science makes it known to us, is the cause of mental phenomenon. In fact, the authors, Crick and Koch[86], who so clearly accept that the discharges of neuronal groups cause mental phenomena, recognize that we have not yet arrived at discovering the exact correlation of mental phenomena."[87]

From here, the Jewish-German philosopher, Hans Jonas, holds that the materialist thesis confronts the absurd characters in their own domain.

In addition to having no evidence (which cannot be) that the brain produces mental states, we even have contrary evidence that it is the whole that acts because of the part and

---

[86] Cf. CRICK and KOCH, "The Problem of Consciousness," 115.

[87] SERANI MERLO, "Dificultades en la Neurofilosofia," editorial translation.

not the part because of the whole. For example, the lung does not breathe, but the animal breathes by means of the lung; therefore, it follows that the brain does not know, but man knows by means of the brain.[88] The soul, in thinking, is served by the brain as an instrument, like a window serves us by letting light enter; the window does not produce the light, but it is the condition for the light to come to us inside the room. From this, we should say that the brain *is the condition* for reasoning, but it is not the cause of reasoning or of the will. Loring cites the neurologist and neuro-surgeon, Wilder Penfield, from the University of Montreal, who dedicated his whole life to the study of the person and the human brain. He explains: "The brain is very much like a computer. However, the mind, the spirit, is something independent from the brain. The mind is a product of the brain. It depends on the brain but it is not the brain, it is not something physiological. No scientist has been able to demonstrate that the mind has a material explanation."[89]

Therefore, we should say that an extremely close relationship, which we still do not understand very well, certainly exists between the mind (soul) and the human brain (corporeal organ) and its study is in the infant stages. Research has to continue, but we should also recognize two things. *First*, the phenomenon of thought (and everything related with thought: consciousness, desires, intentionality, subjectivity, etc.) will never be explained by restricting it to the brain (chemical movements, electrical reactions, etc.). At most we can verify that *when* we think, or are conscious, or love, etc., *there are reactions in our brain*. And it couldn't be any other way, given that the brain is the *instrument* that serves our

---

[88] Cf. SERANI MERLO, "Dificultades en la Neurofilosofia."

[89] LORING, *To Save You*, 66.

soul, and all instruments change with use, but their effect transcends the instrument. For example, the paintbrush moves and oil paint is spread, marvelously combining the colors in a Van Gogh painting, but not even a fool would say that the brush is producing the wonder of a bunch of sunflowers or that it is trying to give us a "mental" message through the sterile forms and the selected colors, even though Van Gogh's genius without the brush would have been as powerless as someone without hands. *Second*, is that the majority of "scientists" who deny the spiritual soul and reduce everything to the mental phenomenon of the brain, are not working with scientific honesty, and usually fall into one of the following errors. Either, they begin, in fact, saying that all mental phenomena are physical phenomena (like Crick did), which is not a starting point; it should be the ending point. Or they make this statement and leave it undemonstrated or evade the question because of its difficulty (and even, instead of leaving it unresolved, they uphold it as if it were proven). Or they simply resort to saying that *the majority of scientists believe that things are this way*, which is not totally true, and even if this were true—even if *everyone believed this*—they forget that the function of science is not to ask us to make acts of faith—because the scientist is not God, nor does he come to the world revealing a supernatural mystery—but that the scientist should either demonstrate what he claims or recognize that is out of his field of study because he cannot prove it. Any attitude beside this would be antiscientific (and it is *precisely* this attitude that such characters take. This attitude has a name: *materialist prejudices*). In any case, a scientist that acts this way does not act scientifically, but behaves like a *founder of a false religion*, who demands faith without doing miracles to prove it—maybe this is what a branch of new science pretends to do. In that case, they would not only be selling you a theory in its infant stages, but "a theory which would need to have its diapers changed."

Keeping this in mind, the words of a true scientist can be understood. John Eccles, winner of the Nobel Prize for Medicine for his work on the brain, has accused materialistic science of *superstition* and has said that "materialism lacks a scientific base, and scientists who defend it are, in reality, believing in a superstition. It leads to a denial of liberty and moral values, since behavior would be the result of material stimuli. It denies love, which ends up being reduced to sexual instinct. This is why Popper said that Freud has been one of the characters who has done the most damage to humanity in the last century. Popper also confirmed that Freud's method is not scientific, after he worked many years ago in Vienna in a clinic where his method was applied. Materialism, if it is carried out to its consequences, denies the most important experiences of human life: 'our personal world' would be impossible."[90]

And also: "Cerebral activity permits us to carry out actions in an automatic way. But we can add a level of consciousness. For example, when I walk, 'I want' to go faster or slower. We can encompass almost anything in the consciousness: 'I want' to walk like Charlie Chaplain concentrating on every step and movement. [...] Monod called me 'animist;' I limit myself to calling him 'superstitious,' because he presents his materialism as if it were scientific, which is not true: it is a belief, and a belief of a superstitious type."[91]

---

[90] JOHN ECCLES, "Prologue," in MARIANO ARTIGAS, *Las Fronteras del Evolucionismo* (Madrid: Palabra, 1985), 171-177, editorial translation.

[91] Ibid.

"The phenomena of the material world are necessary but not sufficient causes for the conscious experiences and for my 'I' in so far as it is subject to conscious experiences. There are important arguments that lead to the religious concept of the soul and its special creation by God. I believe that in my existence there is a fundamental mystery which transcends all biological explanation of the development of my body (including the brain), with its genetic heritage and evolvable origin; and that if this is so, I have to believe the same about each and every one of the other human beings."[92]

Maybe it would be enough to remember a story that Hillaire tells: a positivist was having trouble proving that the soul was physical like the body and a wise man replied: "How much genius have you wasted, Sir, to prove that you are a beast!... As this deals with a personal act we confidently believe in your words..."[93]

d) The soul is immortal

If we want to present a summary of the arguments traditionally used to prove the immortality of the soul, we must cite the following:[94]

a) By its own nature: a being is naturally immortal when it is incorruptible and can live and work independently of another. So, the soul is incorruptible because it is simple and indivisible. It can live and work independently from the body

---

[92] Ibid.

Cf. JOHN ECCLES, *The Wonder of Being Human* (New York: The Free Press, 1984).

[93] HILLAIRE, *La Religión Demostrada*, editorial translation.

[94] They can be seen more fully developed in the already cited work of ALBERT HILLAIRE, *La Religión Demostrada*, in speaking of the human soul.

because it is a spirit. Therefore, it is immortal by nature. A spirit cannot die. Our soul is incorruptible because it does not possess in itself any principle of disintegration or death. This argument is properly metaphysical.

b) The desires and aspirations of the soul also show the immortality of the soul. (This is actually more of an argument of suitability and supposes the acceptance of some truths it contains.) The natural and irresistible desire that we have for perfect happiness and for life without end proves the immortality of the soul. (All men who search their hearts will find in them a deep desire for happiness; this is not an effect of the imagination, we have not given it to ourselves, and it is not in our power to dismiss it. This is not an individual thing, since all men in all places and conditions have experienced this and experience it daily. Therefore, this burning desire springs from the depths of our being and becomes part of man.) This desire cannot be satisfied in the present life and therefore, must be satisfied in the future life. If it is not so, God, the author of our nature, has teased us, giving us aspirations and desires that are always defrauded, never satisfied. This cannot be. Is it possible that God has put in us such an ardent desire that we cannot satisfy? Has he created us for happiness and made it impossible for us to gain it? Obviously not. In this case God would not be the God of truth. God does not deceive the insect's instinct, would he deceive the desire he has infused in our soul? It is inevitable that man will reach perfect happiness sooner or later, if through his own fault he does not oppose it. But this perfect happiness cannot be found on earth: nothing in this life can satisfy our desires; all the finite goods cannot fill the void in our hearts; knowledge, fortune, honor, all types of satisfaction, fall into it as if into an unending abyss. What a strange thing that animals, who have no idea about any happiness superior to sensible goods, are happy with their luck. And man, only man, seeks happiness in vain; this powerful need is carried in the soul. He is never happy, because he desires a complete and endless bliss. Given that he is not happy in this world, happiness will necessarily be found in future life. This reasoning also holds true for our intellectual ambitions. Man thirsts for truth and science, he wants to know everything, and he can never satisfy his desire to know. He has been created, then, to find in God all truth and all knowledge. Just as the body tends towards the earth, the soul tends towards God and towards immortality.

c) The immortality of the soul is demanded by God's wisdom: if God is God, consequently he is the wise and just legislator, rewarding and punishing according to the requirements of the merits and faults of each man. But in the present life we do not see the consequences of the law of God; therefore, it is necessary that it exist in the future life or else we would be led to the false conclusion that God is a legislator without wisdom. The rewards and punishments cannot be limited to remorse or peace of conscience, since the wicked drown out remorse, and peace of conscience is a little thing compared to the sufferings and struggles that virtue requires.

The justice of God is not found in public disregard nor the estimation of men, since we too often see that the greatest offenders are those who enjoy the esteem of men while the just are mocked.

It is not in human justice because justice cannot know thoughts and desires, the sources of evil. There is no reward for virtue, and not all crimes can be discovered since they could be cleverly hoaxed, or blackmailed or intimidated by fear Yes, sometimes the laws of men are avenged and the laws of God are not.

Therefore, it follows that the consequences of the law of God cannot be found anywhere but in the punishments and rewards that await us after death.

This is why J. J. Rousseau himself said: "Had I no other proof of the immaterial nature of the soul, the triumph of the wicked and the oppression of the righteous in this world would be enough to convince me. I should seek to resolve so appalling a discord in the universal harmony. I should say to myself, 'All is not over with life, everything finds its place at death.'"[95] Delille rightly wrote:[96]

---

[95] JEAN-JACQUES ROUSSEAU, *Emile, Or, On Education,* trans. Barbara Foxley (New York: E. P. Dutton and Co., 1911).

[96] W. H. DE PUY, ed., "Jacques Delille," in vol. VI of *The University of Literature* (New York: J. S. Barcus & Co., 1896).

O ye who seize the thunders of
Olympus,
Of law eternal overthrow the altars,
Ye cowards, of the earth the base
oppressors
Tremble! ye are immortal!
O ye who suffer, victims of
oppression
O'er whom God watches with an
eye paternal,
To stranger shores the pilgrims of a
moment.
Rejoice! ye are immortal!

Los que volcáis,
Haciendo a Dios la guerra,
Las aras de las leyes eternales,
Malvados opresores de la
tierra,
¡Temblad! ¡Sois inmortales!
Los que gemís desdichas
pasajeras,
Que vela Dios con ojos
paternales,
Peregrinos de un día a otras
riberas,
¡Calmad vuestro dolor!
¡Sois inmortales!

d) While it is an argument of inferior value to the previous arguments, the acceptance of this truth by all peoples of the world also manifests the immortality of the soul. Ancient and modern history testifies to the fact that all nations in the entire world have acknowledged the immortality of the soul, as proved by the worship of the dead, the religious respect for the ashes of ancestors and the monuments that have been erected over sepulchers.

This constant and universal belief cannot come about except by acknowledging the necessity of future life, or through primitive revelation, made by God to our first parents and transmitted by them to their descendants. This witness, whether from reason or revelation, cannot be anything but the expression of the truth. So, the belief of the peoples is another proof of the immortality of the soul. According to Cicero, when all men share a natural conviction, it is necessarily true. Some modern materialists protest in vain against this axiom of common sense.

But we will try to go deeper into the metaphysical reasons that demonstrate the immortality of the soul.

It is a fact that man dies.[97] Our life is affected by time; in every moment we see the footsteps that time leaves and the moment will come when our material life completely ends. Experience only goes this far; it tells us that at the moment we call death, sensible and vegetative life really come to an end in the human individual, but it goes no further and does not demonstrate that the totality of his being is extinguished with death. If man were reduced to pure matter, we could draw this conclusion, but we have already seen that this is not true. Experience, therefore, does not speak of man's *"non-immortality,"* but of the *mortality* of man's possession of what is material. It is good to establish this, in order to avoid the customary inaccuracies and invasions in this field by those who address these ideas without scientific or philosophical rigor. Experience does not confirm man's total extinction at death, but only the disintegration of his body, since experience cannot go any further than that which is directly able to be experienced. That which is immaterial is not the object of immediate experience; therefore, it cannot be judged based on pure experience. Moreover, it can be said that the sciences which pride themselves on being *experimental* sciences do not have authority to speak about these subjects—just as a blind man cannot express his opinion about colors, nor a deaf man be the judge of a music contest.

We have already said that the soul is simple and spiritual. From this it follows that it is immortal. If the substantial form of the human body—the soul—were only material (this would be proved if the soul were only the origin of sensible and vegetative activity), death would undeniably consist in the extinction of the substantial form of our being since it

---

[97] For this I will take liberty in following the main points explained by ANTONIO MILLÁN-PUELLES, *Léxico Filosófico.*

would not remain if the body that possessed it were not alive. We have already seen that the substantial form of the human body is something more than the origin of our sensible and vegetative actions; it is the source of the particular operations of the intellect and will.

Certainly, it is indispensable that the soul animate the matter so that man may exist and so that the activities of the potencies of his intellect and will may be exercised. But it should not be concluded that these activities can only be accomplished by the spirit when it is united to the matter. The soul has to be united with the body so that man (body and soul) might live and perform his operations, but this union is not required for the spirit to exist in itself or for it to perform its own operations, because "a spirit not united with matter is not missing anything essential. Matter is not any physical part of it or of any of its aspects. The spirit is not matter in any way, although it can inform or animate it and it is necessary for the being and working of man."[98]

"Accordingly, the fact that man dies does not mean that his spirit is also extinguished. Death is the corruption of the human body, but the spirit cannot become corrupted because it does not have parts. It could, nevertheless, extinguish itself if it in some essential way depended on the body; that is to say, if matter was necessary for it to be what it is. But neither is this the case, since it is not material. In fact, when it is united with the matter—as is precisely the case with man—the spirit continues to be immaterial. And we cannot say that in man it is under the 'influence'—if this word is taken in its strictest meaning—of the matter that it animates or vivifies. Insofar as it is a substantial form—as I have already explained—the spirit behaves in an active, not passive way

---

[98] MILLÁN-PUELLES, *Léxico Filosófico*, 366, editorial translation.

with respect to matter. Thus, to speak of an influence of matter on the spirit, the meaning given to 'influence' would have to be that of pure and simple conditioning, which, as has already been clarified, only happens in an extrinsic and indirect manner. That being said, we conclude that this conditioning is necessary only so that the spirit may function in its state of union with matter; however, this state is not a necessity required by the nature of the spirit itself. Consequently, the separation of the spirit with respect to the human body is the death of the body, or more aptly said, that of man. Man dies when he is left without the spirit that enlivens or animates him not only with sensitive or vegetative life but also with another life, which is evidently superior because of its immaterial nature."[99]

Although it is not what principally interests us here, we can add something more: "although by being incorruptible it is immortal, the spirit does not continue living by itself alone. Without the cooperation of God, no finite being would remain in being. Consequently, although the death of man does not in any way imply the extinction of the spirit; neither can it remain in being in virtue of a kind of existential inertia, as if its continuing to be were not due to God. Even if it could have this type of inertia, the spirit would have it as something conferred onto it by God at its implantation in being, which he would still definitively owe to God and not to himself. In no way can it be that the permanence of life of the spirit is something that it imposes, as a necessity, on the being of God."[100] Here I will not enter into another controversial issue argued by theologians, namely whether the substantial unity of the body and soul (that is the proper mode of man's

---

[99] MILLÁN-PUELLES, *Léxico Filosófico*, 367, editorial translation.
[100] Ibid.

existence), does not create a certain unnatural state of the *separated soul* (as occurs at death), and if this, at the same time, does not create a type of a *necessity* for the resurrection. We will not enter into this argument, given that the resurrection of the human body is a dogma of the Christian faith; and we do not wish to detain ourselves in the dogmas of faith but to treat, rather, the philosophical questions that are doubted or denied by the false science of our times.

* * *

Those who deny that human beings have a soul deserve, with every reason, to be called "*soul-less*" and sooner or later they will act as such. From the denial of the soul to the point of "*soul-lessness*" (which, as the dictionary indicates, is the proper term designating inhumanity and perversity) there is not only just one step, but a very short step. Alonso Palencia could give us the title of his fable *Batalla campal de los perros y los lobos* (Pitched Battle between Dogs and Wolves) to properly denominate the world created by those who deny the soul.

One author would suggest that the best way to make them understand that the soul really exists is *to break theirs*; a very effective method, although as Christians we cannot recommend it.

For Further Reading

- Aquinas, St. Thomas. *Commentary on Aristotle's 'De Anima'*. New Haven, Connecticut: Yale University Press, 1999.

Available in Other Languages

- Biot, René. *El Cuerpo y el Alma*. Buenos Aires: Desclée de Brouwer, 1952.
- Büchner, Franz. *Cuerpo y Espíritu en la Medicina Actual*. Madrid: Rialp, 1969.
- Frankl, Víktor. *Homo Patiens*. Buenos Aires: Plantín, 1955.
- ————. *La Idea Psicológica del Hombre*. Madrid: Rialp, 1986.
- Gudin, María. "Cerebro y Persona." *arvo.net,* October 4, 2009. *arvo.net/cerebro-humano/cerebro-y-persona/gmx-niv884-con17556.htm* (accessed September 21, 2014).
- ————. "Cerebro y Afectividad." In *Colección Astrolabio Salud*. Pamplona: EUNSA, 2001.
- Jolivet, Regis. *Tratado de Filosofía: Psicología*. Buenos Aires: Carlos Lohlé, 1956.
- Marín Negueruela, Nicolás. *Dios y el Hombre*. Barcelona: Tipografía Católica Casals, 1936.
- Marmelada, Carlos. "Sobre el origen de la inteligencia humana." *Grupo Ciencia, Razón y Fe de la Universidad de Navarra,* January 20, 2003. *www.unav.es/cryf/origeninteligencia.html* (accessed September 21, 2014).
- Millán-Puelles, Antonio. *Léxico Filosófico*. Madrid: Rialp, 1984.
- Pithod, Abelardo. *El Alma y su Cuerpo*. Buenos Aires: Grupo Editor Latinamericano, 1994.
- Pius XII. "Discursos acerca de ética y psiquiatría." In López Medrano, Carlos, et al. *Pío XII y las Ciencias Médicas*. Buenos Aires: Guadalupe, 1961.
- Rego, Francisco. *La Relación del Alma con el Cuerpo*. Buenos Aires: Gladius, 2001.
- Royo Marín, Antonio. *Teología de la Salvación*, Madrid: BAC, 1965.
- Serani Merlo, Alejandro. "Dificultades en la Neurofilosofía: ¿Dónde Está el Problema en el Problema Mente-Cerebro?" *Persona y*

Bioética 3:7-8 (July 1999). Electronic edition on *arvo.net/cerebro-humano/donde-esta-el-problema-mente-y-cerebro/gmx-niv884-con9968.htm.*

- Velasco Suárez, Carlos. *Psiquiatría y Persona.* Buenos Aires: Educa, 2003.
- Wojtyla, Karol. *El Hombre y su Destino.* Madrid: Palabra, 1998.
- ———. *Mi Visión del Hombre.* Madrid: Palabra, 1997.

4.

THE STOLEN
TRUTH ABOUT
RELIGION

Religion is Something Intrinsic to Every Human Being

When someone tells you that religion is an invention of man or a cultural product, you can be sure of two things: the first is that they want to steal your religion from you, and the second is that they have just laid in your heart the first foundations of a *new* religion. They ask you not to believe in the Church or in God... and to do this you *should* believe in *them*. They do not ask you for a rational or a scientific act; they really ask you for an act of (human) faith in a person who is not credible: a thief of the truth.

It seems to me that the example of the American Protestant theologian Harvey G. Cox, is very enlightening. During the sixties, he wrote a book called *The Secular City*[101] (a bestseller in its time) in which he held that the process of secularization and the progressive decrease of religion in contemporary man was something already completely evident. Among other things, it included the loss of society's interest in any directly supernatural religious aspect, like the ideas related to eschatology, angels and devils, and healings and miracles. Therefore, Cox proposed in his book that instead of fighting against secularization (an enterprise he qualified as impossible and childish), the churches should start to see their new role not as religion but as a predominantly social commitment. It is not strange that Cox, together with others like Vahanian, Juan Luis Segundo, etc., have become known as *theologians of the "death of God."* Cox's book dreadfully influenced those thinkers who are always searching for novelties, causing the loss of faith, abandonment of the priesthood and religious life, politicization of religion and even the spilling of blood on the part of those who understood such a "social commitment" to include "a commitment with an armed subversion." As if

---

[101] Cf. HARVEY COX, *The Secular City* (New York: Macmillan, 1965).

nothing had happened, and with the same irresponsibility of thirty years prior, in the mid-nineties Cox proclaimed the arrival of a civilization without religion. He published another book entitled *Fire from Heaven*[102] in which he affirmed that all he had taught in *The Secular City* was erroneous predictions. In place of a civilization without God, what we have now is a civilization choked with religiosity. Now he considered, "it had become obvious that instead of the 'death of God' some theologians pronounced not many years ago, or the waning of religion that sociologists had extrapolated, something quite different has taken place."[103] We are not going to use his conclusions as sure fact, since you can't teach an old dog new tricks: now as before Cox continues to incorrectly analyze religiosity. (Before he was enthusiastic about an atheistic society, now he is delighted by a society filled with religiosity, which in reality is part of an outbreak of a sentimental religiosity strongly imbued with the New Age spirit). But the example demonstrates the superficiality of the diagnosis of theologians who depart from sound doctrine.

Those in our classrooms who speak inconsiderately against religion and attribute it to human invention are below Cox's academic level, and most of the time, they end up letting themselves be carried away by fads... like Cox.

Instead of accepting these dangerous teachings, it is better to ask ourselves, *why are we religious? Why do all people have their religion, be it true or false?* Religion, which is to say, the *religious act*, is one of the most profound phenomena of our nature (some have even wanted to see it as proof of the existence of God; and in fact, it is not an imprudent method, although it

---

[102] Cf. HARVEY COX, *Fire From Heaven* (Cambridge, Massachusetts: Da Capo Press, 2001).

[103] COX, *Fire From Heaven,* xvi.

does not have the precision of the proofs that we have already seen). Chesterton said in *The Everlasting Man*: "Nature may not have the name of Isis; Isis may not be really looking for Osiris. But it is true that Nature is really looking for something; Nature is always looking for the supernatural."[104] Elsewhere he added "The crux and crisis is that man found it natural to worship; even natural to worship unnatural things. The posture of the idol might be stiff and strange, but the gesture of the worshipper was generous and beautiful. He not only felt freer when he bent; he actually felt taller when he bowed. Henceforth anything that took away the gesture of worship would stunt and even maim him forever. Henceforth being merely secular would be a servitude and an inhibition. If man cannot pray he is gagged; if he cannot kneel he is in irons. We therefore feel throughout the whole of paganism a curious double feeling of trust and distrust. When the man makes the gesture of salutation and of sacrifice, when he pours out the libation or lifts up the sword, he knows he is doing a worthy and a virile thing. He knows he is doing one of the things for which a man was made."[105]

1. THE STEPS OF A CATHOLIC DEMONSTRATION

Our topic here is the reality of the *religious act* or *phenomenon*, not proving the Catholic Church's authenticity or divine origin. The proof of the Church's divine origin (that it is founded by God) pertains to a discipline called *Catholic apologetics,* or also *fundamental theology*. In any case, in order to see the theme in its totality, I would like to present here the steps by which this demonstration—if it can be called that—

---

[104] G.K. CHESTERTON, *The Everlasting Man* (San Francisco: Ignatius Press, 1993), 129.

[105] CHESTERTON, *The Everlasting Man*, 112.

is given. There are fundamentally three: the demonstration of spirituality, Christianity and Catholicity.

a) First stage: spirituality

The first moment consists in demonstrating: the existence of God and his attributes, man and his spirituality (that is to say, that man has a spiritual, free and immortal soul), and religion (the religious act and the necessity—for man—to practice religious worship). This part must also include the refutation of contrary errors: atheism, pantheism, agnosticism and determinism.

We have already taken this step in the chapters dedicated specifically to showing the existence of God and the soul. In this chapter, we will analyze the reality of religion. Here we arrive at the purpose of the book that you have in your hands. But he who wants to demonstrate the authenticity of Catholicism should then cover two more stages, which I will continue to explain.

b) Second stage: Christianity

Once the existence of God, the spirituality of man and the necessity of religion are demonstrated, one must verify whether there is revealed religion (this no longer refers to natural religion) and which is the true religion.

First, the possibility of the revelation of supernatural mysteries, or that God speaks to man about himself, has to be proven. Next, we must analyze the *criteria* through which we can know with certainty that these mysteries are revealed by God and through which we will also be able to discern between true or false religion. As will be demonstrated in this step, there are two criteria: *miracle properly speaking* and *prophecy properly speaking.*

Once made, this step can continue along two different paths. The first—more difficult because of the vast work it requires—is to analyze all the religions which claim to be revealed to see whether or not in each religion the criteria of revelation (what is properly miracle and prophecy) are true and also (which would have been done previously) to verify that their dogmatic and moral teachings contain nothing contrary to the principles of reason and natural law (I say nothing *contrary,* not nothing *superior*). Since if a teaching contradicts the principles of reason (going against the principle of non-contradiction or any other principles) or the natural law (the commandments of natural law, which are *divine,* as we will see later), clearly, it cannot be true, since God is as much the author of supernatural order as of natural order and there cannot be a double truth but only one. (This goes against some philosophers who taught that something could be true for faith and false for philosophy—a theory called *the double truth*). The other path consists in first analyzing Christianity and whether the aforementioned criteria are confirmed in it (with the conclusion that it is of divine origin), limiting ourselves to consider the principal religions that claim to be revealed (although we do not need to study them all, nor with as much attention as we should give to Christianity, since there cannot be two religions *that teach contrary things and are both true*—the principle of non-contradiction would fall). It is this second path that is usually followed, and with every right, since it is in the womb of Christianity that this apologetic discipline was born.

In order to make this study, you must first of all authentically demonstrate the *historicity of Christianity* (that is to say, the historic value of its sources, particularly the Gospels) to determine whether or not what they testify to about Christ and the beginning of Christianity can be accepted as historically true.

Once determined, its historicity proceeds to demonstrate the *legation of Christ* (that Christ is the revealer of divine mysteries) and Christ's divine authority applying the criteria of miracle and prophecy. The fruit of this study is the proof of the absolute credibility of the witness that Christ gives about himself, about the divine mysteries, and about his works. (Also, his divinity will be demonstrated, if *after this process* you can demonstrate that in Christ's trustworthy testimony his claim that *he is God* is also found).

This part must be completed with the study of the principal errors like rationalism and indifferentism. Many studies have carried out this passionate intellectual itinerary; one of the best is that of Leoncio de Grandmaison.

c) Third stage: Catholicism

The third step is to show that Christ founded a Church and to investigate which Church he founded. The investigation can follow three methods:

The first is called the *historical way*. It proceeds by first proving Christ's divine mission, and then it shows that Christ has entrusted the continuation of his redeeming work to a religious society that is the Catholic Church. This method obliges us to go back to the past. Although it is dry, it is consistent and sure, and follows three steps:

1. First, it shows that Jesus Christ intended to found a Church: this is manifested by the promise to build the Church (Mt 16:18); the choosing, instructing and missioning of the Twelve Apostles (Mk 3:13-19, Lk 6:12-17); the "new

covenant" established at the Last Supper (Mt 26:28 and parallels), etc.

2. Then, it shows that Jesus Christ effectively founded a Church and gave it a determined composition and structure. He founded it on the apostles: sending them to preach (Mk 3:14, Lk 9:2, etc.) with the authority to lead all men in his name and to administer the sacraments (Mk 16:16), particularly Baptism, the Eucharist and the forgiveness of sins. Furthermore, he promised and actually gave to just one apostle, Simon Peter, the supreme authority to govern the Universal Church (cf. Mt 16, Jn 21).

3. Finally, it shows that Jesus Christ instituted this Church to endure until the end of the world in the hierarchical form that he gave it in apostolic times. This is established in that it can be clearly seen that he ordained the apostles to have perpetual successors in the triple office of teaching, sanctifying and governing. This is inferred from the promises of Christ about His Church: *"the gates of hell shall not prevail against it"* (Mt 16), the parables of the wheat and the weeds (Mt 13:39), and the commissioning of Peter to confirm his brothers in the future (Lk 22:31). This succession is verified in the bishops, successors of the apostles, and in the Pope, the successor of Peter the Apostle.

The second method is by *way of the marks*, which consists in analyzing the will of Christ and seeing what characteristics (marks or notes) he wanted the Church he founded to have. These marks are four:

the unity in rule of faith and communion;

the sanctity of principles, of members and of means of sanctification;

catholicity or universality of mission, her permanent and simultaneous diffusion across the globe, her preaching to all classes of people and races,

finally, apostolicity, which is to say, the continuity of the apostolic mission (constant successors of the apostles) until the end of the world.

After analyzing the four marks and investigating the different "pretenders" who claim the title of the *church founded by Jesus Christ*, it can be seen that the only one that possesses the four marks in their fullness is the Catholic Church.

The third way is called by some the *way of transcendence* and by others the *empirical or analytical way*. This method begins by looking at the work of the Church, her activity and her action, as it can be clearly seen by all men. The key point of this method is the demonstration that in the historical reality of the Church the *immediate intervention of God* can be seen. In the end, this method is based on the miracle, present in the life of the Church today, more precisely, on: (1) the amazing expansion of the Church in spite of the difficulties, persecutions, and obstacles; (2) the miraculous Catholic unity; (3) the unfailing stability; and (4) the notable holiness and fecundity of the saints.

Clearly, the detailed explanation of any of these ways supposes a development that exceeds the scope of this short book. Therefore, I suggest reading some of the classic studies of Catholic apologetics cited in the final bibliography.

2. THE UNIVERSALITY OF THE RELIGIOUS ACT[106]

We pause here, then, only in the first moment, concretely, in the analysis of religious phenomenon.

Throughout the nineteenth and twentieth centuries, with the advent of atheist ideologies, many philosophers wanted to find a purely natural explanation for religion; however, there is something they could not avoid: the universality of the religious act.

The religious act is found in all peoples. This constant and universal religiosity is based in the moral necessity of religion. Any other way, it would be neither *constant* nor *universal*, as happens with other practices that were unknown in some towns but prevailing in others and those that later disappeared, for example, the system of *closed castes* common among people from India and that of *open castes* among the Egyptians, which are both unknown among the Greeks and Romans.

The religiosity of the *Hebrew people* is known, evidenced, by its law, temple, sacrifices, synagogues, priesthood, Sabbath, tithes, and offerings of the first fruits and circumcision. That of the *Christian people* is known by its admirable dogma, morality and worship. The *Muslim people* worship Allah and have their mosques, santons, prayer, festival days, and Ramadan. All the other nations we can divide into *prehistoric* and *historic*.

In the *prehistoric* peoples, we see certain indications of their religiosity in the *megalithic monuments, tombs, amulets* and *cranial*

---

[106] All these testimonies can be read in NICOLÁS MARÍN NEGUERUELA, *Lecciones de Apologética* (Barcelona: Tipografía Católica Casals, 1944), 19-21, §§15-16.

121

table stands (bones separated from the skull, perforated in their center and arranged near the skeleton).

The *historic* peoples, whether *civilized, primitive* or *savage*, have all practiced religion, professing certain *dogmas, precepts* and *rites.*

Among their *dogmas* we can emphasize: *(a)* Faith in a God superior to man, who cares for him and can help or hurt him, not only in this life, but in the future life. God has been called many different names such as: *Heaven* or *Eminent Emperor* by the Chinese, *Brahma* by the Indians, *Mazda* or *Ormuz* by the Iranians, *Elohim* by the Semites, *Nuter* by the Egyptians, *Zeus* by the Greeks, *Jupiter* by the Romans, *Huitzilopochtli* by the Aztecs, and *Great Spirit* by other indigenous. *(b)* This God is judge of all men. He rewards the good and punishes the bad with *very long or eternal* punishments. Some peoples place other gods, demi-gods and guardian spirits under the authority of the Supreme God.

In respect to their *morality*, we can confirm that all nations demand: *(a) justice* for all; *(b) piety* towards the gods and parents, and *(c) sacrifices* to adore and appease the Supreme God. These sacrifices generally are bloody; sometimes, primarily among the *Semites* and *Americans,* the victim is another person, preferably a child, virgin or prisoner.

Lastly, all the nations have had a *cult* in which they prescribed special formulas or rites in order to give honor to the gods and to receive their benefits. The success of the petition depended on their scrupulous observance. At the end of the nineteenth century, some unprepared or badly educated travelers spoke of the existence of savage peoples that lacked religious ideas, such as Australians, Laplanders, Brazilian Indians or Samoan islanders. Less than fifty years later, based on ethnological studies we can affirm with Schmidt: "In modern ethnology the category *atheistic peoples* has disappeared. The great multitude of peoples that had previously been categorized as such had been reduced to only one: the *kubus* of Sumatra, who were later also eliminated through the observations of von Dongen and Schebesta. The latest attempt to discover *men without God*, recently made by W. Tessmann among the Indians of Ucayali, has also been rejected by ethnological criticism."[107] We should say in passing that even if we were to find some truly atheistic nations or tribes it would not be evidence against the phenomena of the moral universality of the religious act, since it would still deal with isolated cases and exceptions, as the argument about the very existence of such people shows.

Cicero, Plutarch, Seneca, and Maximus of Tyre among the ancients, and Quatrefages and Schneider among the scholars of the twentieth century, could all be asked to give testimony to the idea of universal religiosity. We can content ourselves with just a few assertions. Lactantius said, "religion [...] alone separates us from the brutes".[108] Jean Jacques Rousseau stated, "We should demonstrate to the former [Bayle] that no State has ever been founded without a religious basis".[109] Quatrefages said, "The fact of the universality of religion is so manifest that the most eminent anthropologists do not hesitate to accept religiosity as one of the attributes of the human kingdom."[110] The same eminent wise man asks, "What

---

[107] WILHELM SCHMIDT, *Ursprung und Werden der Religion* (Vienna: 1930), 22, cited in NEGUERUELA, *Lecciones de Apologética*, §§15, 20, editorial translation.

[108] WILLIAM FLETCHER, trans., "Chapter XXXVII: Of Socrates and his contradiction," in vol. II of *The Works of Lactantius* (Edinburgh: T. & T. Clark, 1871), 120.

[109] JEAN-JACQUES ROUSSEAU, *On the Social Contract* (Mineola, New York: Dover Publications, Inc., 2003), 92, book IV, ch. 8.

[110] JEAN LOUIS ARMAND DE QUATREFAGES DE BREAU, *Introduction à l'Étude des Races Humaines,* cited in NEGUERUELA, *Lecciones de Apologética*, §16, editorial translation.

is man? [...] an organized being [...] endowed with morality and religiosity."[111]

Byron Jevons ventures to affirm, "that there never was a time in the history of man when he was without religion [...] is a proposition the falsity of which some writers have endeavoured to demonstrate by producing savage peoples alleged to have no religious ideas whatever. This point we have no intention of discussing, because, as every anthropologist knows, it has now gone to the limbo of dead controversies. Writers approaching the subject from such different points of view as Professor Tylor, Max Müller, Ratzel, de Quatrefages, Tiele, Waitz, Gerland, Peschel, all agree that there are no races, however rude, which are destitute of all idea of religion."[112]

Dutchman C. P. Tiele pointed out that: "The statement that there are nations or tribes which possess no religion, rests either on inaccurate observation, or on a confusion of ideas. [...] It is legitimate, therefore, to call religion in its most general sense a universal phenomenon of humanity."[113] We can close these testimonies with these trustworthy words from Renan: "But nothing can be falser than the dream of certain persons, who, seeking to conceive a perfect humanity, conceive it lacking religion. [...] let us suppose a planet inhabited by a humanity whose intellectual, moral, and physical power is double that of earthly humanity; that humanity would be at least twice as religious as ours. [...] Let

---

[111] EDWARDS PARK and SAMUEL TAYLOR, ed., vol. XIX of *Bibliotheca Sacra and Biblical Repository* (London: Trubner & Co., Paternoster Row, 1862), 611.

[112] FRANK BYRON JEVONS, *An Introduction to the History of Religion* (New York: Macmillan & Co. Limited, 1896), 7.

[113] CORNELIS PETRUS TIELE, *Outlines of the History of Religion to the Spread of the Universal Religions,* 2nd ed., trans. J. Estlin Carpenter (London: Trübner & Co., 1880), 6.

us suppose a humanity ten times stronger than ours; that humanity would be infinitely more religious. [...] Progress, then, will have as its effect the augmentation of religion, not its destruction or diminution."[114]

Therefore, in spite of the passage of time, the words of Eötvös to his fellow Hungarians still apply; "For all the progress that science can make, it will never achieve the elimination of human weakness or its consciousness, with its reasoning. God created our species in such a way that we need support; we need something to bow before. Man will not cease searching for a superior Being, before whom he kneels; and, if the altars of the divinity were demolished, over their ruins they will raise up the thrones of the tyrants."[115] Finally, Russian writer Leo Tolstoy wrote, "If the thought that the conceptions you have about God are not right crosses your mind, or maybe that God does not even exist, do not despair. All of us can pass through such a difficult moment. Do not believe that what causes your incredulity is the fact that God does not exist."[116]

[114] ERNEST RENAN, *The Apostles,* trans. William G. Hutchison (London: Watts & Co., 1905), 136.

[115] EÖTVÖS, quoted in TIHAMÉR TÓTH, *El Joven Observador,* trans. Antonio Sancho Nebot (Madrid, 1963), Ebook edition, 144, *www.scribd.com/doc/57737597/El-joven-observador* (accessed April 5, 2014), editorial translation.

[116] LEO TOLSTOY, quoted in TÓTH, *El Joven Observador,* 142, editorial translation.

3. SOME ATTEMPTS AT EXPLANATION

There really have been many philosophical schools that have tried to explain religious phenomena with purely natural examinations. (I call them 'philosophical,' although they call themselves 'ethnological,' because on this point they involve themselves in an inquiry that touches philosophical problems). Although they have not succeeded (inexplicable difficulties always remain), it is worthwhile to mention them.

Explanation of the mythological school

This school was formed in the middle of the nineteenth century by A. Kuhn and held that religious mythological figures were nothing but personifications of objects and phenomena of nature, especially the great stars. The most famous representative of this school was Frederick Max Müller (1823-1900), founder of the 'History of Religions.' Abusing the philological method, he puts the origin of mythology in the defects of knowledge of the world, the failures of language, and in the confusion and exuberance of words. He explains the origin of religion by the influence of the infinite over the human consciousness: man sees up to a certain point and there he stops. What he does not take in fills him with awe and as he does not have the language to name it and identify it, he calls it God, without specifying whether this God is one or many. Müller never (nor could) explain, however, how it is possible that in all places and among all people, imprecision of language, confusion of words and ignorance, are the point of departure of the most universal act that history records.

This mythological school of thought has had many variations. Some are the aforementioned natural mythology, astral mythology and pan-lunarism; all have the same imperfections.

Explanation of the anthropological school

According to this school, man has the tendency to put something of his own life into the things that surround him: sentiments, passions, etc. The doctrine of this school can be summarized in three undemonstrated hypotheses. The first is a harsh *agnosticism*: we cannot know anything about transcendental causes, since we cannot subject them to experience. Therefore, we should not look for the origin of religion in such metaphysical causes but in ourselves. Reinach said "Unless, then, we admit the gratuitous and childlike hypothesis of a primitive revelation, we must look for the origin of religions in the psychology, not of civilised man, but of man the farthest removed from civilisation." [117] It would be good to know why *his* hypothesis, which is in any case childish and unfounded, is better than the one he refutes. (In the end, he doesn't tell us.) The second hypothesis is the *evolutionist* assumption, which when taken to the greatest universal, concludes that everything evolves from the simple and rudimentary to the complex. Therefore, if we want to find the origin of the religious act, the religion of the most savage peoples needs to be analyzed, since they represent most faithfully the primitive state of humanity. In any case, this would first have to be demonstrated, since these authors will certainly argue as to whether or not a primitive revelation (such as a divine revelation at the beginning of humanity) can be proven. What they cannot do is *deny* it without

---

[117] SALOMON REINACH, *Cults, Myths and Religions*, trans. Elizabeth Frost (London: David Nutt, 1912), v.

demonstration, given that *if God exists, nothing forbids that he reveal himself to man.* If primitive revelation were true, such religiosity would be more perfect by proceeding from a direct revelation of God, while the later forms would correspond to a degeneration of religious sects, which would destroy this hypothesis. The third hypothesis is the *determinist* assumption, according to which the different cults follow each other in a chain, one after another, determined by diverse factors like culture, environment or way of life.

It is clear that the assumptions of those who share this explanation are false and hasty, above all for dismissing, without any proof, all possible primitive revelation and any transcendent explanation. In this manner, they not only shut the door to any supernatural explanation, but to any scientific explanation, since there is nothing more antiscientific then the denial of the Supernatural Cause without proof.

Unfortunately, we do not have space here to expound upon theories that depend on this school. These theories would include, among others *animism* (which explains the origin of religion by the belief that primitive peoples had in the individual soul and in spirits); *manism* (the hypothesis that holds that the worship of the souls of the dead—or *manes*— is the origin of religion); *magism* (founded by James George Frázer who said that the religious act derived from magic or the communication of man with a mysterious power or energy that responding to his invocations and rites satisfies his desires); *fetishism* (worship of *fetishes,* that is to say, of a representation of wood, clay or stone consecrated to various spirits or idols—Auguste Comte, founder of positivism in the nineteenth century, supposed that this was man's first "religious" stage); *totemism*, which holds that the origin of religion comes from the worship given the totems, preferably animals (the totem is a material object that the pagan looks to with superstitious respect, believing that between him and each member of the clan who is represented in the totem there is an intimate and special relationship).

Explanation of the sociological school

For this school, society mechanically imposes the religious act on each one of the individuals that makes up that society. Therefore, society creates the religious notion; religious ideas spontaneously spring from the individuals as soon as they interact with each other and live a social life. Afterwards, this religion slowly goes on purifying and idealizing itself. The motive is that society needs an ideal in order to live. Society creates and presents to all of the individual members an ideal under the aspect of the *sacred* and the majesty of the *divine*. This theory can be credited for recognizing the religious phenomenon and affirming, against Comte, that it is not an artificial creation but a spontaneous one. It can also be given credit for teaching that religion is *the social act par excellence* from which all others derive; in other words, it is the strongest social link, the principal cohesive factor among the members of a society. The idea of God, even in sociology, is the only idea that can inspire and maintain an individual spirit of sacrifice for the sake of the rest of the society (that this is accepted says a lot). This school can also be given credit for recognizing that religion has a social aspect; that it is not a purely individual phenomenon (as liberalism claims). Sociologists recognize that we need a religious tradition, that a religious sociology is legitimate, that religion is a perpetual and permanent act, and that there is agreement between social changes and religious doctrines or practices... but the foundations of their explanation is wrong. For Durkheim, the main spokesman of this school, man is born a beast, and it is society that makes him man; therefore, what is human in him is only a reflection of society, even his religious dimension is only an echo of society. It is evident that such an explanation is viciously false. In some moments, there have been individuals who ended up forming a society and—at least in that moment—the process had to necessarily be the reverse of that expounded by the sociological school, since the individuals projected their values onto the society that they formed. With this, the principal on which the whole theory is based, falls and with it fall all the explanations of how one conceives of acts, including religious ones.

Explanation of the psychological school

For this school, begun by William James, in his book *The Varieties of the Religious Experience: A Study of Human Nature*, the religious act consists first in an *affective attitude*. For this author, feelings, associated with the will, are essential in religion. Feelings are the true religious states; they reduce religious experiences of trust in the divine, joy, exaltations, and ecstasy to optimism and reduce the feelings of sin, remorse, and repentance to pessimism. The religious phenomenon is nothing more than a projection of the subconscious. These very ideas entered Catholicism through the *modernist* movement that reduced religion and faith to a *need for the divine*. Therefore, there is no objective religion, revelation or faith in a God who actually speaks to man, but only a subconscious projection of our needs for protection and security that we alleviate with an idea of God that we ourselves create without knowing it.

This school and its theories can also be given some credit. They recognize the reality of religious experience and acts of the conscience, partly separating itself from the gross materialism of other theories. They do not reduce these acts to philosophical laws (James ridicules the materialist doctors who explain moral conversion as a crisis of the sexual instinct or categorize St. Teresa of Jesus as a hysteric). They recognize the multiplicity of religious experiences and proclaim the higher value of religious life, considering holiness as an essential factor in the social good and counting the saints among the greatest benefactors of humanity. But they are wrong on some fundamental points: they reduce all religious phenomena to the affective sphere, and do not count the intellectual elements (beliefs, dogmas, truths) that are fundamental in all religion. The error of agnosticism comes with it and discards all its explanations about everything that is superior to man. As Faguet pointed out, "James does not say one word, or if he did, it was so short that I missed it, about St. Thomas Aquinas, Bossuet, or St. Francis de Sales. But many unbalanced men who have various kinds of brain defects find a home in this book."[118] Furthermore, the psychological school neglects the principal element of religion, *adoration*, precisely because this supposes a personal reality apart from man to which he should submit, accepting its teachings, obeying its commands, and appeasing it through certain practices or acts of worship.

Conclusions

The research made by important philosophers and ethnologists, disentangled from prejudice, helps us to arrive

---

[118] ÉMILE FAGUET, "L'Expérience Religieuse," *La Revue Latine* 7:8 (August 1908): 450, quoted in NEGUERUELA, *Lecciones de Apologética*, §89, editorial translation.

at certain conclusions about the religious act that we can summarize in the following:[119]

1. *In the history of humanity, there is no irreligious period.* "No wise man of any renown would dare to deny it."[120] The affirmation of Lubbock, Letourneau, Mortillet, Hovelacque, Le Bon and others that the origins of humanity are irreligious is in opposition to the facts. In all areas man shows himself religious, whether we are looking how he has appeared in history, how he has been observed by ethnography or reconstituted by prehistory.

2. *There is no religion separate in its origin from morality; therefore, there are no primitive amoral states.* Wherever we go, if we pay attention to the native people, we see a morality intimately linked to religious dogmas and rights. The greater part of the amoral practices are united, not with religion, but with magic, its enemy and imitator, which claims to obtain without God and against Him results that man is incapable to produce.

3. *Morality is purer and more dependent on religion in the most primitive peoples.* "The Africans who are in the first steps of progress have speculative and practical morals certainly superior to numerous relatively civilized African populations."[121]

4. *Nations do not exist without determined family organization.* Moreover, what the proponents of Monist evolution suppose is false: namely, common promiscuity (or that everyone lived together sexually without matrimony or family) at the beginning of mankind. Darwin himself wrote: "The

---

[119] These can be seen in NEGUERUELA, *Lecciones de Apologética*, §105.

[120] SCHMIDT, *Ursprung und Werden der Religion*, 57, cited in NEGUERUELA, *Lecciones de Apologética*, §105, editorial translation.

[121] LE ROY, "Les Populations de Culture Inférieure," in *Christus*, 96-97, cited in NEGUERUELA, *Lecciones de Apologética*, §105, editorial translation.

hypothesis that presents promiscuity as a general phase in the history of humanity is one of the most foolish in the world of sociological sciences."[122]

5. *As opposed to the evolutionist plan, the religious progress of humanity is not unilinear, rectilinear or progressive.* Contrary to evolutionist claims, the point of departure for religions is characterized by religious morality and monotheism, and in many verified cases they have then fallen into polytheism. The evolutionists themselves have not been able to agree on the religious stages. Thus, the religious stages vary, conforming to the biases of each author. Commonly, religious evolution has happened by degradation: animism has replaced monotheism and a coarse morality for a purer morality. Therefore, the religious evolution of Tylor, Spencer, Reville and other authors fails.

6. *There is no parallelism or synchronism between religious and mythological evolutions.* Usually, in every people, two elements coexist: *religion* and *mythology*. The superior element, religion, believes in a being superior to man who is father and creator of things; the inferior element, mythology, is coarse and often obscene. These two elements inversely evolve. Suffocated by mythology, the religious element loses purity and dignity. Le Roy speaks of "the Romans and Greeks with a religion more elaborate but less pure than that of the Assyro-Chaldeans, the latter with beliefs less elevated than those of the Egyptians, the Egyptians with practices more multiplied and systems more complex but an ensemble less easy to penetrate than that of the Hamitic, Nigritian, or Bantu tribes. We find these last with religious data more complete but more diffuse than those of our humble little Pygmies whose poor imagination

---

[122] DARWIN, quoted in NEGUERUELA, *Lecciones de Apologética,* §100, editorial translation.

found nothing to enrich the dogmatic and moral foundation which they bore with them in their wandering life. Nevertheless it has maintained them through the long series of centuries past and gone."[123]

7. *No religion exists without relation to superior beings.* Magic, which would be the starting point of religious evolution for King, Hartland, Marett and others, is unknown in the Indian and Egyptian religions; moreover, ethnography shows us that in the primitive peoples, greater worship of a Supreme Being means the presence of less magic. The sense of dependence that comes with every religion presupposes belief in superior and personal beings.

8. *The religion of the truly primitive people was monotheism.* This conclusion from the history of religions is a practical confirmation of the philosophical thesis about the possibility of knowing God. The primitive peoples, despite the cultural limits or lack of civilization that we suppose, have rational souls; they have ideas made by looking at the things that surround them; ideas that are not exclusive to civilized man. From the contemplation of the things they see, they deduce the existence of the Sovereign Creator. A. Lang himself (1844-1912), previously the most brilliant defender of religious evolution became an intrepid defender of primitive monotheism, upon closely examining peoples of Australia and Oceania. The cradle of humanity has heard the most majestic name: *God*; and this name was the most beloved to man, who called God *his Father*.

9. *Analysis of the religious act offers us evident scientific proof of the existence of God.* If we deny God, the religious act is an impenetrable enigma.

[123] ALEXANDER LE ROY, *The Religion of the Primitives* (New York: The Macmillan Company, 1922), 278.

4. WHY IS RELIGION NECESSARY?[124]

We have already said that we have a soul, and that the soul is just as capable of knowing what God is as it is capable of knowing what man is. This knowledge obligates us to practice religion, which unites man with God as his beginning and ultimate end.

In effect, religion is the totality of the duties that man should perform for the Supreme Being—his Creator, his Benefactor and his Lord—and through them he is united with God.[125]

These obligations include: truths to believe, precepts to practice and a cult to pay homage to God.

As natural and sacred bonds exist between parents and children, they also exist between God, Creator and Father of man, and man, the creature and son of God. The bond that unites man to God is stronger than that which unites a son with his father. Why? Because we owe much more to God than a son owes to his father. God is our Creator and our ultimate end; our parents are not. Thus, our obligations to God are much holier than those of children to parents.

Natural religion has to be distinguished from supernatural, or revealed, religion.

Natural religion is that which is known by the natural lights of reason and is based on the necessary relations between the Creator and the creature. This natural religion is an absolute obligation to all men, in all times and all places, because it proceeds from the nature of God and the nature of man. It contains in itself the truths and precepts that man can know by reason, even though, in fact, he has known them through revelation: the existence of God, spirituality, the soul's liberty and immortality, natural law's first

---

[124] Cf. HILLAIRE, *La Religión Demostrada*.

[125] According to some, the word "religion" comes from *religare*: to bind tightly. According to others, it comes from *reeligere*: to choose God again. That is to say: man should bind himself freely to God as his beginning, and should choose God as his ultimate end.

principles, the existence of a future life and its rewards or punishments.

Supernatural or revealed religion is that which God has made known to man since the beginning of the world. The Creator gave to the first man truths to believe, such as man's supernatural end, the necessity of grace to reach this sublime end, and hope of the Redeemer; and obligations to fulfill such as the Sabbath rest, the offering of sacrifices, and others.

The intention of these pages is not, as I have said above, to speak about revealed religion or to prove that the Catholic religion is true; on this point we have limited ourselves to indicating the ways to demonstrate it. Therefore, the objective is to present only the motives for which man needs religion as a fish needs water. Religion is necessary to man because it is founded on the nature of God and on the nature of man, and is based on the necessary relationships between God and man. Only God has the right to impose religion; practicing religion is man's duty: God is the Creator, man should adore him. God is the Lord, man should serve him. God is the Benefactor, man should thank him. God is the Father, man should love him. God is the Legislator; man should keep his laws. God is the source of all good; man should direct all his pleas to him. All these duties of man towards God are necessary and obligatory, and together they make up religion. Therefore, religion is necessary.

It is so vital that God cannot exempt man from the religious obligation. God cannot renounce his rights as Creator, as Lord, as ultimate end. As a father cannot excuse his sons from owing him respect, submission and love, likewise, God cannot excuse us from practicing religion.

God, who is infinite wisdom and supreme justice, must necessarily prescribe order, and order requires that inferior beings be subordinate to the Supreme Being, so that creatures glorify their Creator, each one in conformity with its nature. Therefore, order requires that the intelligent and free man render to God:

1. Homage of his *dependence*, because He is his Creator and Lord;
2. Homage of his *gratitude*, because He is his benefactor;
3. Homage of his *love*, because He is his Father and Sovereign Good;
4. Homage of his *expiations*, because He is his legislator and judge;
5. Homage of his *prayers*, because He is the source and infinite ocean of all goods. God cannot, then, renounce this essential right of requiring our homage, because he would not be God if he did not love order and justice.

God could have not created us, but from the moment we are the work of his hands, his dominion is inalienable.

Religion is also necessary to man because *man cannot be happy without religion.* Man is not happy in this world if his faculties are not fully satisfied, and only religion can give serenity of spirit, peace of heart, rectitude and strength of will. Therefore, without religion, man cannot be happy in this world. Neither can he be happy in the future life, because without religion he cannot reach happiness which is the possession of God, the Sovereign Good.

Man cannot be happy without that religion which allows him to properly know God and to love him. This can be clearly seen in the following ways:

1. Intelligence needs the truth—the entire truth. The pieces of truth scattered about by creatures cannot be enough to fulfill man; he needs infinite truth, which only can be found in God. Consequently, before all else, the intelligence needs the knowledge of God, its beginning and end. Since religion is the only thing that offers clear, precise and fully satisfactory solutions to all the questions that man cannot ignore, we must conclude that religion is necessary. This is why all the wise men truly worthy of the name have been profoundly religious. Time has proven Bacon's statement to be true: "a little philosophy inclineth Man's mind to

atheism, but depth in philosophy bringeth men's minds about to religion."[126]

2. Man's heart needs the love of God because it has been made for God and cannot find rest or happiness without loving God, his supreme Good. Neither gold nor pleasures nor glory will ever be able to satisfy man's heart; his desires are so big that all these finite and passing things will not be enough to fulfill them. This is why all saints, all noble hearts, all men find in religion a joy—a fullness of happiness that all the sensible pleasures and all the worldly joys will never be able to give.

3. Man's will needs a sure rule in order to direct himself towards the good and towards motives capable of encouraging him to bravely face the passions that must be conquered, the duties that must be fulfilled, and the sacrifices that must be made. Only religion can give the will this strength, this superior energy, showing God to man as the one who rewards virtue and punishes crime. If there were not the healthy deterrent of the fear of God, man would abandon himself to all the passions and cast himself headlong into an abyss of miseries.

4. Finally, religion prepares for us consolation in prayer, remedy in hope, joy in the love of God, help and strength in resignation, and, furthermore, gives us a glimpse of a complete and unending happiness after this life. The religious man is always the happiest or, at least, the most consoled.

On the other hand, the man without religion is most unfortunate, even in this world.

Religion is also *necessary to society*. Since all societies need: (1) from those who govern, justice and a willing disposition to serve and protect others; (2) from the citizens, obedience to the laws; and (3) from all, social virtues. Now, only religion can inspire leaders to enact justice and sacrifice themselves for the good of their subjects, inspire others to obedience and respect for power,

---

[126] FRANCIS BACON, "Essay XVI. Of Atheism," in *Bacon's Essays* (London: John W. Parker and Son, West Strand, 1856), 135.

and inspire all to social virtues—justice, charity, unity, harmony and sacrificial spirit for the good of others. Therefore, religion is necessary to society.

The foundation, the base of all society, is the right to command of those who govern and the obligation of those who are governed to obey. The impious Voltaire recognized this: "I should not wish to come in the way of an atheistical prince, whose interest it should be to have me pounded in a mortar; I am quite sure that I should be so pounded."[127] He adds, "If [...] the world were ever to be governed by Atheists, we might as well be under the empire of those infernal beings who are represented to us as savagely tormenting their victims."[128] In fact, today in many countries governed by atheists, this Voltairian observation is realized. Where does this right to command, which constitutes social authority, come from? It cannot come from man, even taken collectively, given that all men are equal by nature, and therefore no one is superior to his fellow man. This right cannot come from anywhere but from God, who, in creating man as a social being, has in fact created society. Therefore, to justify this right, he has to have recourse to God, the supreme authority from which all authority proceeds. "He who fears and hates religion, is like the savage beast that growls and bites the chain, which prevents his flying on the passenger"[129] writes Montesquieu. Skeptical Rousseau confesses, "I do not mean by this that one can be virtuous without religion; I held this erroneous opinion for a long time but am now only too disabused of it."[130]

---

[127] VOLTAIRE, "A Philosophical Dictionary," in vol. VI of *The Works of Voltaire* (New York: E. R. DuMont, 1901), 125.

[128] "Art. VI. Göthe's Festival," in vol. XCII of *The Edinburgh Review* (London: 1850), 195.

[129] MONTESQUIEU, vol. II of *The Spirit of the Laws,* trans. Thomas Nugent (Cincinnati: Robert Clarke & Co., 1873), 120.

[130] BLOOM, trans., *Letter to M. d'Alembert* (Ithaca: Cornell University Press, 1960), 97, note.

Furthermore, the necessity of religion is proven by *our own experience.* "In all stages of history" says Le Play, "one has observed that nations, pervaded with a most firm belief in God and in the future life, have become rapidly lifted above others as well through virtue and talent, as through power and wealth".[131]

Crimes multiply in a nation insofar as religion decreases. This is why the worst enemies of society are those who try to destroy religion in a nation, undermining society's foundation. Plutarch said: "a city might sooner be built without any ground to fix it on, than a commonweal be constituted altogether void of any religion and opinion of the gods".[132] Plato wrote: "That which destroys religion destroys the foundations of all human society, because without religion there is no possible society."[133] Napoleon I said, "Without religion, men would slaughter themselves for anything of insignificance whatsoever."[134] When all is said and done, we just have to look at the new irreligious societies... and watch our backs.

This is why all nations have recognized the necessity of religion. All nations in every period of history have had temples and altars. As unpretentious Hume said, "A State was never founded without religion serving as its basis. Look for a nation without religion, and if you find it, you can be sure that it will be no different from the animals."[135]

* * *

In considering these ideas, we can show that many have constructed theories as if they were new towers of Babel, capable of reaching heaven and challenging God himself. Yet in a short

---

[131] EDWARD SODERINI, *Socialism and Catholicism,* trans. Richard Jenery-Shee (New York: Longmans, Green, & Co., 1896), 313.

[132] WILLIAM GOODWIN, ed., vol. V of *Plutarch's Morals* (Boston: Little, Brown, and Company, 1874), 380.

[133] PLATO, quoted in HILLAIRE, *La Religión Demostrada*, editorial translation.

[134] NAPOLEON I, quoted in HILLAIRE, *La Religión Demostrada*, editorial translation.

[135] HUME, quoted in HILLAIRE, *La Religión Demostrada*, editorial translation.

time we have seen them fall like the walls of Jericho. In fact, in the majority of the cases, a trumpet blast is not even needed; a low whistle is enough.

For Further Reading

- Chesterton, G. K. *The Everlasting Man.* Garden City, New York: Image Books, 1955.

Available in Other Languages

- De Grandmaison, Leoncio. *Jesucristo.* Barcelona: Litúrgica Española, 1941. Re-edited by Madrid: Edibesa, 2000.
- Francisco Vizmanos and Ignacio Riudor. *Teología Fundamental para Seglares.* Madrid: BAC, 1963.
- Hillaire, Albert. *La Religión Demostrada.* Barcelona: Luis Gili, 1955.
- Lang, Albert. Vols. 1-2 of *Teología Fundamental.* Madrid: Rialp, 1977.
- Marín Negueruela, Nicolás. *Lecciones de Apologética.* Barcelona: Tipografía Católica Casals, 1944.
- ———. *¿Por qué soy católico?* Buenos Aires: Poblet, 1956.

5.

THE STOLEN
TRUTH ABOUT
OUR DIGNITY
AND ORIGIN

The Truths and Limits of Evolutionism

If you are told that the Church's doctrine clashes with the indisputable theory of evolution, then you are being cheated out of many truths. First of all, they are not dealing with only one theory but many different ones. And many of these cases are not worthy of the name "theory," and the ones that can be taken seriously do not disagree with any Catholic truth.

It is understandable, in any case, that we should talk about this topic. Everyone is intrigued by man's origin, where man comes from, and his history, given that man's end (his purpose or destiny) depends on it as well. Are we the result of an unexpected accident, of evolution or of the work of a Creator? The different possible answers imply many different concepts about man and the world, and they translate into very different attitudes about life (for example, the difference between hope and anxiety in the face of death). The Church, with Bible in hand, teaches us an answer: man has been created by God, who formed his body from a material element, and created his soul in a direct manner. This process continues to repeat itself for each person who comes into the world: he receives his body from his parents, but his spiritual and immortal soul is created by God. Do the teachings of evolution (which are just as much about the origin of the universe as about the origin of man) contradict this teaching? Not all theories of evolution do. Furthermore, are the theories of evolution that contradict this teaching credible, or do they have their scientific "black holes" which cut them off at the knees? We will see in this chapter.

1. THE PRESENT STATE OF THE THEORIES OF EVOLUTION

We will see, first of all, and with the simplicity that our work (and capacity) requires, what the current state of the theories of evolution is (regarding both the origin of the universe as well as life and man in particular). I will continue on this point with the valuable work of Dr. Mariano Artigas.[136]

When speaking of evolution, Darwin immediately comes to mind, but already before him and his work *The Origin of Species* (1859), there had been other attempts to scientifically explain evolution. Lamarck in particular, in 1809, proposed explaining evolution through the inheritance of acquired characteristics. According to Artigas, Aristotle, when he explained the existence of finality in nature, offered an explanation almost identical to Darwin's. He taught that the explanation of the parts of a living organism would be that among the different products of nature, only the most well adapted ones would be preserved.[137] Darwin made evolution famous and influential, occupying himself first with the origin of species, and subsequently with the origin of man, and, in passing, with the origin of the first living beings. With time, evolutionist thought has expanded to the origin of the universe and its subsequent evolution. We will look at the present state of each one of these points.

a) About the origin of the universe

Albert Einstein formulated the theory of general relativity in 1915 and applied it to the study of the entire universe in 1917. His theory presupposed a changing universe. Displeased with this idea, he introduced into his formulas a "cosmological constant," with the goal of achieving a static universe. Later he said that this had been the worst mistake of his life. Willem de Sitter (1916-1917) and

---

136 Cf. MARIANO ARTIGAS, "Evolución, Fe y Teología: Desarrollos recientes en evolución y su repercusión para la fe y la teología," *Scripta Theologica* 32 (2000): 249-273. It can be seen on the *Grupo de Investigación sobre Ciencia, Razón y Fe* (CRYF) webpage: *www.unav.es/cryf/desarrollosenevolucionyrepercusiones.html.* Artigas himself has also dealt with the topic at further length in *Las Fronteras del Evolucionismo* (Madrid: MC, 1986).

137 Cf. ARISTOTLE, *Physics*, II, 8, 198b 23-32, cited in ARTIGAS, "Evolución, Fe y Teología."

Alfred Friedmann (1922-1924) developed Einstein's theory in the framework of a dynamic universe, an idea that was corroborated in 1929, when Edwin Hubble formulated the law that postulated that the universe is expanding and the galaxies are separating one from the other with a velocity that is proportionate to their mutual distance.

In 1927, the priest Georges Lemaître proposed his theory of the *primitive atom* which, after being reformulated by Georges Gamow in 1948, is known as the *Big Bang* theory or the "great explosion." According to this theory, about 15 billion years ago all the material and energy of the universe, which was concentrated in conditions of enormous temperature and density, experienced an expansion. This expansion, after a successive decrease of temperature and localized concentrations, produced a radiation that can still be observed today. The detection of this fossil radiation in 1964 by Arno Penzias and Robert Wilson brought about general acceptance of the theory. However, like all physical theories, it contains problematic aspects that many have tried to solve with other theories, such as the theory of *cosmic inflation* given by Alan Guth, according to which the universe, in the first moments of its existence and during a very small lapse of time, would have experienced an enormous expansion. In 1992, the observations of background radiation made by the satellite COBE (Cosmic Background Explorer) exposed the existence of the fluctuations in the early universe, which would explain the irregular distribution of matter necessary to produce the local condensations that gave rise to the stars and planets.

The model of the Big Bang has been widely accepted but raises important questions. Among other equally important things *we ignore* (from an exclusively scientific point of view): *the question of why there was a Big Bang.*

b) About the origin of life

Scientists calculate that the age of the Earth is some 4.5 billion years. The oldest fossils date back 3.8 billion years. Scientists suppose therefore, that primitive living things appeared in the interval between these two dates. Various theories exist that claim to explain the origin of life on Earth. One of the first was Alexander Oparin's proposition in 1922 that life emerged in the water of the oceans. In a famous experiment carried out in 1953 in Chicago, Stanley Miller simulated the conditions of the primitive atmosphere (ammonia, methane, hydrogen, and water vapor, excited by electric discharges) and obtained some amino-acids, which are the building blocks that compose proteins. It seemed that the problem about the origin of life could be solved, at least at first. However, there continue to be serious difficulties. The life that exists now on earth is based on the mutual interaction between nucleic acids (DNA and RNA) and proteins, but the nucleic acids are necessary to make proteins, and vice-versa. Also, these macromolecules are extremely complex, which makes it difficult to believe that they originated in a spontaneous manner.

At the end of the 1960s, Carl R. Woese, Francis Crick, and Leslie E. Orgel proposed what is now known as the theory of the *RNA World*, according to which primitive life was based on RNA.[138] They propose that this nucleic acid had two properties that it now lacks: it could self-replicate without needing proteins and it could catalyze the synthesis of these proteins. However, they do not know how it could do this, much less how RNA itself formed, which is also extremely complex. Furthermore it is all based on "*they suppose*," which for any scientific theory is very weak.

Others, such as Graham Cairns-Smith, have proposed more radical theories: according to him, the first system with the capacity to replicate itself was inorganic and was based on clay crystals. Another approach stated that the origin of life took place in thermal springs in the ocean depths. However, there are still enormous difficulties. Just think that the DNA of bacteria, one of the simplest living organisms, can have some two million

138 Cf. LESLIE E. ORGE, "The Origin of Life on Earth," *Scientific American* (Oct. 1994).

nucleotides, on whose organization the DNA depends in order to function and be able to direct the production of more than a thousand different proteins. In view of this, some scientists, such as Juan Oró, Fred Hoyle and Chandra Wickramansinghe, have postulated that complex precursors of life have existed in other parts of space and have come to Earth, for example, by collisions with meteors. Thus, they eliminate the problem of the origin of life on earth, *transferring it to another place in the universe*. (How did it emerge there?)

The enigmas surrounding the origin of life are very great, in spite of the existence of different theories that have tried to explain it.

c) About the origin of species

Darwin proposed in 1859 that natural selection, acting upon hereditary variations, primarily principle motor of evolution, but he knew nothing about the nature of these variations. Starting with the works of the Augustinian monk Gregor Mendel, published in 1866 and rediscovered in 1900, genetics became an essential part of evolutionary theory. In the early 1940s, the incorporation of genetics into Darwinism led to the formation of *neo-Darwinism* or the "Modern Evolutionary Synthesis" theory which continues to consider natural selection as the main factor to explain evolution.

A typical objection to neo-Darwinism is that it does not explain macroevolution, the origin of new species or types of living organisms. Darwinism insists on gradualism and affirms that major changes are the results of the accumulation of many small changes, but others have formed alternative proposals. Stephen Jay Gould and Niles Eldredge uphold that evolution is not gradual, but that it works in jumps (the theory of "punctuated equilibrium"). They held that there would be great periods of stability interrupted by brief intervals in which big and violent evolutionary changes would take place. (This is how they would explain why they do not find *intermediate links* in the fossil registry.) This theory (of punctuated equilibrium) proposes explanations that are not Darwinist but that are evolutionary (the discussion centers around the mechanisms of evolution, not around its existence).

In 1967, Motoo Kimura proposed another theory: *neutralism*, which denied that evolution had anything to do with natural selection. For him the evolutionary changes would be due to the "genetic drift" of genetic mutations. Kimura also did not dispute evolution but only its mechanisms.

One of the biggest difficulties of evolutionism is explaining new types of organization that require multiple, complex and coordinated changes. In order to solve this problem, theories have been proposed that, for the moment, are very hypothetical, since they are based on data that is still quite insufficiently known.

Many of the theories we have mentioned are presented in opposition to Darwinism. Darwinists, however, claim that they do fit within their theory, and that, in any case, these new theories are not critical of evolutionism but are attempts to furnish more profound explanations for evolution.

d) About the origin of man

Since the publication of Darwin's theory, attention has been centered on the biological explanation of the origin of man. Here began the search for the intermediate links between man and other primates that has driven the common classification of modern man's ancestors: the *australopithecus africanus* (between 4.5 and 2 million years ago), followed by *homo habilis* (since 2.3 to 1.5 million years ago), the *homo erectus* (or *homo ergaster* in Africa, between 1 and 2 million years, and of *homo erectus* in Asia), and the different variations of *homo sapiens*. This enters territory where many uncertainties exist, and novelties which oblige theorists to change diagrams are frequently introduced.

In the last few decades, new methods of molecular biology have been applied to the study of evolution, which sometimes reach different conclusions than those derived from studying fossils, giving rise to differences between molecular biologists and

150

paleontologists. Thus, in agreement with molecular biology, the supposed common ancestor of chimpanzees and humans would be placed between 5 and 6 million years ago, much more recent than the previous estimate, which goes back some 20 million years. It is thought that the lineage of this common ancestor had probably already separated from gorillas.

The supposed determination of modern man's origin through the study of mitochondrial DNA, passed on from the mother, has gained particular attention in this field. According to some molecular biologists, all modern human beings descended from one woman who lived between 100,000 and 200,000 years ago in Africa. This theory has received the expressive title "mitochondrial Eve." It has to be noted, nevertheless, that those who ascribe to this theory do not claim to have scientifically proven monogenism.[139] Also, their claims are not accepted by everyone; in particular, some paleontologists have reservations, especially with respect to the use of what these molecular biologists have called the "molecular clock."[140]

Two different opinions about the presumed origin of modern man are the "multiregional hypothesis" and the "Recent African Origin" model. The multiregional hypothesis holds that the very primitive species *homo erectus*, which includes *homo ergaster,* is nothing more than an ancient deviation of *homo sapiens.* Furthermore, it defends that in the history of our lineage over the last two million years, this species' intertwined populations evolved in all the regions of the Old World, each one adapting to the local conditions, although still firmly linked by genetic exchange. The variation that we see today between the principal geographic populations would be, in accord with this model, the last permutation of the long process.

---

[139] Cf. ALLAN C. WILSON and REBECCA L. CANN, "The Recent African Genesis of Humans," *Scientific American* (April 1992): 70.

[140] ALAN G. THORNE and MILFORD H. WOLPOFF, "Multiregional Evolution of Humans," *Scientific American* (April 1992): 76.

On the other hand, the Recent African Origin model asserts that 100,000 years ago a new type of human being originated in Africa and completely took the place of the previous species.

Also, studies of Y chromosome, inherited exclusively from the father, have been carried out and the results are in accord with the Recent African Origin model.

In regard to the most recent era, it seems that for the last 30,000 years, only the present modern man remained, although he may have coexisted for thousands of years with other types of human ancestors (like the Neanderthal man). There is not unanimous agreement about the origin of the different human groups that exist today.

In the midst of many uncertainties, it is customary to claim that modern humanity proceeds from some relatively recent ancestors that appeared in Africa, or perhaps the Middle East, and dispersed throughout the world.

e) The two fundamental variations of evolutionism

We have mentioned different theories and proposals from the philo-evolutionist field. Another key element that is interwoven with these theories of evolution and their more or less scientific arguments, which transcends the strictly scientific field, must be taken into account: the acceptance or rejection of a supernatural cause in the process of evolution.

I say that it is an element that transcends the field proper to the disciplines that propose evolutionism (physics, chemistry, biology, or paleontology) given that here we enter into a metaphysical and also (although not exclusively) theological plane. It is the key point, given that some think that the evolutionists who deny the intervention of a supernatural cause (God) in the process of evolution are making a claim that falls within the field of their science. But this is not so. It is invading the realm of philosophy, as we have already clarified when we spoke of the existence of God and the competencies of all scientists with respect to it.

When we consider the positions of evolutionist scientists' on the possibility of supernatural intervention in the origin of the cosmos, life and man, we find ourselves with essentially two different variants: radical evolutionism and mitigated evolutionism.

"Radical," "crude," or "absolute" evolutionism grants to matter a potentiality from which all beings emerge through evolution in its almost infinite virtualities. On a universal level, it attributes to an initial chaos or a first particle—or whatever it might be—the capacity of expanding, bursting, or reacting (according to each of the different explanations of each theory) and thus causing the origin of the present universe. Applied to the origin of life, "it supposes that, without exception, living beings originated from one first elemental living organism, or even from a prime matter or particular non-living materials, which would have given rise to the first living organism, and would then have gone on reproducing and diversifying itself through various mutations into different species."[141] Oparin spoke, for example, of a "primordial soup" from which all life emerged with a powerful electric energy discharged at its root.[142] This is not science but "a mythological and literary conception of life."[143]

This evolutionism has been upheld by authors like Lamarck, Spencer, Darwin, Oparin, and many others who sometimes profess blatant, barefaced atheism. This can be seen in the explicit declaration of many of the defenders of this theory. For example, Darwin addressed Thomas Huxley as "My good and kind agent for the propagation of the Gospel—i.e. the devil's gospel."[144] "God

---

[141] J. MORALES MARÍN, "Evolución. Filosofía y Visión de Conjunto," in *Gran Enciclopedia Rialp* (Madrid: Ediciones Rialp, 1991), editorial translation.

[142] Cf. ALEKSANDR IVANOVICH OPARIN, *The Origin of Life*, trans. Sergius Morgulis (New York: The Macmillan Company, 1938).

[143] C. VELASCO SUÁREZ, *Psiquiatría y Persona* (Buenos Aires: Educa, 2003), 29, editorial translation.

[144] C. DARWIN to T. H. Huxley, August 8, 1860 in vol. II of *The Life and Letters of Charles Darwin,* ed. Francis Darwin (New York: D. Appleton and Company, 1911), 124.

is", said Haeckel, "a 'gaseous vertebrate.'"[145] And Lemoine confessed, "Evolution is the dogma of the antichurch."[146] In the words of Thomas Huxley, "the doctrine of evolution [...] occupies a position of complete and irreconcilable antagonism to [...] the Catholic Church."[147] When speaking of this crude evolutionism, there is no doubt that Huxley's conclusions are in fact the case; however, it is also clear that this crude evolutionism is not a *scientific theory* but a *prescientific dogma* or better yet a *pseudoscientific faith* adorned with scientific elements. Actually, this type of evolutionist explanation has been contested by various sciences. Mathematicians doubt that there would have been sufficient time for natural selection and the laws applied by theories of evolution to have caused the phenomena that are observed in nature. Biochemists answer that random and simple evolution unguided by an Intelligence cannot explain the perfect organization of life in its present state, nor the origin and operation of living organisms starting from a purely material state. Philosophy demonstrates that more cannot come from less, speaking of the qualitative jumps of form, not purely accidental, and above all that the spiritual cannot proceed from the material, and that nothing comes from nothing; in no way can intellectual, moral and spiritual life be deduced from biological processes. In spite of all this, radical evolutionism was assimilated as the basis for other philosophical systems, which adapted it for other designs. For example, Hegel applied evolution to the Absolute Spirit, and Marx and Engels applied it to society and history driven by a dialectic evolution. The stability of other systems, which senselessly erected themselves on Darwin's foundations and depend on his validity, provides the current validity of the extravagant Darwinian claims.

---

[145] ERNST HAECKEL, *The History of Creation* (New York: D. Appleton and Company, 1906), 71.

[146] E. DÍAZ ARAUJO, *Evolución y Evolucionismo* (Guadalajara: Universidad Autónoma de Guadalajara, 2000), 19, editorial translation.

[147] THOMAS HUXLEY, "Mr. Darwin's Critics," in *Darwiniana: Essays* (New York: D. Appleton and Company, 1912), 147.

On the other hand, we have *relative* or *mitigated* evolutionism, which accepts an evolution, both of the universe and of life, without excluding from it divine action. This divine action would both providentially direct the organic evolution itself and, in a given moment, infuse creation with the spiritual soul. In spite of the fact that it is *mitigated*, we should not forget the scientific arguments, on which the diverse theories of evolution are based, do not resolve all the problems and among them there are notable discrepancies.

f) *In synthesis*

As we can see, among all of these theories that drive current science, many important questions exist. The Big Bang theory appears well situated, but cannot be considered as definitively established and contains many unresolved questions. Many very different hypotheses about the origin of life exist. With respect to the evolution of living beings, although it is commonly admitted that the combination of genetic variation and natural selection play an important role, there is a need to search for explanations that go beyond this plan. Finally, the origin of man continues to be surrounded with a sea of doubts and arguments, even among the evolutionists themselves.

In spite of this, the work on evolution, in its general characteristics, has many solid elements. On the other hand, the same cannot be said about the concrete explanations of this work (or better, of the many acts included in the entirety of evolution). Arguments taken from different specialties appear to support the vast evolutionary process that has produced nature in its current state, although many questions and discrepancies exist in regard to particular aspects.

This should at least cause us to reflect a great deal when people speak about the "theory of evolution" as if referring to a concrete and accurate theory. We are very far from that; the value of the universe's evolutionary explanation is distinct from that of man and of life. There are *many* different explanations, and many theories are contradictory among themselves (and therefore are hostile and restrictive) to the point that if one is true the other soundly falls. Any one of these theories (on any point) *does not explain all the facts* that it presents (loopholes always remain, through which the knot which could seal the explanation with certainty slips out; in other words, there is no theory that completely closes the issue). Even so, we are going to give these theories a certain value, at least in reference to the *fact* of evolution in general.

2. WHAT DOES THE CHURCH TEACH ABOUT THESE TOPICS AND WHAT DOES SHE SAY ABOUT THESE THEORIES?

To see if it is true that the theories of evolution exclude or discredit what the Catholic faith teaches about the origin of the world, life and man, we must clearly spell out what exactly the Catholic faith teaches.[148]

The principal source of Catholic doctrine is Sacred Scripture (the story of the creation of the universe and man is in the book of Genesis, although not exclusively, since there are other passages that can complement it) and the documents of the Magisterium, where the Church has determined with her doctrinal authority what should be believed by faith on these points. According to the Catholic faith these are the sources in which Divine Revelation is contained.

In the creation story of Genesis (Chapters 1-3), there are many elements that should be understood correctly, since they are written in a special and unique style, relating true acts in a language adapted to the mindset of its first audience. Therefore, in a historic sense, it does not correspond to the canons of history to which we

---

[148] There are many bibliographies about this; I will follow in broad strokes an old but valuable study by NICOLÁS MARÍN NEGUERUELA, *Con la Razón y la Fe o Problemas Apologéticos* (Barcelona: Tipografía Católica Casals, 1941), 20ff.

are now accustomed. However, neither can it be considered as a *fable* taken from the mythologies and cosmogonies of ancient peoples and adapted to monotheistic doctrine (faith in one God) by the sacred author, first purging all polytheistic (belief in multiple gods) errors. It deals neither with *allegories* nor with symbols void of all real and objective foundations, proposed in historic form, to instill philosophical and religious truths. Neither does it deal with *legends*, partly historical and partly fictional, freely composed for the instruction and edification of listeners and readers.

However, on the other hand, it also does not deal with *history* the way it is understood by Greek and Latin and modern historians.[149] There are strictly historical elements and elements that relate *metaphorically* to historic acts. What are the elements that we should understand with a literal historic sense? The main ones are:[150]

1. The creation of all things by God
2. The particular creation of man
3. The formation of the first woman from the first man
4. The unity of human lineage
5. The original happiness of our first parents in the state of justice, integrity and immortality
6. The commandment imposed by God to test our obedience
7. The transgression, by the persuasion of the devil
8. The loss of the primitive state of innocence
9. The promise of the future Redeemer.

---

[149] The encyclical, *Humani Generis* (August 12, 1950) affirmed that the first eleven chapters of Genesis, "although properly speaking not conforming to the historical method used by the best Greek and Latin writers or by competent authors of our time, do nevertheless pertain to history in a true sense, which however must be further studied and determined by exegetes." (PIUS XII, *Humani Generis* (Boston: St. Paul Editions: 1950), no. 38.)

[150] Cf. PONTIFICAL BIBLICAL COMMISSION, "The Historical Character of the Earlier Chapters of Genesis" (1909), in HENRY DENZINGER, *The Sources of Catholic Dogma*, trans. Roy Deferrari (Fitzwilliam, New Hamshire: Loreto Publications, 1955), no. 2123.

Therefore, it is fair for Catholic doctrine to examine and follow the judgment that appears most well-founded for each one of those points where there is no formal interpretation on the part of the Magisterium and that has been examined by serious authors, beginning with the Fathers of the Church and the doctors of all times; as long as the interpretation does not contradict or distort some other truth of faith. (This follows the affirmation made in the documents of the Church that *the judgment of the Church and the analogy of faith should be saved.*) The document of the 1909 Biblical Commission expressly gave the liberty to consider and offer different interpretations in respect to: many of the words and phrases used in this story (especially those that clearly have a metaphorical or anthropomorphic sense); some passages can be interpreted in an allegorical or prophetic manner (as was done by many of the Holy Fathers); this story should not be understood as if it were a scientific declaration; in particular, exegetes should be left free to argue about the significance of the term "day" (*Yôm*, used for the days of creation).

The Church, basing itself principally on the Biblical narrative, teaches that God has created all things freely, out of nothing. Also, all that he has created is good. (God did not make evil; it was introduced by his creatures: first, by the angels in heaven, who rebelled, and then, by men, instigated by the rebellious angels, disobeyed God.) Furthermore, man has been created by God in a particular way, different from other creatures, and the first woman comes from the first man (the unique origin of the human genus).[151]

Some dispute this last point, saying that this unique origin of the first couple, Adam and Eve—the doctrine called *monogenism*— is not a teaching of faith. For them, the only teaching of faith would be *that God has created man*, but he could have created various

---

[151] All these teachings can be seen in the *Catechism of the Catholic Church* (CCC), 2nd ed. (Washington, DC: Libreria Editrice Vaticana-United States Conference of Catholic Bishops, 2000), nos. 325-421; there you will find the references to previous documents of the Magisterium.

human couples—a doctrine named *polygenism*. Other authors say that if monogenism is not a teaching of faith, at least it is *proximate truth of faith*, which means that without affirming this truth, we cannot understand other truths of faith, and, therefore, it can be considered *implied* in other truths. In particular, the Catholic truths that can be most compromised if monogenism is not accepted are: first of all, the dogma of original sin (a sin committed by the first parents, transmitted to all men that come into this world), and, consequently, the dogma of Christ's universal redemption (that Christ has redeemed *all men* from original sin) which is a truly Biblical teaching, as can be seen in the passage of St. Paul's letter to the Romans (5:12-21) and parallel passages.[152] Pope Pius XII, in the encyclical *Humani Generis*, limits himself to saying that "When there is a question of another conjectural opinion, namely, of polygenism so-called, then the sons of the Church in no way enjoy such freedom. For the faithful in Christ cannot accept this view, which holds that either after Adam there existed on this earth, who did not receive their origin by natural generation from him, the first parent of all; or that Adam signifies some kind of multitude of first parents; for it is by no means apparent how such an opinion can be reconciled with what the sources of revealed truth and the acts of the Magisterium of the Church teach about original sin, which proceeds from a sin truly committed by one Adam, and which is transmitted to all by generation, and exists in each one as his own."[153]

3. IS THERE REALLY OPPOSITION?

a) *Opposition with the extremist systems*

The opposition with the extremist systems is evident. This would include all the theories of evolution that, alongside the data

---

[152] See the excellent criticism regarding this, by ARAUJO, *Evolución y Evolucionismo*, 419-432.

[153] DENZINGER, *The Sources of Catholic Dogma*, no. 2328.

used to formulate the theories, not only *freely add* what is unscientific, but also include the scientifically and philosophically imbued presupposition of the non-existence (and therefore, non-intervention) of a Supernatural Power. Not much needs to be added. This position, however, falls on its own, if we keep in mind what was already said about the existence of God and the existence of the soul. *If they steal these two truths from you (God and the spiritual soul), as a consequence, they will also steal from you the truth of your dignity, reducing you to a little bit of "miraculously" evolved matter. (Do not doubt that the atheistic evolutionists believe in miracles; at least they believe in this singular and astonishing miracle that something came from nothing and that from something material, life emerged, and that from biological life, the spirit emerged. It has not been proved yet, but indubitably the first one to demonstrate it will be canonized immediately.)*

b) Possible agreement with moderate systems

All the moderate evolutionist systems also need to be demonstrated, which we are still far from achieving. In any case, they have in their favor a collection of more or less certain data; however, this data is unified by theories that are difficult to demonstrate and conflict with other theories within the same scientific field. At least they have the merit of not leaving the confines of the object and method prescribed by their specialty; they do not jump from geological, biological, or archeological data to metaphysical conclusions. In this sense, their hypotheses are works in progress and deserve to be considered by philosophy and theology, always taken into account with respect to their scientific status (examined as hypothesis and not considered as already proven).

Keep in mind that, due to the nature of this book, it is not my purpose to directly debate any of the theories or hypotheses but to take into account those that *from the scientific point of view* can be discussed and debated to see if they can really call into question the Catholic Faith (as many pseudo-scientists and spokespersons of high schools and universities claim). In any case, although only briefly, I want to note here that, according to some authors, we are living the historic moment of possible *transition* regarding the value of some scientific theories, particularly those referring to the origin of life and man. It is what some, like Carlos Javier Alonso, call the "crisis of the Darwinist paradigm."[154] It does not mean that this crisis in this "model of explanation" will cause those involved to leave the realm of evolutionist thought (since they will find other evolutionist schools like the various types of neo-Darwinism); however, the weakness of the theories has been revealed. "To this very day, a scientifically acceptable theory about the origin of life does not exist; there is only a series of highly speculative conjectures. All the biogenetic knowledge has been ballasted by hypotheses without sufficient foundation; and currently there is nothing about the origin of life that is not an unjustified assertion or ventured supposition whose level of credibility we cannot even evaluate,"[155] maintains Alonso. Also with respect to the question about human evolution (*anthropogenesis*), "too many problems without solutions exist and they lack plentiful evidence to be able to claim—as some distinguished neo-Darwinists have done—that the search for human origins has been concluded with success. The specialists not only do not have a sufficient number of well differentiated fossils with which to work, but they also do not agree on how to classify the few types of fossils that are available. The origin of the hominid primate is still a scientific enigma whose precise explanation constitutes a fascinating adventure. The search must continue, although in view of preceding missing links that were never verified and the following temptation to cover up the lack of evidence with generalizations, the best policy in an area as sensitive as human origins should be that of caution and moderation."[156] If all this is kept in mind, it will be understood that we are not accepting any evolutionist hypothesis—or theory, if you

---

[154] CARLOS JAVIER ALONSO, *El Evolucionismo y Otros Mitos: La Crisis del Paradigma Darwinista* (Pamplona: EUNSA, 2004), editorial translation.

[155] Ibid.

[156] ALONSO, *El Evolucionismo y Otros Mitos,* ch. 8, editorial translation.

like—but analyzing them, without losing sight of their hypothetical quality, to find the possible difficulties for faith.

If we take into consideration the theories about the universe and its evolution, be it the Big Bang or any other, it must be said that they are theories about the origin of the development of the universe, not about *why* the universe has this beginning or any other. They do not in any way exclude causality on God's part, whether it started with a "great explosion" of a "primordial nucleus," as Georges Lemaître supposed and the majority of today's scientists admit, or any other explanation. The universe *is* (it exists) instead of *not being* (not existing); that is the point. Science can try to explain what the beginning was like, but it cannot explain *why it is* in place of *not having been*.

To highlight the point that there is no conflict between the theories of the origin of the universe (at least those that conceive of it as an expanding universe), it does not hurt to remember that Georges Lemaître, one of the founders of the great explosion theory, was also a Belgian priest (1894-1966). The term "big bang," coined by the British astronomer, Fred Hoyle (supporter of an eternal universe for philosophical reasons), is sarcastic and mocking in order to ridicule the ideas developed by Lemaître. Hoyle thought that Lemaître was trying to scientifically justify the Biblical creation of the world with his theory. However, Lemaître's scientific convictions were not founded on his faith (he always knew how to avoid all confusion between science and belief), but on solid mathematical and physical arguments.[157]

With regard to the evolution of our planet, scientists distinguish two clearly different moments: the first was the abiotic era (*a-bios*: without life) and the second is the biotic era (ever since the origin

---

[157] This can be seen with respect to DOMINIQUE LAMBERT, "El Universo de Georges Lemaître," *Investigación y Ciencia* 307 (April 2002); also available online at *arvo.net/fe-y-ciencias/el-universo-de-georges-lema-tr/gmx-niv90-con10046.htm*. Lambert is a doctor of physical sciences and philosophy from the Catholic University of Louvain and gives classes in philosophy and history of science in the Higher Institute of Notre-Dame de la Paix, in Namur.

of life). This second era is generally divided into various time periods like: the Primary (Cambrian, Silurian, Devonian, Carboniferous, and Permian Periods), the Secondary (Triassic, Jurassic, Cretaceous), the Tertiary (Eocene, Oligocene, Miocene, Pleistocene), and the Quaternary Period (Diluvial and Alluvial). The appearance of man is placed in this last period.

Throughout the history of Christianity, there have been different attempts to reconcile these periods (as science progressively defined them) with the Biblical narratives. These attempts have led to the appearance of conciliatory systems that are divided into three groups: *the historical or reconciling system* (which wants to reconcile the Biblical narrative with the objective order of things as science claims to establish them); *the allegorical system* (represented, for example, by St. Augustine, which claims that the biblical narrative is not a historic narrative but is the manner in which the inspired author had knowledge of the events or an allegorical description of the events); and *the historical-allegorical system* (which holds that the narrative contains objective truth but recognizes a certain literary artifice in the narration). It is clear that all of the reconciling systems (in vogue in the nineteenth and beginning of the twentieth centuries) fall into artificial explanations and do not keep in mind that the biblical narrative is not a scientific explanation. The problem of the allegorical systems—although they have been presented by some Fathers of the Church—is that they do not preserve sufficient certainty about the historic character of the first chapter of Genesis (although they do not deny it). So, the most adequate solution is to sustain that the correct interpretation should take the narrative as partly historical and partly allegorical. I think that, in spite of the passage of time, we can take the primary foundations of interpretation indicated by Father Prado in his exposition on the Old Testament, distinguishing between the clearly historical and doctrinal elements and those elements pertinent to the literary form[158]:

---

[158] Cf. JUAN PRADO, Liber 1 of *Vetus Testamentum* (Taurini: Marietta, 1934), 27-28.

1. The following pertain to history and doctrine, among other things:

   a. The creation of all things, made by God at the beginning of time;

   b. The goodness of all the works of God, as far as they respond to the divine idea and will;

   c. Certain gradation or progression and succession in the production of things, beginning with the creation of the first elements and ending with the formation of man;

   d. The totally singular creation of man in the image of God (necessarily implying the creation of a spiritual element).

2. The literary form can include:

   a. The anthropomorphic images that represent God speaking or working;

   b. The description of heaven, sea, rain, plants and animals, in which non-scientific descriptions make use of appearances, and the ideas and the manner of speaking of that time;

   c. The order of the narration (such as, a week); etc.

It is clear that if we make these distinctions, there are no problems with harmonizing the Biblical narrative with the facts that science uses (as long as these are kept within their limits). Therefore, when we are asked if science's descriptions of the origin and evolution of our planet and the stages of development of life in it (prehistoric fossils, continental drift, or distant cataclysms) can be taken as objections to the veracity of the Biblical narrative or of the Judeo-Christian faith, we have to respond that no such difficulty exists. It could be interesting to read what Mariano Delgado (Doctor in Biology and Theology) has written about this topic in *Concordancia del Génesis con la ciencia moderna: Adán, Eva y el Hombre Prehistórico* [Concordance of Genesis with Modern Science: Adam, Eve and Prehistoric Man].[159]

The same can be said with respect to the origin of man. We have already stated the indisputable biblical information about the origin of man from the point of view of faith. It can be reduced to the following: the singular creation of man, the essential difference between man and all other living beings (that is, the creation of his spiritual and immortal soul) and the facts surrounding original sin. I am inclined to think that the unity of the human genus (monogenism) pertains to these truths of faith as well (although there are theologians who say that polygenism does not present difficulties in understanding the dogma of original sin and universal redemption accomplished by Christ, I sincerely cannot come to see this "absence of difficulties.")

With respect to these truths, there are no true objections about a possible evolution of some animal species into man, or even about the existence of the diverse races that humanity is divided into today.

We begin with this last idea. The different human races have been the pretext for some writers to deny the unity of the human species at some point (especially in order to defend polygenism). There are three principal human races: white or Caucasian, yellow or Mongolian, and black or Ethiopian. They certainly have different characteristics with regards to pigmentation and physical traits (principally facial features). Actually, the three are only the principal races, but the numerous sub-races in which they can be divided will have to be pointed out if you wish to be precise. In reality, these differences are not sufficient differences to defend polygenism, because: (1) *skin coloration* is a physical phenomenon of little importance and of no specific value, easily produced by the

---

[159] Cf. MARIANO DELGADO, *Adán y Eva y el Hombre Prehistórico* (Madrid: Palabra, 1995), 604. It touches upon the themes of the universe in the biblical narration, similarities and differences between the Genesis story and the myths of neighboring towns, Adam and Eve and their children, history and prehistory, fossil data, data from molecular biology, etc.

influence of the environment and nutrition; (2) *hair*, which according to Hackel differentiates human species, being so changeable that the individual himself can easily change the form and color, totally lacks value and presents much less profound variations than the fur of an animal classified as the same species; (3) the anatomical differences are not so exclusive to one race that they cannot be found in individuals of others; likewise we see more pronounced anatomical characteristics in individual animals of the same breed; (4) the intellectual differences are not exclusive to the races, but fundamentally depend on the individuals (there are both high and low intellectual coefficients in all); and (5) the linguistic differences are even less, since we also find completely different languages among the individuals of the same race (as occurs in some African tribes of the Western Sahara).

On the other hand, the different races coincide at fundamental points: the same genetic makeup to the point of finding the *same* mitochondrial DNA, transmitted exclusively maternally, in all women of the human race. This has brought some scientists to postulate the existence of one same original mother, the mitochondrial Eve, which is a disputed subject at the moment. In addition to this, the anatomical, physical, and psychological similarities are remarkable. *Anatomically*, all races have the same organs, the same anatomical structure, and the same interdependence of organs. *Physiologically*, the phenomenon of organic and sensible life is identical in all races, while they differ highly between the animal breeds. Animals that produce fertile offspring are considered to pertain to the same species and to be descendants of the same common family tree. On the other hand, those animals whose mating is sterile or whose offspring is infertile are considered to pertain to different species. However, ever since time began, the human races have intersected, begetting generations and generations of healthy fertile individuals. *Psychologically*, there are accidental psychological diversities between the races (some more dry and reserved, others more talkative and open, others more credulous and superstitious, others more skeptical) and among the individuals of the same race; however, all healthy men, regardless of their race, possess an articulate language, have a sense of good and evil, are by nature religious, progress in all orders, and are industrious.

With all this said, we can clearly see none of it presents a difficulty for maintaining the unity of the human genus; on the contrary, it sustains it. We leave the arguments about how the races became diverse and what factors influenced this process to other experts.

Another theme related in a certain way could also be mentioned here. Could another humanity have existed before our own that had already disappeared before the creation of Adam? In the past, some proposed the doctrine of *pre-adamism* (supported by Isaac de la Peyrère in 1655). However, this theory did not speak of the extinction of the pre-adamites but maintains that the pagans descended from them, while only the Jews descended from Adam (evidently Isaac de la Peyrère was a Jew). The theory failed two years later after the conversion of its author. The encyclopedists of the eighteenth century repeated it. Maybe someone will propose it to explain archeological findings that do not appear to fit in the human species (*homo sapiens*). We would have to say that we do not have information to biblically support this theory, but there would not be difficulties in accepting it (except for the fact that *it should be proven and not only presented in a hypothetical way*) as long as we maintain that these sub-humans, pre-humans, para-humans or humans before Adam, disappeared or subsisted together with the human race without mixing and afterwards perished. This is purely hypothetical and does not touch that which is essential to the dogma: the creation of the human race by divine intervention and the singularity of this (for the aforementioned reasons).

In regard to a possible animal evolution that would have ended in modern man, it must be said that, allowing for providential direction over this evolution and the creation of the spiritual soul and its infusion at a given moment—in this case—in the individual that would start what is properly the human race, in itself there is no specific clash with the teachings of the Christian faith.

On this topic, I return to the previously cited article of M. Artigas: "In 1950, in the encyclical, *Humani Generis*, Pope Pius XII

167

declared that 'the Teaching Authority of the Church does not forbid that, in conformity with the present state of human sciences and sacred theology, research and discussions, on the part of men experienced in both fields, take place with regard to the doctrine of evolutionism, in as far as it inquires into the origin of the human body as coming from pre-existent and living matter—for the Catholic faith obliges us to hold that souls are immediately created by God.'[160] In a speech in 1985, directed to participants in a symposium about Christian faith and evolution, Pope John Paul II recalled the words of the teaching of Pius XII, affirming that, 'on the basis of such remarks made by my predecessor, no obstacles are created by a properly conceived faith in creation or by a properly understood teaching on evolution'.[161] [...] It is clear that 'understanding properly' means admitting that the spiritual dimensions of the human person require a special intervention on the part of God, an immediate creation of the spiritual soul; but this deals with some dimensions and an action which, on principle, fall outside the direct object of natural science and do not contradict it in any way. Keeping in mind the previously marked out limitations and referring again to the teaching of Pius XII, John Paul II taught in his 1986 catechesis: 'It can therefore be said that, from the viewpoint of the doctrine of the faith, there are no difficulties in explaining the origin of man in regard to the body, by means of the theory of evolution. But it must be added that this hypothesis proposes only a probability, not a scientific certainty. However, the doctrine of faith invariably affirms that man's spiritual soul is created directly by God. According to the hypothesis mentioned, it is possible that the human body, following the order impressed by the Creator on the energies of life, could have been gradually prepared in the forms of antecedent living beings. However, the human soul, on which man's humanity

[160] PIUS XII, *Humani Generis*, no. 36.

[161] ST. JOHN PAUL II, "Address to the Symposium 'Christian Faith and the Theory of Evolution', Rome," April 26, 1985, trans. Paolo Zanna, *Interdisciplinary Encyclopedia of Religion & Science, inters.org/John-Paul-II-Faith-Evolution-1985* (accessed January 9, 2015).

definitively depends, cannot emerge from matter, since the soul is of a spiritual nature.'[162] In 1996, John Paul II delivered a message to the Pontifical Academy of Sciences, gathered in a meeting of the plenary assembly. Again he alluded to the teaching of Pius XII about evolution, saying that: 'Taking into account the scientific research of the era, and also the proper requirements of theology, the encyclical *Humani Generis* treated the doctrine of 'evolutionism' as a serious hypothesis, worthy of investigation and serious study, alongside the opposite hypothesis.'[163] And a little later he adds some reflections of great interest because they echo the progress of science in the realm of evolution in recent times: 'Today, more than a half-century after the appearance of that encyclical, some new findings lead us toward the recognition of evolution as more than an hypothesis. In fact it is remarkable that this theory has had progressively greater influence on the spirit of researchers, following a series of discoveries in different scholarly disciplines. The convergence in the results of these independent studies—which was neither planned nor sought—constitutes in itself a significant argument in favor of the theory.'[164] These words should not be interpreted as an uncritical acceptance of any theory of evolution whatsoever. In fact, immediately after these words, John Paul II adds important reflections about the extent or reach of the evolutionary theories, about their different variations, and about the philosophies that can be implicit in them. Especially interesting are the extensive reflections that the Pope dedicates to the evolutionary ideas applied to the human being. It could even be said that this is the nucleus of the Pope's document [...] In this context, he recalls textually the words of Pius XII in the encyclical

---

[162] St. JOHN PAUL II, "Man is a Spiritual and Corporeal Being," General Audience, April 16, 1986,
www.vatican.va/holy_father/john_paul_ii/audiences/alpha/data/aud19860416en.html (accessed October 26, 2014).

[163] St. JOHN PAUL II, "Message to the Pontifical Academy of Sciences: On Evolution" (October 22, 1996), no. 4, *www.ewtn.com/library/papaldoc/jp961022.htm* (accessed January 11, 2015).

[164] Ibid.

Humani Generis, according to which the spiritual human soul is created immediately by God, and extracts the following consequence: 'As a result, the theories of evolution which, because of the philosophies which inspire them, regard the spirit either as emerging from the forces of living matter, or as a simple epiphenomenon of that matter, are incompatible with the truth about man. They are therefore unable to serve as the basis for the dignity of the human person.'[165] [...] John Paul II affirms that 'With man, we find ourselves facing a different ontological order—an ontological leap,'[166] and he asks if this ontological discontinuity does not contradict the physical continuity supposed by evolution. His reply is that science and metaphysics use two different perspectives, and experience on the metaphysical level gives evidence of the existence of dimensions situated on a superior ontological level, such as self-consciousness and self-awareness, moral conscience, liberty, aesthetic and religious experience. He adds, finally, that 'theology seeks to clarify the ultimate meaning of the Creator's designs.'[167]"[168]

4. BY WAY OF CONCLUSION

"Scientific activity supposes that a natural order exists," says Artigas, to whom this whole paragraph is attributed. "Experimental science searches to know this order and all its achievements are a particular manifestation of natural order. It can be said in a illustrative manner that the more science there is, the more order: as science progresses, we better understand the order that exists in nature, although obviously we understand it in our own way, through representations that are not always simply

---

[165] St. JOHN PAUL II, "Message to the Pontifical Academy of Sciences: On Evolution," no. 5.

[166] St. JOHN PAUL II, "Message to the Pontifical Academy of Sciences: On Evolution," no. 6.

[167] Ibid.

[168] ARTIGAS, *Evolución, Fe y Teología,* editorial translation.

photographs of reality [...] When we reflect on this current worldview that is permeated with subtlety and rationality, it results as unlikely or improbable to reduce nature to the result of blind and accidental forces. It is much more logical to admit that the rationality of nature reflects the action of a personal God who has created it, imprinting in it some tendencies that explain the prodigious capacity to form successive organizations, enormously complex and sophisticated, on different levels, reaching the point of complexity necessary for the existence of human beings.

"I will not resist commenting here on a type of definition proposed by Thomas Aquinas, which appears to me more complete and profound than the usual definitions. At the end of one of his commentaries on Aristotle's Physics, Thomas Aquinas goes much further than his teacher and writes: 'Hence, it is clear that nature is nothing but a certain kind of art, i.e., the divine art, impressed upon things, by which these things are moved to a determinate end. It is as if the shipbuilder were able to give to timbers that by which they would move themselves to take the form of a ship.'[169]

"The comparison in the example is much more applicable today than in the eighth century; then it was no more than a simple comparison, while now it could actually become reality. Contemplated under the theist perspective, nature does not lose anything of what is its own; on the contrary, its dynamism and its potentialities appear to be stones in their proper place of a radical foundation—none other than divine action—which explains nature's existence and notable properties. All of nature appears as the unfolding of divine wisdom and power, which directs the course of events in agreement with His plans, not only respecting nature, but also giving it being and allowing it to possess the characteristic proper to nature. God is at the same time both transcendent to nature (because He is distinct from it and gives it

---

[169] ST. THOMAS AQUINAS, *Commentary on Aristotle's Physics*, trans. Richard J. Blackwell (Notre Dame: Dumb Ox Books, 1999), 134, book II, lecture 14, no. 268.

being) and immanent to nature (because his action extends to all that nature is, to the most intimate part of its being).

"This perspective shows that the presumed or alleged opposition between evolution and divine action is lacking from the start. Naturalism claims to remove God from the world in the name of science, but to do so theorists must close their eyes to the real dimensions of scientific enterprise. 'Integral naturalism' can be mentioned, which, in line with previous reflections, contemplates natural science together with its suppositions and its implications; this analysis reaches the doors of metaphysics and theology.

"Many scientists on the front lines admit that evolution and divine action are compatible. For example, Francisco Ayala, currently one of the principle representatives of neo-Darwinism, has written that creation from nothing 'is one notion that, in its very nature, remains and always will remain outside of the borders of science', and then 'other notions outside the borders of science are the existence of God and of spirits, and whatever activity or process is strictly defined as immaterial.'[170] In effect, in order for something to be studied by science, it must include material dimensions that can be subjected to controllable or closed experiments. This is not possible with the spirit, or with God, or with the action of God. On the other hand, Ayala recalls the opinions of the theologians who say: 'Divine existence and creation are compatible with evolution and other natural processes. The solution resides in accepting the idea that God operates through intermediate causes: that a person is a divine creature is not incompatible with the notion that he has been conceived in the womb of his mother and that he lives and grows through means of nutrients... Evolution can also be considered as a natural process through which God brings living species to existence in accordance with His plan...'[171]

---

[170] FRANCISCO AYALA, *La Teoría de la Evolución: De Darwin a los Últimos Avances de la Genética* (Madrid: Ediciones Temas de Hoy, 1994), 147, editorial translation.

[171] AYALA, *La Teoría de la Evolución,* 21-22, editorial translation.

"Catholic doctrine affirms that all depends on God, and that 'Creation has its own goodness and proper perfection, but it did not spring forth complete from the hands of the Creator. The universe was created *in a state of journeying* (*in statu viae*) toward an ultimate perfection yet to be attained, to which God has destined it. We call 'divine providence' the dispositions by which God guides his creation toward this perfection. By his providence God protects and governs all things which he has made, 'reaching mightily from one end of the earth to the other, and ordering all things well.' For 'all are open and laid bare to his eyes,' even those things which are yet to come into existence through the free action of creatures.'[172] This perspective speaks of God as the First Cause of being for all that exists, and of creatures as second causes whose existence and activity always suppose divine action: 'The truth that God is at work in all the actions of his creatures is inseparable from faith in God the Creator. God is the first cause who operates in and through secondary causes... Far from diminishing the creature's dignity, this truth enhances it.'[173] It is not only that God is simply the first in a series of causes of the same type: his action is the foundation of the activity of creatures that could not exist nor act without the permanent influx of divine action.

"According to naturalism the existence of God and his action in nature is unnecessary. Nature, including man, would be the result of blind forces. Darwinism is often used in this context to claim that Darwin has made it possible to be an atheist in an intellectually legitimate way, because Darwinism shows that it is not necessary to admit to divine action in order to explain the order that exists in the world.[174] It is also claimed that Darwinism allows us to demonstrate that the hierarchy of ideas which places God on the top and interprets everything starting from God must be renounced. The Darwinist explanation would give a type of general

---

[172] CCC 302.

[173] CCC 308.

[174] Cf. RICHARD DAWKINS, *The Blind Watchmaker* (New York: W. W. Norton & Company, 1996).

algorithm that explains, in an advantageous way, what was previously attempted with recourse to divine action.[175]

"These naturalist doctrines often fall into a basic philosophical error: concretely, these scientists often take it as a given that divine action and the action of natural causes are on the same level. If they admit this, all natural actions would be understood to exclude divine action; thus, it would seem that scientific progress, which claims an ever growing knowledge of natural activity, is constantly putting itself farther within the limits of metaphysics and theology. Seen in this light, evolution seems to effectively make divine action unnecessary. However, *this naturalist reasoning forgets that the scientific perspective, which is both legitimate and important, is only one perspective. This one perspective should not oppose metaphysical and theological perspectives, but better yet should presuppose them, at least if one wants to obtain a complete idea of the problems.* As we have previously noted, philosophical reflection about the suppositions and implications of the progress of science becomes fully coherent within a theist perspective. On the other hand, the naturalist perspective is decisively incomplete, given that it contents itself with the explanations of experimental sciences, as if reason and human experiences could go no farther, and renounces the exercise of metaphysical reasoning, which is one of the specific characteristics of human beings and is also crucial to scientific progress.

"Pope John Paul II, in a speech at the Pontifical Academy of Sciences, expressed this idea in the following manner: 'The Bible itself speaks to us of the origin of the universe and its make-up, not in order to provide us with a scientific treatise, but in order to state the correct relationships of man with God and with the universe. Sacred Scripture wishes simply to declare that the world was created by God, and in order to teach this truth it expresses itself in the terms of the cosmology in use at the time of the writer. The Sacred Book likewise wishes to tell men that the world was

---

[175] Cf. DANIEL DENNETT, *Darwin's Dangerous Idea* (London: Penguin Books, 1996).

not created as the seat of the gods, as was taught by other cosmogonies and cosmologies, but was rather created for the service of man and the glory of God. Any other teaching about the origin and make-up of the universe is alien to the intentions of the Bible, which does not wish to teach how heaven was made but how one goes to heaven. Any scientific hypothesis on the origin of the world, such as the hypothesis of a primitive atom from which derived the whole of the physical universe, leaves open the problem concerning the universe's beginning. Science cannot of itself solve this question: there is needed that human knowledge that rises above physics and astrophysics and which is called metaphysics; there is needed above all the knowledge that comes from God's revelation.'[176]

"God does not compete with nature. Any problems that are raised which oppose God to nature are based on a metaphysical error: the failure to realize that the existence and the activity of second causes, rather than making the existence and activity of the First Cause unnecessary, is unintelligible and impossible without this fundamental foundation. Certainly, thinking in terms of First Cause and second causes requires situating oneself in a metaphysical perspective; those who think that experimental science exhausts the types of questions and answers accessible to the human being will adopt these terms with difficulty. But, however trivial this seems, it must be remembered that any reflection on science, even when it denies the legitimacy of any knowledge that surpasses it, supposes accepting a certain dose of meta-scientific thought [...] All too often, in dealing with evolutionism, God and creatures are considered as causes that compete on the same level, ignoring the distinction between First Cause, which is the cause of the being of all that exists, and the second created causes, which act on something that preexists and modify it, necessitating the constant assistance of the First Cause

---

[176] ST. JOHN PAUL II, "Cosmology and Fundamental Physics," in *Discourses of the Popes from Pius XI to John Paul II to the Pontifical Academy of Sciences 1936-1986* (Vatican City: Pontifica Academia Scientiarum, 1986), 161-164, no. 2.

to exist and act in every moment. In such cases, when this distinction is ignored, the following alternative is presented: either God or natural causes. This gives an impoverished idea of God, which ends up becoming a *deus ex machina* introduced merely to explain particular problems, especially the order or agreement between different parts of nature [...]

"They should not formulate the problem as a type of 'competition' between God and evolution to explain the natural end [...] The current scientific worldview is very coherent with the claim that divine action serves as the foundation of all that exists. God is different from nature and completely transcends it, but, at the same time, as the First Cause, He is immanent to nature, is present wherever the creature exists and acts, making its acting and existence possible. Furthermore, in carrying out his plans, God counts on secondary causes, and so evolution is consistent with this systematic action of God with creatures."[177]

* * *

Therefore, we leave the scientists with their arguments about the origin and development of the cosmos, life, and man (asking them only to behave professionally like true men of science and to demonstrate what they claim and to doubt what is doubtful). And if you get the chance (and you have the calling), be a man of science and carefully examine what you are told is already settled. When a person with a seductive and attractive voice wants to sell you a horse saying that it is young, first look in the horse's mouth and you will find that behind the mesmerizing charm, signs of a fraud are hidden.

---

[177] ARTIGAS, *Evolución, Fe y Teología,* editorial translation.

For Further Reading

- Chesterton, G. K. *The Everlasting Man*. Garden City, New York: Image Books, 1955.
- Gilson, Etienne. *From Aristotle to Darwin & Back Again: A Journey in Final Causality, Species and Evolution*. San Francisco: Ignatius Press, 2002.
- St. John Paul II, "Address to the Symposium 'Christian Faith and the Theory of Evolution', Rome." April 26, 1985. Translated by Paolo Zanna. *Interdisciplinary Encyclopedia of Religion & Science, inters.org/John-Paul-II-Faith-Evolution-1985* (accessed January 9, 2015).
- ————. "Cosmology and Fundamental Physics." In *Discourses of the Popes from Pius XI to John Paul II to the Pontifical Academy of Sciences 1936-1986*. Vatican City: Pontifica Academia Scientiarum, 1986.
- ————. "Man is a Spiritual and Corporeal Being." General Audience. April 16, 1986. In *God, Father and Creator*. Boston: Pauline Books & Media, 1996.
- ————. "Message to the Pontifical Academy of Sciences: On Evolution." October 22, 1996. *www.ewtn.com/library/papaldoc/jp961022.htm* (accessed January 11, 2015).
- Wasmann, Erich. "Catholics and Evolution." In vol. V of *The Catholic Encyclopedia*. New York: Robert Appleton Company, 1909.

Available in Other Languages

- Artigas, Mariano. "Evolución, Fe y Teología: Desarrollos recientes en evolución y su repercusión para la fe y la teología." *Scripta Theologica* 32 (2000): 249-273. Electronic edition by *Grupo de Investigación sobre Ciencia, Razón y Fe* (CRYF), *www.unav.es/cryf/desarrollosenevolucionyrepercusiones.html*.
- ————. *Las Fronteras del Evolucionismo*. Madrid: MC, 1986.
- Díaz Araujo, Enrique. *Evolución y Evolucionismo*. Guadalajara: Universidad Autónoma de Guadalajara, 2000.
- Delgado, Mariano. *Adán, Eva y el Hombre Prehistórico*. Madrid: Palabra, 1995.

- Javier Alonso, Carlos. *El Evolucionismo y Otros Mitos: La Crisis del Paradigma Darwinista*. Pamplona: EUNSA, 2004.
- Lambert, Dominique. "El Universo de Georges Lemaître." *Investigación y Ciencia* 307 (April 2002). Electronic edition on *arvo.net/fe-y-ciencias/el-universo-de-georges-lema-tr/gmx-niv90-con10046.htm*.
- Marín Negueruela, Nicolás. *Con la Razón y la Fe o Problemas Apologéticos*. Barcelona: Tipografía Católica Casals, 1941.
- Morales Marín, J. "Evolución: Filosofía y Visión de Conjunto." *Gran Enciclopedia Rialp*. Madrid: Ediciones Rialp, 1991.

6.

THE STOLEN
TRUTH ABOUT
HUMAN LIFE

When does a human being begin to be a human being?

If you study medicine, biology, embryology, pharmacy, nursing, or some related sciences, it would not be strange for you to hear the most absurd things about the moment a human being begins to be a human being. Maybe you will hear it said that this occurs only two weeks after conception, or maybe in the moment of implantation (and only if this takes place), or even later. From these theories some logical conclusions can be drawn: before this moment "determined" by science there is no human being; and therefore, no harm is done to a human being in investigating and harming "this," the fruit of conception, nor is it murder if it is destroyed, nor is there any sinister action if it is used as a deposit of cells, etc. Be careful, they are preparing you to hand yourself over to the macabre game of destroying your fellow creatures and taking the title of human being away from them before you do it. Not only are they stealing from you this truth that has been part of your life (you were also an embryo and you are reading this because from the very first moment you were treated as a human being), but they ask your complacency in the face of the daily massacre that our modern world carries out, or they invite you to consort with the modern slaughterhouses.

This chapter has such importance that I will try to deal with it in the clearest manner possible, although you will have to make an effort to read many technical terms that are necessary to make this truth clear. However, in spite of the complexity of language, you will see that this truth is not so difficult to assimilate.

1. THE BIOLOGICAL NATURE OF AN EMBRYO

In the first place I would like to give an account of the commentary by two Italian authors, A. L. Vescovi, and L. Spinardi, members of the "National Stem Cell Consortium" of Italy, who invite us to follow—with the facts from current science—the different moments of a human embryo's development in order for us to draw our own conclusions about the moment it begins to be

181

human.[178] At the root of the debate about "artificial" fertilization, use of stem cells, cloning, etc., these two authors establish the biological basis to also offer a biological response to the debate about the beginning of life. The key question that should precede all discussion of the subject is this: When—if it is possible to determine—does human life properly begin? They respond that biologically and logically it can be established with certainty, but before looking at their reply, we follow their exposition. We will restrict ourselves only to the embryonic process (that is until two months old, when the term "embryo" is replaced with "fetus") this will be enough for our purposes. Some authors use the term "embryo" to refer to the thing that develops in the womb of a woman "after implantation in the womb." For ideological reasons, they use other terms, like "pre-embryo," zygote or other similar terms for the events prior to implantation. This is an abuse of language that comes with bad intentions. It is enough for our objective, that by simplifying the language we will allow ourselves to use "embryo" for the process that goes from the moment of conception to two months.

For those who find some of the next pages dry, I remind you of the importance of being aware of the steps that describe embryonic development (a strictly scientific question), in order to have a true and correct basis for the moment in which philosophical (and also theological) questions are argued. Man cannot be cured if one does not know what a man is, or, in the words of Gustave Thibon, the medical technician cannot know what a sick person has if he does not know what a sick person is. It was not for nothing that they attributed to Galileo (c. 130 BC) the expression: "the best doctor is also a philosopher."

---

[178] A. L. VESCOVI and L. SPINARDI, "La Natura Biologica dell'Embrione," *Medicina e Morale* (January 2004): 53-63. I will follow this article almost to the letter, adding a few things to clarify the concepts and summarizing others. For this reason and in order not to make the reading more difficult, the authors' literal text will not be in quotes.

a) The embryo and its origin

The development of a human being begins with an encounter during which a single sperm cell (male cell) unites with an egg cell, ovum (female cell), after a sexual act carried out during a woman's fertile period. This is called *fertilization*. *Fertilization* includes a series of successive events: from the penetration of the sperm into the ovum, to the *fusion* of the cell membranes (what some call *syngamy*), to the union of the pronuclei of the two cells (each one of which has 23 chromosomes) in order to create a new cell with a complete genome (called *diploid*) of 46 chromosomes. We remember that our body's cells are divided into two main groups. *All types of cells* (nervous, muscular, epithelial, and skeletal cells) *except one* have 46 chromosomes, that is to say, the complete patrimony with our genetic information (for this reason they are called *diploids*). The *only* one that does not share these characteristics is the sexual cell or *germ* cell (thus called because it is destined to be the seed of a new being; it is the sperm in the man, and the ovum in the woman) that has only half of this genome (23 chromosomes; male germs can contain either X or Y chromosomes because the diploid male is XY: an ovum contains X because the female diploid is XX) because they are destined to unite, forming one new being with a complete genome, half contributed by the father and half by the mother.[179]

The ovum fertilized by the sperm is a new cellular entity called the *zygote*. This zygote will begin to divide itself, first into two cells, then in four, etc. The two cells that came from the first cell division appear to possess different characteristics that then persist in successive cell divisions. Therefore, the embryo comes from the progeny of one of the cells and the embryonic membranes (among which is the placenta) come from the progeny of the other.

---

[179] From this you can also deduce that nature itself only has two sexes, since the germinal cell are complementary one (that of the woman) with the other (that of the man). There is not a third cell that is complementary with the cells of its same class. Therefore there is not a third sex; homosexuality is not natural, as can already be deduced from this genetic argument.

However, it's not worth talking about the cell's "destination," because, if one of the first cells is removed, those remaining are in a condition to compensate for its absence.

After fertilization, the first cell divisions of the zygote occur slowly in a process called *segmentation* that, beginning from one cell, carries out the formation of two, four, eight, and sixteen cells. The cells formed in this way are called *blastomeres* and the organism as a whole is called *morula* (named such because of its resemblance to a mulberry). Many zygotes do not get past this stage of development and die by spontaneous abortion (therefore, before arriving at implantation). When the morula reaches the uterus it is made up of 32 cells and begins to swell, absorbing liquids between the blastomeres. The spaces that contain the liquids come together causing a cavity. When this cavity can be detected, the whole organism is called the blastocyst. The outer most cells of the *blastocyst*, above all those that surround the cavity, assume a flat form, and give rise to the cells of the trophoblast. These cells will contribute to the formation of the embryonic membranes. The internal cells of the blastocyst give rise to the cells of the inner mass: these make up the formation of the new organism. The inner mass cells can give rise to all types of cells present in the adult individual. This is why they are called *pluripotent*—it is not correct, however, to call them, as some do, *totipotent,* because they are not capable of giving rise to the cells that make up the embryonic membranes (that come exclusively from trophoblasts). These embryonic stem cells (mother cells) are separated, precisely, from the cells of the inner mass cells.

In the uterus, the blastocyst grows and adheres to the endometrium (this is the name for the inner wall of the uterus) by means of the trophoblasts. This act is called *implantation* of the blastocyst and occurs six days after fertilization. The embryo begins the second week of development. The implantation of the blastocyst is completed in three or four days and is generally finished before day twelve. During implantation, the trophoblast cells actively make contact with the surface of the endometrium and totally penetrate the epithelium. At the point of contact with the uterine mucous, it develops a *primitive circulatory system* that provides nutrition to the implanted blastocyst and to the embryonic membranes that it is forming. The blastocyst's cavity tends to expand and give definitive separation between the inner mass cells and the trophoblasts. In this way it forms the first embryonic membrane called the *amniotic cavity*. From the trophoblast, another embryonic membrane is generated called the *chorion* (the membrane that enfolds the embryo and keeps it apart from the uterine wall) from which the chorionic villus are successively derived, and finally the placenta. The blastocyst is thus completely nestled in the rich endometrium or uterine wall and irrigated by the maternal blood. When the fetal circulation system is developed, the fetal and the maternal blood remain separate and nutritive, carrying oxygen and waste products in the proper direction through the barrier of the placenta.

b) From implantation to gastrulation

During the phases of implantation in the uterus, the trophoblasts differentiate themselves in a way that anticipates the cells of the inner cell mass, in order to guarantee the nutrition of the embryo. However, the cells of the inner cell mass also undergo a series of changes. First of all they divide in order to generate 2 layers: the outer epiblast (or primitive ectoderm) and the more inner hypoblast (or primitive endoderm). The supportive embryonic membranes are external to the embryo that begins to develop independently, although they remain in close continuity with them.

At the beginning of the third week of development, the epiblast cells thicken and give rise to a structure called *primitive streak* that extends from the principal extremity to the system of the embryonic disc, thus defining the anteoposterior axis and the bilateral symmetry of the embryo. Some epiblast cells emigrate and will end up giving rise to the three layers called ectoderm, mesoderm, and endoderm. This whole process is called *gastrulation*. It must be noted that all the tissues of the future organism are derived from epiblast. As of today, it appears that the hypoblast does not contribute to the formation of any embryonic structures; it seems that it would have a transitory function to protect the epiblast.

Gastrulation is a crucial point in the embryo's development; during this process an essentially spherical blastocyst transforms into a cylindrical structure with head, tail, and three distinct embryonic walls or layers. The ectoderm gives rise to the skin, the nervous system, and the sensory structures of the eyes, nose, and mouth. The mesoderm gives rise to the skeletal, muscular, and circulatory systems. The endoderm gives rise to the epithelium lining of a number of systems including the digestive tract and the respiratory system.

c) From the formation of the central nervous system to genesis of organs

The term *neurulation* indicates a series of processes leading to the formation of the central nervous system in the embryo. From the cranial extremity (rostrum) of the primitive line, a large structure that extends further in the rostral direction develops in the mesoderm. This structure is called *notochord* and constitutes the anteoposterior axis of the embryo. Over the sides of the notochord the vertebral column will develop. In this stage of development, the *neural plate* is brought about when the notochord and the adjacent tissues exert induction upon the ectoderm. The edges of the neural plate are elevated to form the neural folds. The nueral folds unite themselves, forming the neural tube, starting from the center and moving toward the two extremities with a mechanism similar to a zipper. This process is completed by the third week of embryonic development. The mesoderm, that confines the neural tube, is differentiated by a series of structures called *somites*. The first pair of somites appears in the cranial part of the neural tube by the twentieth day after conception. The other somites are formed little by little in the tail end until day thirty. The mesenquimal stem cells, cells that arise from the somites, give origin to the major part of the skeletal structure and the muscular system.

The formation of the fetal circulatory system begins in the embryo three weeks after conception, even though fetal blood is not produced till the fifth week. The heart looks like a big cup of blood that folds on itself to produce the atrio and ventricles that will become its final form. Nevertheless, in its first structure with its tube form, the plasmatic membranes of some of its cells possess an electric potential and a contractible capability to make the heart start beating by the third week, forming a primitive circulatory system.

The principal structures of the organism and the connections between the various organs and systems are formed between the fourth and eighth weeks of embryonic development. First the embryo folds itself many times, transforming the linear and flat structure of the neural tube and the somites into a "C" shaped structure. This structural change gives the cerebrum, the intestines and other organs a more suitable position for the formation of anatomical connections. During the fourth week the extremities of the neural tube close, delimiting what would become the central nervous system and also throughout this time the first cartilage of the limbs appears. During the closing of the neural tube, the primordial structures of the cerebrum begin to develop. In this stage, the cranial nerves, like those of the eyes and the muscles of the face, also begin to develop. The embryonic cerebrum starts to develop in the fifth week, along with the appearance of the optic vesicle and the retina of the eye. Development continues as various organs emerge: the skeletal structure, the limbs and the face. All this happens following the eighth week after conception, when the embryo is already called a *fetus*. Once the basic elements of the process have been established, during the development of the embryo, the full development of the main body and the infinite connections among all the bodily structures develop during the fetal stage and continue even after birth.

187

2. SOME CONSIDERATIONS

Keeping in mind what we have just explained following Vescovi and Spinardi (which is similar to what can be found in the human embryology chapter of any medical or biology book) we can draw some conclusions of enormous importance.

a) The nature of the embryo

The first question the authors themselves rightly raised: "The principal problem of the debate about the nature of the embryo centers on one fundamental point: Where is it licit, from a strictly biological point of view, to draw the line between life and 'non-life'?"[180] Or, can we determine a moment in this process when we can say that before there was no human life and afterwards there is? "The answer," they continue, "is in reality dramatically simple. And it is this, the beginning of life coincides with the act of forming a biological entity that contains and is gifted with the entire program of growth and with the information necessary to unfold and progress through all the stages of development that characterize a human being and that are an integral part of his natural history—zygote, morula, blastocyst, embryo, fetus, neonate, child, adolescent, man—until death. This end coincides with the loss and/or destruction of such information and/or capacity. Based on this, it is evident that the beginning of life in a human being coincides with the act of fusion between the sperm and the ovum, which brings about the creation of a zygote and the chain of events that culminates in the birth of a newborn baby."[181]

These authors also propose making the analysis from the other perspective: starting from the adult individual. We try to travel backwards in his biological history, looking for a *"break in*

---

[180] VESCOVI and SPINARDI, "La Natura Biologica dell'Embrione," editorial translation.

[181] Ibid.

continuity," (that is to say, an *interruption*) in its vital process. "We immediately note that such a break of continuity occurs only in the act of fertilization."[182] In all other stages of development life is present (and this refers to autonomous life, advanced, and directed *from the embryo itself*). This allows us to see that "the different stages commonly suggested as the boundaries between life and non-life— implantation in the uterus, development of the brain, self-consciousness—appear arbitrary. These stages merely represent the boundaries between different phases of vital development, but are all contained within this development, and do not represent the boundary of vital development itself."[183]

Therefore they conclude by saying that all of the attempts to reduce the embryo to an entity devoid of life are not viable and incorrect biologically and logically.

Thus, holding—as some authors have claimed—for example, that the embryo is not a living being because it is incapable of "communicating" (connecting with others) is absurd because the embryo *communicates with his mother* from the first stages of development. He does this through the exchange of very specific chemical molecules. The discrimination between life and non-life, therefore, is not based on the inability to communicate but on the *form of communication* used: *chemical* for the embryo, *mechanical* (sound, the vibration of air) in the adult. For those who deny the embryo the title of human their problem with it is that it communicates with his mother without using the voice or gestures of the face and hands.

We find the same fallacy in those who deny the embryo the category of human being because he would be incapable of elaborating information or of acting in a self-conscious way. If this were the case, we could come to categorize as non-living a significant number of those affected by important pathologies, for

---

[182] Ibid. [*Editor's Note:* For a clearer understanding of "break in continuity," see the *Vocabulary* section.]

[183] Ibid.

example, those suffering from Alzheimer's, a disease that can totally disable the cognitive faculties.[184]

b) The moment of passive conception

In speaking of the human soul we have said that a human being is such because he has a spiritual soul. If we say that the embryo is a human being, we have to affirm at the same time that he has a soul; that which does not have a spiritual soul is not human. Now, from what moment is the embryo a human person, that is to say, has a human (or spiritual) soul?

We are not going to return to considering the answers that many thinkers give with respect to the human being; it is enough that we just keep them in mind. Some hold that man is the result of chance or accident (that is to say, from the unplanned convergence of factors that produced not a piece of marble or a grain of wheat, but a man). Those that respond in this way, sooner or later conclude that man is absurd (Sartre dared to say clearly that for him, "man is a useless passion"[185], "condemned to be free [...] thrown into the world"[186], and destined for nothing). But it is not possible to (seriously) think this way, and even less to work out the consequence of this claim. In effect, that which is born by chance lives by chance and is utterly given to chance, without law or any end, and no man can live with this perspective. With respect to this Basso writes: "More concretely, it is fitting to ask: Could it be that life, with its distinctive perfections (the complexity of its

---

[184] For the arguments about what is called the "biological state of the embryo" (or its "nature"—"what is" the embryo), see the interesting and well-documented article by JESÚS BALLESTEROS, "El Estatuto de Embrión," *Fundación Introamericana Ciencia y Vida, www.ulia.org/ficv.*

[185] JEAN-PAUL SARTRE, *Being and Nothingness: An Essay on Phenomenological Ontology* (1943), trans. Hazel Barnes (New York: Washington Square Press, 1956), 784.

[186] JEAN-PAUL SARTRE, *Essays in Existentialism* (New York: Citadel Press, 1993), 41.

mechanisms, its remote preparations and its proximate arrangements) is a simple product of chance? If one has made, be it only once, the approximate calculation of the mathematically infinite number of fortuitous coincidences necessary to bring together a miniscule cell of four microns by two (the sperm) twenty three chromosomes with their 50,000 perfectly programmed genes, he will come down on the affirmative side of the aforementioned question. Believing in chance to such an extreme could even be called faith!"[187]

Others have claimed that the human being in an embryonic state is potentially human "biological matter" and that it only acquires the title of person through his free recognition and free acceptance on the part of the adult society.[188] For example, René Frydman claimed that embryos do not possess the attributes of a human person, but only their potential. In order to acquire these attributes, the embryo must be desired by an adult and must surmount the concrete difficulties of development. In this manner, the person would be a social construct, the artificial product of selective and arbitrary social adoption. From this reasoning they will logically conclude that one can then renounce his personhood by desiring to not live. Therefore, taking away life from someone who no longer wants to relate with others or from those who are set apart from his society . . . would not be murder (now we have made euthanasia legitimate!).

We have already said that man begins to be a person, a human being, upon receiving from God the spiritual soul that takes the function of form in the complex human being. The Catholic Doctrine affirms this, saying: "'*God created man in his own image, in the image of God he created him, male and female he created them*' (Gen 1:27). Man occupies a unique place in creation: (I) he is *'in the image of God'*; (II) in his own nature he unites the spiritual and material

---

[187] DOMINGO BASSO, *Nacer y Morir con Dignidad* (Buenos Aires: Consorcio de Médicos Católicos, 1989), 20.

[188] Cf. ANGEL RODRIQUEZ LUÑO, "El Concepto de Respeto en la Instrucción 'Donum Vitae'," *Anthropotes* 2 (1988): 261-272.

worlds; (III) he is created *'male and female'*; and (IV) God established him in his friendship. Of all visible creatures only man is 'able to know and love his creator.' He is 'the only creature on earth that God has willed for its own sake,' and he alone is called to share, by knowledge and love, in God's own life. It was for this end that he was created, and this is the fundamental reason for his dignity; St. Catherine of Siena asked God: What made you establish man in so great a dignity? Certainly the incalculable love by which you have looked on your creature in yourself! You are taken with love for her; for by love indeed you created her, by love you have given her a being capable of tasting your eternal Good. Being in the image of God the human individual possesses the dignity of a person, who is not just something, but someone. He is capable of self-knowledge, of self-possession and of freely giving himself and entering into communion with other persons. And he is called by grace to a covenant with his Creator, to offer him a response of faith and love that no other creature can give in his stead."[189]

We have already dealt with this theme in the chapter about the soul; what we bring up now is precisely something that the previous chapter left hanging: When does the soul begin to be present in this being, which begins to have life at conception and will end with his natural death (maybe upon reaching an old age)?

It is clear that those who say that man is the result of chance will say that he began to be a person when so produced by happenstance, and therefore this will depend on chance in every case. Those that hold the relational theory will say that it is when society accepts the new individual (therefore, an embryo not accepted as a person or an "unwanted" pregnancy makes this "thing" something other than a human person). But those who hold that everything began with God's creative intervention of the soul (passive conception) will have to conclude that the new being begins to be a person when God infuses the human soul into the organism capable to receive it.

---

[189] CCC 355-357.

Accepting that the soul is created and infused by God, we encounter a curious fact of historical interest: the theory of *delayed hominization*. This theory was defended in antiquity not only by pagan philosophers like Aristotle (with his theory known as *epigenisis*, a term coined in 1651 by William Harvey and not used by Aristotle himself) but also a few centuries later by the great Christian thinkers, both men of science and theologians, including those along the lines of St. Albert the Great and St. Thomas Aquinas.[190] Aristotle's theory is that the formation of living organisms is achieved through a slow process in which they gradually acquire their definitive form, progressively replacing imperfect forms with other more perfect ones until the definitive form is reached.[191] Aristotle held and defended this against Democritus who had defended the theory of implicit pre-formation, precursor to all the preformationist theories (the preformationists held—I don't know if anyone would argue this today—that the organs of the whole organism were already pre-formed in the ovum or sperm; we would have—in the case of man—a type of microscopic perfect little man or *homunculus* as some called it which can been seen in the Goethe's literary work, *Faust*). The danger that medieval scientists and theologians wanted to prevent in returning to Aristotelian delayed hominization was precisely this preformationism that some Augustinian theologians defended. Against this, St. Thomas—who, like all the thinkers, could not rely on any data other than what was offered by the science of his time—defended delayed hominization, saying that the "body is formed and progressively goes preparing itself in view of the soul," receiving a series of "souls" (not spiritual but imperfect, and therefore, like those that non-human beings have) that go on replacing themselves, in such a way that "when it is imperfectly disposed, it receives an imperfect soul; and when it is perfectly disposed, it receives the perfect soul," that is, the spiritual

---

[190] The discussion on this topic and how the dispute evolved can be seen in BASSO, *Nacer y Morir con Dignidad,* 89-108.

[191] Cf. ARISTOTLE, *De Generatione Animalium,* II, 734a.

one.[192] St. Thomas expounds this doctrine for the purpose of explaining the case of Christ; He was an exception given that his "body, on account of the infinite power of the agent, was perfectly disposed instantaneously. Wherefore, at once and in the first instant it received a perfect form, that is, the rational soul."[193] I want to emphasize two things in this theory.

1. The first is that the supporters of delayed hominization condemned abortion as a crime, although they admitted that the embryo received the spiritual and immortal soul only in the last stages of its formation. There was some hesitation with respect to this by some theologians like Peter Lombard.[194] Nevertheless, the same authors maintained that abortion of still inanimate embryos, *although it was not homicide, was equally illicit.* In any case, the doctrine of the Church and that of the majority of the theologians did not support this. I want to clarify that the debate about the subject did not center on the approval of abortion in these cases, but around *decriminalization* (that is, not imposing canonical penalties) in the case when a fetus was not yet human.[195] It is interesting that the majority of ancient authors, whether accepting—as certain or possible—delayed hominization or not, they always adhered to the gravity of abortion in whatever stage of development.[196] Those who have studied the implications of St.

---

[192] AQUINAS, *Summa Theologica,* III, Q. 33, Art. 2, ad. 3.

[193] Ibid.

[194] In any case, let us note that Peter Lombard and those who followed him based themselves in the doctrine of Aristotle and in a biblical text (the passage from Exodus 21:22) which they thought affirmed that it was not homicide if a woman's miscarriage resulted from the blows of a fight, and *that the fetus did not yet have a soul nor a form.* However, they later found out that the text was altered by the Greek version of the Bible, and that the original does not say this.

[195] This can be seen in the arguments' documents in BASSO, *Nacer y Morir con Dignidad,* 104-105.

[196] See SACRED CONGREGATION FOR THE DOCTRINE OF THE FAITH, "Declaration on Procured Abortion," November 18, 1974, no. 7, *www.vatican.va/roman_curia/congregations/cfaith/documents/rc_con_cfaith_doc_1974111 8_declaration-abortion_en.html* (accessed October 5, 2014). Summarizing, it says: "In the course of history, the Fathers of the Church, her Pastors and her

Thomas's doctrine on this subject affirm that he, although supporting delayed hominization, did not accept abortion as licit in any phase for the principal reason that he held that "what nature intends, God intends through her."[197] Therefore, interrupting the biological process of a human being tries to prevent the appearance of a human life desired by God, and thus will be an attempt against a human life, be it direct (if the soul has already been infused) or indirect (if it had not yet been infused). In this, St. Thomas and the ancient moralists were guided by the principle, "probable life, certain life," wishing to say that while there is the probability of personal, human life, it must be treated as if it existed with certainty, because the risk implies exposing oneself to consciously committing murder.[198]

2. This discussion is also valuable because it was elaborated with insufficient scientific information about the embryo. The solution of these scientists, philosophers, and theologians would have been different if they had possessed the data of current bio-genetics. Modern bio-genetics make us aware of how the members and definitive organs are not actually present in the sperm, nor in the ovum, nor in the embryo—as preformationism ignorantly proposed—but neither is it necessary to wait for a moment late in the evolution of the embryo to see the given conditions of matter—body—adequately disposed to receive the soul, since in the very moment of conception the totality of the genome is given. This complete genome perfectly contains all the capabilities that the embryo, the fetus, the child, and the future adult will develop with the passage of time, *always beginning with the orders emanating*

Doctors have taught the same doctrine [the illicitness of abortion]—the various opinions on the infusion of the spiritual soul did not introduce any doubt about the illicitness of abortion."

[197] ST. THOMAS AQUINAS, quoted in BASSO, *Nacer y Morir Con Dignidad*, 107-108, editorial translation.

[198] On this position of St. Thomas, see BASSO, *Nacer y Morir con Dignidad*, 107-108;

GIOVANNI DI GIANNATALE, "La Posizione di S. Tommaso sull'Aborto," *Doctor Communis* 34:3 (1981): 296-311.

from the embryo itself. St. Thomas accepted that God could prepare a body that was perfect from the first moment and *in such a case* it would receive the soul immediately (for him this was the case with Christ). I am sure that if St. Thomas had known what the embryo really was, its genome and capacity to self-direct the process of gestation, he would have considered such a state as the state of (relative) perfection necessary in order to judge the matter disposed for the soul and would not have had to distinguish the case of Christ from other men insofar as the moment of his passive conception.

I expressly point out that the past discussion about delayed hominization is very valuable—not as some erroneously think as an *objection* to the Catholic doctrine from *its own theologians*—but because it shows us that: (a) Supporting delayed hominization (like many modern scientists, although they do not speak of passive conception but of hominization or personalization) is an error linked to a lack of knowledge about the embryo's biological nature. If the scientists, philosophers and theologians of the past fell into this error, it cannot happen in our time with the knowledge we have of genetics and embryology. (b) It shows us that in spite of what they believed about such delayed hominization, the moral attitude will always be one of absolute respect for the embryo.

Now, we should be conscious that since we cannot have direct, experimental knowledge of either the soul or the divine creative act, we cannot give a "direct" response to the question about *the moment in which the infusion of the soul takes place.* However, with what we have said above about the embryo's biological development, we can attempt an "indirect" response. This indirect response is based on an *absolutely objective* truth that permits us to confirm with certainty the moment in which this new being *is already given the conditions* to be a human person. If such conditions are verified, then we should conclude that it is a human person (or at least have to conclude that *the contrary cannot be said, that "it is not a human person"*). This fact, reinforced today by genetic studies, is established: in the whole process (from the sexual act between a man and a woman, fertilization, its embryonic development, birth, growth, adulthood, old age, and death) there is only one objective truth that permits us to say: "*biologically in this moment there is a new being.*" That moment is the conception or fertilization that results in a new fully individualized being, different from the cells that give it origin and different from the maternal organism that nurtures it.[199]

I want to demonstrate this by citing a few pages of a very valuable study by Professor Angelo Serra, a prestigious geneticist. It deals with the point in which this author, after having described the embryo's biological development in a manner very similar to what we have done above, proceeds to what he calls "biological induction," meaning, the process by which a scientist, starting from the experimental data that science gives, reaches proven conclusions. The text says: "So far we have very briefly described the first stages of human embryonic development, and hinted at its genomic control. We had not intended either to verify or to falsify any particular hypotheses. The aim was to offer a basic knowledge of the complex biological process of the development of a human being. This knowledge is the premise to an answer to the questions: '*What is the status of an early human embryo*', and '*When does a human being start its own life cycle*'. In order to answer these questions, there

---

[199] Angelo Serra affirms: "Now the first cell of the new being results from the fusion of two gametes, cells are marvelously ordered to one another. There are two complex and different biological systems, which between the two give origin to a third system that is different from the first two. *Two seconds after* the moment in which the two germinal cells meet, the third cell already has its own identity: the PH is modified, the DNA remodeled, the division of chromosomes is initiated and the first messenger RNA begins to form. Two seconds removed from moment 'x,' the embryo has a new identity with a well-marked genome, that is to say, with the distinctive human qualities imprinted, unique and unrepeatable. Therefore, the first phase of suspension, between the already and the not yet, is represented in those first two initial seconds, which are nevertheless, only theoretically revealed." All subsequent mutations and changes, up to the individual's moment of death from old age, with respect to this change, are accidental and secondary. (Report of Angelo Serra, S.J., one of the most eminent Italian geneticists at the end of the 20th century, by DANIELE NARDI, "La Via," *Sì Alla Vita* (May 1991), editorial translation.)

is no need to make new hypotheses, but simply to approach our data inductively."[200]

He then continues to point out how no moment other than that of fertilization can be pinpointed as its beginning and the acquisition of the definitive title of human being (that is, when it starts to be a person, and from our point of view, the moment of the soul's infusion, respectively). This is because from this moment three fundamental properties are found in this being that indicate that we have an autonomous and complete individual (in regards to individuation), although it has not developed all of its capabilities. Those three properties are coordination, continuity, and graduality. Serra continues, saying:

"[a.] Coordination

"The first property is *coordination*. Embryonic development, from the moment of the fusion of the gametes up to the formation of the embryonic disc around 14 days from syngamy, and still more patently afterwards, is a process where there is an evidently coordinated sequence and interaction of molecular and cellular activities, under the control of the new genome, that is modulated by an uninterrupted cascade of signals which are transmitted from cell to cell, and from the external and/or internal environment to the single cells.

"Precisely this undeniable property *implies* and, even more, *requires* a rigorous *unity* of the being that is steadily developing. The more research advances, the more this unity appears guaranteed by the new genome, where a great number of regulator genes assure the exact time, the precise location, and the specificity of the morphogenetic events. J. Van Blerkom underscores this property in concluding an analysis of the nature of the developmental

---

[200] ANGELO SERRA and ROBERTO COLOMBO, "Identity and Status of the Human Embryo: The Contribution of Biology," in *Identity and Statute of Human Embryo,* ed. Juan de Dios Vial Correa and Elio Sgreccia (Vatican City: Libreria Editrice Vaticana, 1998), 162-163.

program of the first stages of mammalian embryos: 'Available evidence suggests that developmental events in the maturing oocytes and early embryo follow a schedule directed by an intrinsic program. The apparent autonomy of such a program indicates interdependence and coordination at the molecular and cellular levels to result in the expression of a cascade of developmental events'. [201]

"All this leads to the conclusion that the human embryo—like any other embryo—even in the earliest stages *is not*, as N. M. Ford states, 'only a cluster of cells', 'each of which is a distinct ontological individual',[202] but that the whole embryo *is a real individual*—in the sense declared in the first section—where the single cells are strictly *integrated* in a process through which it *autonomously* translates, moment after moment, its own *genetic space* onto its own *organismic space*.

"[b.] Continuity

"The second property is *continuity*. It seems undeniable, on the basis of the data presented above, that a new life cycle starts at syngamy. 'The final function of the sperm cell is to fuse with the egg plasma membrane. At the moment of fusion [*i.e.* syngamy] it ceases to be a sperm and becomes part of a newly formed cell, the zygote'.[203] The zygote is the *primordium* of the new organism, which

---

[201] JONATHAN VAN BLERKOM, "Extragenomic regulation and autonomous expression of a developmental program in the early mammalian embryo," *Annals of the New York Academy of Sciences* 442:58-72 (1985): 61.

[202] NORMAN FORD, *When did I begin? Conception of the human individual in history, philosophy, and science* (Cambridge: Cambridge University Press, 1988), 145. "As new cytological and molecular data on early mammalian embryo become available, there is little evidence for Ford's statement 'that at least up to the eight-cell stage in the human embryo there are eight distinct individuals rather than one multicellular individual' (FORD, *When did I begin?*, 137)." (SERRA AND COLOMBO, "Identity and Status of the Human Embryo," 164, note 91.)

[203] DIANA MYLES and PAUL PRIMAKOFF, "Why Did the Sperm Cross the Cumulus? To Get to the Oocyte. Functions of the Sperm Surface Proteins PH-

is at the very beginning of its life cycle. If one considers the dynamic profile of this cycle in time, it clearly appears to proceed without interruptions: the first cycle does not end at the embryonic disc, nor does another cycle start from that point on. A single event, such as cell multiplication, or the appearance of the various tissues and organs, might appear discontinuous to our eyes; however, each one of them is the final expression at a given instant of an uninterrupted succession of, so to speak, infinitesimal events connected one to the other without a break in continuity

"This property *implies* and *establishes* the *unicity* or *oneness* of the new human being: from syngamy it is always *the same identical human individual who is being autonomously built up* according to a strictly defined plan, while passing through stages that are qualitatively ever more complex.

"[c.] Graduality

"The third property is *graduality*. The *final form* is reached *gradually*: it is an *ontogenetic law*, a constant of the reproductive process. This law of the gradual building up of the final form through many steps, starting from the zygote, *implies* and *claims* a regulation that must be intrinsic to any given embryo and keeps the development permanently oriented in the direction of the final form. It is precisely because of this *intrinsic epigenetic law*, which is written in the genome and begins to operate from the fusion of the gametes, that any embryo—and, therefore, the human embryo as well—permanently maintains its own *identity*, *individuality* and *unicity*, being uninterruptedly the *same identical individual* during the whole process of development, from syngamy onwards, notwithstanding the ever *increasing complexity of its totality*.

"W. J. Gehring clearly recognized this law while foreseeing the future advances of developmental genetics: 'Organisms develop according to a precise developmental program that specifies their

---

20 and Fertilin in Arriving at, and Fusing with, the Egg," *Biology of Reproduction* 56:320-327 (1997).

body plan in great detail and also determines the sequence and timing of the developmental events. This developmental information is stored in the nucleotide sequences of the DNA [...] The developmental program consists of a precise spatial and temporal pattern of expression of these structural genes that forms the basis of development. Normal development requires the coordinate expression of thousands of structural genes in concerted fashion. Since independent control of the individual structural genes would lead to a chaotic development, we might predict that there are controlling genes that regulate the activity of groups of structural genes coordinately'.[204]"[205]

And Serra concludes with "the answer" that these facts give us: "It is unmistakably clear that the above three properties, when truly dispassionately considered, perfectly meet the essential criteria established by the meta-biological reflexion for the definition of an '*individual*'.

"Thus, the logical induction from the data afforded by the experimental sciences leads to the unique possible conclusion, that apart from fortuitous disturbances, *at the fusion of two gametes, a new real human individual initiates its own existence, or life cycle*, during which—given all the necessary and sufficient conditions—it will autonomously realize all the potentialities with which he is intrinsically endowed.

"The embryo, therefore, from the time the gametes fuse, *is* a *real human individual*, not a *potential human individual*.

"We believe that the insightful statements of the *Instruction on Respect for Human Life in its Origin and on the Dignity of Procreation*, published by the Congregation for the Doctrine of the Faith in 1987, are scientifically correct. They read: 'Recent findings of human biological science [...] recognize that in the zygote resulting

---

[204] WALTER GEHRING, "Homeo-boxes in the study of development," *Science* 236 (1987): 1245.

[205] SERRA AND COLOMBO, "Identity and Status of the Human Embryo," 163-165.

from fertilization the biological identity of a new human individual is already constituted'.[206][207] Here ends the study of Angelo Serra.

In any case, we insist that if someone does not accept this scientific truth as determining the moment of passive conception, that fact would not leave him authorized by any other data to choose another moment as the beginning of the human person, since all other moments (suggestions have been implantation, the end of two weeks, two months, etc.) would not present any essential change from the moment just prior and would then deal with an arbitrary determination. Moreover, it would be like saying, "Not being able to confirm experimentally at what moment the creating intervention of God occurs, *I decide* that it occurs at this moment." For this reason, the term "pre-embryo," coined to designate the time prior to these arbitrary determinations is as arbitrary and biased as the determinations themselves. On this point, the Declaration on abortion says: "From a moral point of view this is certain: even if a doubt existed concerning whether the fruit of conception is already a human person, it is objectively a grave sin to dare to risk murder. 'The one who will be a man is already one' (Tertullian)."[208]

*   *   *

What we have embarked upon in this chapter has major importance for our lives, especially for the life of a scientist or a student in the careers related to life. From the principles we have set out, it can be understood that the following are illicit: some techniques of human reproduction (like *in vitro* fertilization), embryonic experimentation, cloning and above all abortion (in any of its surgical or chemical forms).

---

[206] CONGREGATION FOR THE DOCTRINE OF THE FAITH, "Instruction on Respect for Human Life in Its Origin and on the Dignity of Procreation 'Donum Vitae'" (February 22, 1987), *Acta Apostolicae Sedis*, 80:70-102 (1988): 82.

[207] SERRA AND COLOMBO, "Identity and Status of the Human Embryo," 165-166.

[208] SACRED CONGREGATION FOR THE DOCTRINE OF THE FAITH, "Declaration on Procured Abortion," no. 13.

If these principles are denied, one can fall into accepting the most deviant experimental practices (techniques very similar to those that our society condemned in *Nazism*): eugenics (killing children born with disabilities or who simply do not meet the expectations of their parents), the creation of organ banks (banks of human beings stored in the embryonic state, destroyed for their cells and organs when such are needed by an adult) and all manners of abortion and infanticide.

Do not be surprised by this and do not be deceived by the titles or achievements that a scientist may have; those who deny the humanity of an embryo can come to defend the most criminal positions. To show this, just read the chilling declarations of Dr. James Watson, winner of the Nobel Prize for Medicine and Physiology (famous for his discovery of the structure of DNA together with Francis Crick): "Many malformations and series of defects are only seen after the creature is born, frequently because not all the unborn can be subject to pre-natal diagnostics. This is why I agree with my colleague and friend, Francis Crick, in favor of *not declaring newborns 'alive' until three days after they come into the world,* giving the parents, during this time, the possibility of preventing the incurable child a life full of suffering."[209] Yes, you have just read the vindication of infanticide by the two scientists who discovered the structure of DNA, one of the greatest achievements in biogenetics. If you are reading these pages, you must be grateful to your parents, for they did not lend their ears to these and other authors who propose the possibility of becoming modern Herods, and for yourself, not to be one more of the innumerable members of the legion of *holy innocents.*

---

[209] EGMONT KOCH and WOLFGANG KESSLER, *¿Al Fin un Hombre Nuevo?* (Barcelona: Plaza & Janés, 1979), 95, editorial translation.

For Further Reading

- Bedate, Carlos Alonso and Robert C. Cefalo. *The Zygote: To Be or Not Be a Person. Journal of Medicine and Philosophy* 14:6 (1989): 641-645.
- Serra, Angelo and Roberto Colombo. "Identity and Status of the Human Embryo: The Contribution of Biology." In *Identity and Statute of Human Embryo.* Edited by Juan de Dios Vial Correa and Elio Sgreccia. Vatican City: Libreria Editrice Vaticana, 1998.

Available in Other Languages

- Ballesteros, Jesús. "El Estatuto del Embrión." *Fundación Interamericana Ciencia y Vida. www.ulia.org/ficv.*
- Blázquez, Niceto and Luis Miguel Pastor. *Bioética Fundamental.* Madrid: Editorial Católica, 1996.
- Castilla, Blanca. "Comienzo de la Vida Humana: Aspectos Filosóficos." *Cuadernos de Bioética* 8:31 (1997): 1113-1118.
- Colombo, Roberto. "Statuto biologico e statuto ontologico dellé embrione e del feto umano." *Anthropotes* XI (1996): 132ff.
- De Santiago, Manuel. "Estatuto Biológico, Antropológico y Ético del Embrión Humano." *Bioetica. www.bioeticaweb.com/estatuto-biolasgico-antropolasgico-y-atico-del-embriasn-humano-dr-manuel-de-santiago* (accessed January 11, 2015).
- López Moratalla, Natalia and María J. Iraburu Elizalde. *Los Quince Primeros Días de Una Vida Humana.* Pamplona: EUNSA, 2004.
- Melina, Livio. *El Embrión Humano: Estatuto Biológico, Antropológico y Jurídico.* Madrid: Rialp, 2000.
- Monge, Fernando. *Persona Humana y Procreación Artificia.* Madrid: Palabra, 1998.
- Orrego Vicuña, Fernando. "Acerca de la Infusión del Alma Espiritual." *arvo.net* (accessed 2005).
- Possenti, Vittorio. "¿Es el embrión persona? Sobre el estatuto ontológico del embrión." In C. I. Massini and P. Serna, ed. *El Derecho a la Vida.* Pamplona: EUNSA, 1998.
- Sgreccia, Elio. *Manuale di Bioetica.* 2 vols. Milan: Vita e Pensiero, 1998.

7.

THE STOLEN
TRUTH ABOUT
NATURAL LAW

There is a natural law and it does make us free!

I wouldn't be surprised if you have often heard the word law and the word freedom; however, I have sufficient reason to fear you have not been presented with the true meaning of either one.

Today freedom is highly praised without the explanations that correspond to it; and the law is only spoken of in an impoverished sense. The majority of our contemporaries probably form an idea of these two concepts like two boxers throwing punches in the ring of our consciences. If I want to be free, the law stops me; if I try to enforce the law, I restrict my freedom and that of my fellow men. With such an idea those who want to speak with me about God's commandments will not have much of a chance. And what will you think about me if I come to tell you that God's commandments *free you and open up unknown horizons to you*! Will you believe me or will you think that I am speaking like *a prudish priest imposing his ideas on others*?

Nevertheless, I would like to call your attention to this point. Because if you do not understand the liberating potential of the commandments and of the law (natural and divine), I assure you that you are not being released from any chains, but actually, the legs of your true liberty are being cut off.

Before continuing, I would like to clarify one point so we do not confuse ourselves. To simplify, I will speak in general terms about God's commandments (the *Decalogue, meaning ten words or laws;* that is, the *Ten Commandments*) and natural law as if they were the same thing. They are not, but they substantially agree with each other. Natural law is the law written in our hearts from the moment we were created (all beings have this engraved in their nature). The Decalogue has been revealed by God at various times. The most formal was God's revelation to Moses on Mount Sinai, but what's more,

Our Lord repeats it many times in the Gospels. In reality, the Decalogue is a privileged expression of "natural law." As the substance of the commandments pertains to natural law, it can be said that even though they were revealed, they are actually intelligible to our reason. Thus, in revealing them, God has done nothing but remind us of them (adding, certainly, some strictly revealed precisions or applications). "[St. Irenaeus of Lyons said:] 'From the beginning, God had implanted in the heart of man the precepts of the natural law. Then he was content to remind him of them. This was the Decalogue.'[210] [...] Sinful humanity needed this revelation [as St. Bonaventure says]: 'A full explanation of the commandments of the Decalogue became necessary in the state of sin because the light of reason was obscured and the will had gone astray.'[211] We know God's commandments through the divine revelation proposed to us in the Church, and through the voice of moral conscience."[212]

---

[210] ST. IRENAEUS, *Adversus Haereses*, 4, 15, 1, quoted in CCC 2070.

[211] ST. BONAVENTURE, *In Libros Sententiarum*, 4, 37, 1, 3, quoted in CCC 2071.

[212] CCC 2070-2071.

If we compare the Ten Commandments of the Old Law, the Law of Christ, and the natural law we see this correlation:

Old Law (Dt 5:6-21)	Law of Christ	Natural Law
I am the Lord your God, who brought you out of the land of Egypt, out of the house of bondage. You shall have no other gods before me.	You shall love the Lord, your God, with all your heart, with all your soul, and with all your mind. (Mt 22: 37) It is written, 'You shall worship the Lord your God and him only shall you serve.' (Mt 4:10)	You shall love God above all things.
You shall not take the name of the Lord your God in vain.	Again you have heard that it was said to the men of old, 'You shall not swear falsely [...] But I say to you, do not swear at all. (Mt 5:33-34)	You shall not take the name of God in vain.
Observe the sabbath day, to keep it holy.	And he said to them, 'The Sabbath was made for man, not man for the Sabbath; so the Son of man is lord even of the Sabbath.' (Mk 2:27-28)	You shall keep feast days holy.
Honor your father and your mother.	For Moses said, 'Honor your father and your mother,' and, 'Whoever curses father or mother shall die.' (Mk 7:10)	Honor your father and your mother.
You shall not kill.	You have heard that it was said to your ancestors, 'You shall not kill; and whoever kills shall be liable to judgment.' But I say to you that everyone who is angry with his brother shall be liable to judgment (Mt 5:21-22)	You shall not kill.
Neither shall you commit adultery.	You have heard that it was said, 'You shall not commit adultery.' But I say to you that every one who looks at a woman lustfully has already committed adultery with her in his heart. (Mt 5:27-28)	You shall not commit impure acts.
Neither shall you steal.	You shall not steal. (Mt 19:18)	You shall not steal.
Neither shall you bear false witness against your neighbor.	Again you have heard that is was said to your ancestors, 'Do not take a false oath, but make good to the Lord all that you vow.' (Mt 5:33)	You shall not bear false witness nor lie.
Neither shall you covet your neighbor's wife.	But I say to you that everyone who looks at a woman lustfully has already committed adultery with her in his heart. (Mt 5:28)	You shall not consent to impure thoughts or desires.
You shall not desire [...] anything that is your neighbor's.	For where your treasure is, there will your heart be also. (Mt 6:21)	You shall not covet your neighbors' goods.

As we can see, the precepts contained in natural law, which all men can discover with their intelligence, have also been revealed by God in the Old Testament and the New Testament. And, as we will continue to explain, natural law comes from God; and as such, it is in a sense "divine." Therefore, referring to both things, we will speak of the divine commandments in general terms.

1. WHAT IS A NATURAL LAW?

In an address to the Congregation for the Doctrine of the Faith on February 6, 2004, Pope John Paul II clearly pointed out the following: "Another important and urgent topic I would like to call to your attention is that of natural moral law. This law belongs to the great heritage of human wisdom. Revelation, with its light, has contributed to further purifying and developing it. Natural law, in itself accessible to every rational creature, points to the first essential norms that regulate moral life. On the basis of this law it is possible to construct a platform of shared values around which can be developed a constructive dialogue with all people of good will and, more generally, with secular society.

"Today, as a result of the crisis of metaphysics, people in many spheres no longer recognize a truth engraved on every human heart. On the one hand, therefore, we are witnessing the spread of a fideistic morality among believers, and on the other, the lack of an objective reference point for legislation, which is often based merely on social consensus, making it more and more difficult to establish an ethical foundation common to all humanity."[213]

---

[213] ST. JOHN PAUL II, "Address to the Participants in the Biannual Plenary Assembly of the Congregation for the Doctrine of the Faith" (February 6, 2004), no. 5,

a) A "natural" law exists

The *existence of a natural law* is presumed for the same reason. If we accept the existence of God and the creation of everything that exists by God, we should accept the existence of God's eternal plan for all creation. Consequently, a certain correlation among creatures themselves follows, since all rules and standards are in some way found in that which regulates and that which is regulated. This is reinforced by the universal conviction, also found among pagan nations, of a moral duty and of the possibility of knowing and discerning good and evil. We also see it in considering the absurdity to which the denial of natural law would lead; for example, all moral opinions would be admissible, and therefore, the vices could be virtues and the virtues vices, according to man's diverse arbitrary conceptions. For a believer, we can add to these arguments the testimony of Revelation.

This is why it is said that natural law is actually the eternal law participated in beings gifted with reason,[214] or, as it is often defined: *the rational creature's participation in the eternal law.*[215] It has been rightly called a "participated theonomy," that is to say, the divine ordering of the rational creature

---

www.vatican.va/holy_father/john_paul_ii/speeches/2004/february/documents/hf_jp-ii_spe_20040206_congr-faith_en.html (accessed November 9, 2014).

[214] "The natural law," says the encyclical *Veritatis Splendor,* "is written and engraved in the heart of each and every man, since it is none other than human reason itself which commands us to do good and counsels us not to sin [...] the natural law is itself the eternal law, implanted in beings endowed with reason, and inclining them towards their right action and end; it is none other than the eternal reason of the Creator and Ruler of the universe." (ST. JOHN PAUL II, *Veritatis Splendor (The Splendor of Truth)* (VS) (Boston: St. Paul Books & Media, 1993), no. 44.)

[215] In Latin: *Participatio legis aeternae in creatura rationali.* (ST. THOMAS AQUINAS, *Summa Theologiae* (Lander, Wyoming: The Aquinas Institute, 2012), I-II, Q. 91, Art. 2, ad. 3.)

toward his ultimate end, written in human nature and perceived by the light of reason.[216]

This law is present in all beings. However, in man there is something particular. Irrational creatures are driven by blind instincts; they look for the goods that perfect them, but they do not understand that these are good nor that they are looking for them—they simply look. They do not consciously look; they are just drawn on. They defend themselves when they are attacked because they instinctively love their life and do not want to lose it, but they do not understand what life is. They mate and reproduce and then feed and defend their young because they blindly love the good of the species; although, they do not understand what the sensible love they feel is nor what the species is (therefore, when their young do not need them any more, they forget about them). They live in the herd because they take pleasure in living with those of their own species, but they do not understand its significance. They enjoy being together, but they do not have friendships. Instincts are the invisible threads that make them move themselves about on the stage of the world like marionettes in a child's puppet theater.

With man there is a profound difference. He also carries the Plan of God written in his being. But his are not blind instincts. From God he also receives the light of reason that permits him to discover and read this Plan, and the liberty to carry it out. Doing this is his prerogative. God sends him to the great theater of the world with a script full of wisdom and

---

[216] The term, "participated theonomy" (from the Greek words *theos,* meaning "God"; and *nomos,* meaning "law"; therefore, "theonomy" means "divine law"), appears in the encyclical *Veritatis Splendor:* "Others speak, and rightly so, of theonomy, or participated theonomy, since man's free obedience to God's law effectively implies that human reason and human will participate in God's wisdom and providence." (No. 41.)

with spiritual eyes to read and understand; to love this plan and carry it out (this is the natural law). The Second Vatican Council affirms: "In the depths of his conscience, man detects a law which he does not impose upon himself, but which holds him to obedience. Always summoning him to love good and avoid evil, the voice of conscience when necessary speaks to his heart: do this, shun that. For man has in his heart a law written by God; to obey it is the very dignity of man; according to it he will be judged. (Cf. Rom 2:14-16.)"[217] "At the same time this code of morality is written in yet another form. It is inscribed in the moral conscience of humanity in such a way that those who do not know the commandments, in other words, the law revealed by God, *are a law to themselves'* [Rom 2:14]. Thus writes St. Paul in his Letter to the Romans, and he immediately adds: *They show that what the law requires is written on their hearts, while their conscience also bears witness'* [Rom 2:15]."[218]

Therefore, it deals with *divine law* because it has been desired and promulgated directly by God. It is called natural not in opposition to supernatural law but in opposition to positive law (divine or human). Its proper name is "natural divine law."

Why is it called natural? First of all, because it does not impose things other than what is within the reach of natural human reason, commanded because they are good in themselves (like truth or the love of God), or prohibited because they are bad in themselves (like blasphemy or lies). Furthermore, because it is known by the interior light of our

---

[217] *Gaudium et Spes (Pastoral Consitution on the Church in the Modern World)*, promulgated by PAUL VI (Boston: St. Paul Editions, 1965), no. 16.

[218] ST. JOHN PAUL II, *Apostolic Letter To the Youth of the World on the Occasion of the International Youth Year (Dilecti Amici)*, (Vatican: Vatican Polyglot Press, 1985), no. 6.

reason, independent of all acquired science, all positive law, and even all revelation (although God in his mercy also reveals this to us). Such light permits us to distinguish between good and evil by comparing our inclinations with their proper ends. This is why the foundation of determining an objective universal morality for human actions is established through the light of reason.

That we have this law written in our hearts means that our reason is capable of reading in our own nature the end for which we exist (the end that is our true perfection and happiness) and can discover that all other beings in relation with this end are nothing but the means with which to arrive at the end. At the moment that each human being, reaching the age of reason, recognizes that he has a final end and an efficient cause on which he depends, he makes each law his own in a sort of individual and subjective promulgation. [219]

b) What is the content of this law (that is to say, what does it command)?[220]

Analyzing our nature and the natural or spontaneous inclinations that we find within ourselves, we can come to formulate the things that natural law commands or prohibits.

---

[219] "Thus Saint Thomas, commenting on a verse of Psalm 4, writes: 'After saying: *Offer right sacrifices* (Ps 4:5), as if some had then asked him what right works were, the Psalmist adds: *There are many who say: Who will make us see good?* And in reply to the question he says: *The light of your face, Lord, is signed upon us*, thereby implying that the light of natural reason whereby we discern good from evil, which is the function of the natural law, is nothing else but an imprint on us of the divine light.' It also becomes clear why this law is called the natural law: it receives this name not because it refers to the nature of irrational beings but because the reason which promulgates it is proper to human nature." (VS, no. 42.)

[220] Cf. AQUINAS, *Summa Theologica*, I-II, Q. 94, Art. 2-3.

It more properly deals with a type of "reading" that we do in our nature.

First of all, we find a fundamental precept. The first thing that we grasp in the practical order is the notion of the *good*: good is that which all beings desire. And so, our reason grasps a first principle: good should be worked for and bad should be avoided. Sometimes it takes on other forms (for example, "observe the order of being," "always do your duty," etc.), but these are nothing more than formulations derived from or equivalent to the first principle upon which all the others are based. We should not reduce this perception that good *must be* done or that bad *must be* avoided in the sense given by Kant (for him this only had sense of a simple *obligation* that we cannot escape). In reality it is infinitely richer than this. What our intelligence comprehends in perceiving the good is the *attraction* that it exerts over all being. We understand this, then, in the sense that good is really what attracts us—with irresistible force, like love—and evil causes authentic and deeply rooted aversion.

The immediate conclusions. In saying that our nature is inclined toward good and flees from evil, we are still speaking in general terms. What good? What evil? Our reason, analyzing the proper inclination of our nature will be able, therefore, to define what is good (or what are those goods) that attract us with their irresistible force (because in them is our perfection). Then from this our reason will be able to express in the form of precept or commandment, the first precepts of natural law, also called *immediate conclusions* because they are the conclusions reached starting from the first precept. St. Thomas discovered in our very nature three fundamental tendencies of man: that which corresponds to us as substances (remote genus of the human being), that which corresponds to us as animals (proximate genus) and that which corresponds to us as rational beings (that is our specific difference from the rest of the animal genus). This last tendency reveals two complementary facets, since we see that there are goods that will perfect us spiritually, while others will perfect us socially.[221] Let us look at each one of these.

The first inclination is the *inclination to preserve our being* (being, existing, is the first good that perfects us, which is why we desire it). We have this inclination in common with all beings and it produces in us the desire to live. This natural inclination is the basis, for example, of the right of self defense, and also of the prohibition of the murder of innocents (being is my perfection, and, therefore, I have the

---

[221] Cf. AQUINAS, *Summa Theologica*, I-II, Q. 100, Art. 2.

The encyclical *Veritatis Splendor* says: "This capability [of ordering to the good] is grasped by reason in the very being of man, considered in his integral truth, and therefore in his natural inclinations, his motivations and his finalities, which always have a spiritual dimension as well. It is precisely these which are the contents of the natural law and hence that ordered complex of 'personal goods' which serve the 'good of the person': the good which is the person himself and his perfection. These are the goods safeguarded by the commandments, which, according to Saint Thomas, contain the whole natural law." (No. 79.)

"The 'divine and natural' law shows man the way to follow so as to practice the good and attain his end. The natural law states the first and essential precepts which govern the moral life. It hinges upon the desire for God and submission to him, who is the source and judge of all that is good, as well as upon the sense that the other is one's equal. Its principal precepts are expressed in the Decalogue. This law is called 'natural,' not in reference to the nature of irrational beings, but because reason which decrees it properly belongs to human nature: *'Where then are these rules written, if not in the book of that light we call the truth? In it is written every just law; from it the law passes into the heart of the man who does justice, not that it migrates into it, but that it places its imprint on it, like a seal on a ring that passes onto wax, without leaving the ring. The natural law is nothing other than the light of understanding placed in us by God; through it we know what we must do and what we must avoid. God has given this light or law at the creation.'* [St. Augustine, *De Trin.*]" (CCC 1955.)

right to not have it unjustly taken away, and I am obligated to do the same for my fellow men). This inclination is also the source of spontaneous and natural self-love; it forms in ourselves the love of natural goods, such as life and health; it inclines us to seek all that is useful for our subsistence: food, clothing, and housing; it inclines us to action and also to necessary rest. This inclination is developed and strengthened by natural virtues, in particular hope and fortitude.

The second is the *sexual and familial inclination*. It deals with the proper inclination of our animal dimension, and this inclination directs us towards perpetuating our species. We are not talking about merely sexual attraction but, more exactly, a tendency toward love between a man and a woman and affection between parents and children. It is the foundation of the right to be married and also the duty of responsibly assuming the connected and complementary obligations: the gift of transmitting life, mutual support, education of children who are the fruit of this inclination, and the duty to respect other marriages. The false kinds of sexuality can be deduced upon examining this inclination: homosexuality, masturbation, deliberately infertile heterosexuality (contraception), and unstable heterosexuality (having concubines and fornication, including pre-marital sex). This inclination is naturally perfected by the virtue of chastity, which assures dominion over our sexuality in view of natural, spiritual, and familial growth.

The third inclination is the *inclination to know the truth*. It is born of our spiritual nature, and translates into a spontaneous instinct to search for the truth. It is so natural to man that it is intrinsic to his intelligence; this is why even though no one teaches a child to ask *the why* of things, all children, as soon as they begin to use their intelligence, want to know everything and want everything to be explained to them.

Sometimes we call them *question machines*; more precisely they are *devourers of the truth*. Love of the truth is the most particularly human desire and is the origin of all knowledge. This inclination is the basis for the natural right of each man to receive what is necessary to develop his intelligence, that is, his right to instruction. But, on the other hand, this also imposes the fundamental obligation to search for truth and to improve the intelligence, especially in the domain of the moral and fundamental truth, that is, the truth about God.[222]

This same third spiritual inclination has another goal: the *inclination to live in society*. Aristotle had already qualified man as a social and political animal. This inclination is based as much on motives of the material order (the impossibility of the individual to subsist by himself) as on spiritual reasons (the inclination towards and the necessity of friendship, affection, and human love). This inclination is the foundation of all social rights and puts limits on arbitrarily conceived liberty. For example, from this inclination the abnormality of lies, theft, or the unjust distribution of natural goods can be established. The virtue of justice correctly perfects and guards this natural inclination of man.

The secondary precepts of natural law. Working with the fundamental principle of natural law and the first precepts of natural law, our reason, which now works in a more refined manner, discovers other ends which perfect us but are not immediately evident like the first ones. Rather they

---

[222] "It is in accordance with their dignity as persons—that is, beings endowed with reason and free will [...] all men should be at once impelled by nature and also bound by a moral obligation to seek the truth, especially religious truth. They are also bound to adhere to the truth, once it is known, and to order their whole lives in accord with the demands of truth." (WALTER ABBOTT, ed., "Dignitatis Humanae (Declaration on Religious Freedom)," in *The Documents of Vatican II* (New York: Guild Press, 1966), no. 2.)

are the fruit of a reasoning which is generally scientific.[223] These ends have been given different names: applied, special, secondary, or derived natural law. For example, the illicitness of personal revenge or the indissolubility of marriage pertains to this level of principles.[224]

c) What is this natural law?

This natural law has various characteristics; the most important three are that it is universal, immutable, and indispensable.

Universality. Natural law is valid for all men.[225] All those who defend some type of cultural or geographic relativism (those who hold that moral and ethical principles depend exclusively on each culture or region; thus, those who say that homicide or adultery do not have the same moral value in our western culture as among the Hottentots) deny this truth. In the end, these relativisms confuse the objective value of natural law with possible ignorance on the part of some men. Natural law is valid for all human beings because it is deduced, as we have already indicated, from man's natural inclinations. Because of the essential unity of mankind, the precepts must necessarily be universal. Man, with these fundamental structures of his nature, is the measure,

---

[223] St. Thomas writes, "And there are certain things which, after a more careful consideration, wise men deem obligatory. Such belong to the law of nature, yet so that they need to be inculcated, the wiser teaching the less wise." (AQUINAS, *Summa Theologica*, I-II, Q. 100, Art. 1.)

[224] Cf. ST. THOMAS AQUINAS, "Supplement" to the Third Part of the *Summa Theologica* (Westminster, Maryland: Christian Classics, 1981), Q. 65.

[225] Cf. CCC 1956, 2261.

condition, and basis of all culture.[226] Despite this truth, it is
another thing that all men *know* these precepts. In this sense
philosophers and theologians distinguish between the
different levels of law. There is no room for doubting the
most universal precept because it is intrinsically evident.
Concerning the first precepts, there is the possibility of
ignoring some of them (although they can't be ignored
forever); this is intensified by the actual situation of fallen
man (but they say it is impossible to ignore them altogether).
Finally, about the remote conclusions, there are greater
possibilities of inculpable ignorance, of the darkening of the
intellect due to sin and of error in the processes of practical
reasoning. We note in passing that this supposes the moral
necessity of grace and revelation for the religious and moral
truths to be known by all, without difficulty, with certitude,
and without the admixture of error.[227]

Immutability. Natural law is also immutable. That means
that it endures throughout the changes of history. It subsists
under the movement of ideas and customs and sustains their
progress.[228] Historic relativism, or ethical evolutionism, is in
opposition to this truth, maintaining that morality is subject
to constant change (that is to say, the morality of our time is

---

[226] "It must certainly be admitted that man always exists in a particular
culture, but it must also be admitted that man is not exhaustively defined by that
same culture. Moreover, the very progress of cultures demonstrates that there is
something in man which transcends those cultures. This "something" is
precisely human nature: this nature is itself the measure of culture and the
condition ensuring that man does not become the prisoner of any of his
cultures, but rather asserts his personal dignity by living in accordance with the
profound truth of his being. To call into question the permanent structural
elements of man which are connected with his own bodily dimension would
[…] conflict with common experience". (VS, no. 53.)

[227] Cf. PIUS XII, *Humani Generis*, no. 3; CCC 1960.

[228] Cf. CCC 1958, 2072.

one thing and the morality in the time of Christ another, and the next century's morality will be yet another). Again, we are faced with a confusion among points of view. We can distinguish between an objective immutability and a subjective immutability. Objectively speaking natural law admits a certain quantitative change in the sense that it can achieve over time a greater expression of the precepts contained in it. But this does not mean that it truly changes, only that its ordinances become more explicit, more concrete and more known. From the point of view of the subjects, natural law is immutable in so much as it cannot be erased from the heart of man, in the same way man cannot lose his nature.

Indispensability. Natural law does not permit exceptions. The only possibility of exemption from some precept of *secondary natural law* accepted by St. Thomas is that made by God himself (in so far as he is the author of nature), and only when a greater good requires it and given that this safeguards only the secondary ends of nature. This is the case in the Old Testament, for example, regarding the permission for polygamy and divorce.[229] But there is never an exception nor dispensation from any first precept.[230] Therefore,

---

[229] St. Thomas interprets in this way the permission for the polygamy of the patriarchs and the declaration of divorce for the Jews. (Cf. AQUINAS, "Supplement," Q. 65-67.) In the case of the bill of divorce, the grave motive was to prevent the crime of murdering one's spouse or one's wife (uxoricide), which the Jews, in the hardness of their hearts, would have transgressed without hesitation. Some Fathers (St. John Chrysostom, St. Jerome, St. Augustine) and St. Thomas himself deduced that it is this hardness to which Christ refers, based on these very words: "If a man after marrying a woman and having relations with her comes to dislike her" (Dt 22:13). In the case of polygamy, the primary motive was the perpetuation of the Chosen People in the order of worship of the True God.

[230] This is why the Old Testament, while permitting a bill of divorce and polygamy, condemns having concubines, because this contradicts natural law in

morality admits of apparent exceptions in the case of theft and homicide, but they are not true exceptions to natural law, but authentic interpretations that respond to the true idea of the law.[231]

---

its first principles: it contradicts the primary end intended by nature which is the perpetuation of the species. (Cf. AQUINAS, "Supplement," Q. 65, Art. 3-5.)

[231] Thus, for example, "you shall not kill," must be adequately interpreted as "you shall not commit an unjust homicide." Therefore, the licitness of the legitimate defense is not an exception to the precept. They say the same about the apparent contradiction between the precept of "no stealing" and the licitness of the use of other's goods in the case of extreme necessity.

2. OUR MISCONCEPTION ABOUT THE COMMANDMENTS

Happy are those who observe God's decrees…
May my ways be firm
in the observance of your laws!
…teach me your laws…!

These are words from the Bible, taken from Psalm 119, titled "A Prayer to the Divine Law." Attentive reading of this psalm will never cease to surprise one who thinks of the law as "raining on a parade." In fact, what is the common concept that we have of divine laws? We can say that the majority of Christians think of them as if they were a barbed wire fence. This is to say we think that the commandments put "limits" on our actions, that they indicate the permissible minimum, and that whoever trespasses beyond them "sins." So they are like a fence that you cannot trespass.

Many good people also think this way, or at least their subconscious works this way.

Just look at the kinds of questions that a priest often hears. Businessmen ask: "What is the minimum one must declare in paying taxes?" Others ask: "How late can I come to Mass without disobeying the precept?" "Does it count if I come after the homily?" "What if we arrive after the Creed?" From some engaged couples they hear, "What is licit for couples during engagement?" "How far can you go without sinning?" We could make an endless list of such questions!

In the end, what are we asking? We are asking them to indicate for us the minimum of morality! Or could it be that we are bartering with God; we are asking him for a "discount" on the commandments.

Those who think this way also tend to say with great self-confidence, "I am not a bad person. I am not saying that I follow *all* the commandments, but I follow the *majority*."

What idea of natural law and God's commandments has been formed in us? It is like a fence with eight strings of barbed wire that prevents us from going into our neighbor's yard, which always appears greener than our own! But what happens when we see it this way? The same thing that happens to cows enclosed in a withered pasture, separated by a barbed wire fence from another field full of enticing greenery with a fragrant smell: they spend all day up against the fence nibbling the alfalfa that pokes through the wires and looking with listless hope at the neighboring pasture.

Something similar happens to Christians who see the commandments in this way—they spend life flirting with sin and envying those who live without scruples as libertines. Pemán reminds them:

> ¡Qué mal equilibrio es éste   What unsteadiness is this
> de andar pies tras pies por   to be walking step by step
> la orilla de un volcán![232]   upon the edge of a
> volcano!

This manner of understanding the law and the commandments is foreign to our faith. Or, better said, it is contrary to it. It began with an idea spread by a wayward friar named William of Ockham, who thought that God arbitrarily commanded things. Ockham recognized that in order to save ourselves we have to follow what God commands, but he also said that God could perfectly well change his opinion and demand the contrary to what he is commanding of us

---

[232] JOSÉ MARÍA PEMÁN, "El Divino Impaciente," in book IV of *Teatro: Obras Completas* (Madrid: Escelicer: 1950), 112.

now, making what is now vice become virtue and what is now virtue into vice. He even said that if, instead of commanding that we love him above all things, God demanded that we hate him, then hating God would be virtuous and obligatory![233] Ockham founded pure voluntarism, which claimed that the will determines good and evil, independently from the intelligence. For centuries now we have been paying for his mistake. All those who believe that an evil action (like contraception, sterilization, or abortion) is licit because the law permits it, are legitimate children of Ockham. At the Earth Charter celebrated in Río de Janeiro in 1997, an offspring of Ockham said that a new ethic must be elaborated for a new world, a new universal code of conduct, replacing the ten commandments with the eighteen principles of this letter. And these eighteen principles did nothing but affirm the licitness of contraception, abortion, the right to sterilization, the right of homosexuals and lesbians to get married and adopt children, and the right to give contraceptives to minors, etc. [234]

Things in reality are quite different, and we should keep this idea clear, but also fresh, in our minds. The divine commandments, similar to the natural law in which they are contained, do not only emanate from His Divine Will, but

---

[233] Cf. WILLIAM OF OCKHAM (GUILLELMI DE OCKHAM), *Quaestiones in Librum Secundum Sententiarum (Reportatio),* in book V of *Opera Philosophica et Theologica,* ed. Gedeon Gál (New York: Franciscan Institute Publications, 1981), Q. 19, 1: "I say that hatred of God, theft, adultery and other similar actions of the common law have a circumstantial evil attached to them when performed by those who are obliged by divine precept to do the opposite. However, in their absolute being (*esse absolutum*) those actions could be given by God without the circumstance of evil attached, and they could even be performed meritoriously by earthly pilgrims if they were to fall within divine precept." (Editorial translation.)

[234] Cf. SALVADOR ARGUEDAS, "La Cumbre de la Tierra," *Agencia Informativa Católica Argentina* (AICA-DOC 2106), April 30, 1997, editorial translation.

fundamentally from His Intelligence. As Scripture, Tradition, the Magisterium, Theology and common sense, all of which are forgotten by Ockham, teach: divine law is the *plan* of the Wisdom of God. This is why Psalm 107, mentioning the attitude of sinners, says: *"For they had rebelled against the commandments of God, and spurned the plan of the Most High"* (Ps 107:11). This is the Plan according to which He has created the entire universe and directs and cares for it. It is the Plan according to which He has done all things in a determined manner. As Scripture says: *"But thou hast arranged all things by measure and number and weight"* (Wis 11:20).

Each determined nature can only be perfected by determined ideals; just as every lock has only one key and if I use the wrong key, I break the lock. For this reason, in every being in the universe, including man, we find natural inclinations towards the goods that perfect them. Looking for these goods, therefore, is not only an obligation but also a "desire," a "tendency" of nature, and a "vocation." Because good attracts the one for whom it is good.

We already said that this law is condensed by what is expressed in the Ten Commandments. Therefore, the commandments do not do anything but indicate the "goods" that perfect us and help us to take precautions against the evils that degrade and lower us, ruining our nature. We also said that these commandments are both written in our nature and have also been revealed. Why? Because man lost his moral and religious orientation and dulled his conscience with sin. He was left with the script, but reading it makes him myopic, as if he were nearsighted, trying to read in dim light. This is why when Moses descended Mount Sinai where God had revealed his law to him, he actually brought with him the mercy of God carved on two stone tablets. God reiterated the divine commands to a mankind that was deaf and blind.

In his turn, Jesus Christ, by instituting the New Law, internalized and elevated this same law through grace, frequently repeating the necessity of following the commandments of God. In the Sermon on the Mount, Jesus revealed—or you can say, unveiled—the original meaning of the Ten Commandments, demonstrating all of their requirements and giving them complete fulfillment. In this way, Jesus unveiled God's primordial design for man. Therefore, the Psalm is fulfilled: *"All thy commandments are true"* (Ps 119:86). This is the truth about man.

The divine law is then a lighthouse, a splendid light that lights the path ahead of us.

"How can a young man keep his way pure?
By guarding it according to thy word." (Ps 119:9)

To walk "pure" is to walk safely. What better education can there be than making the wisdom hidden in the commandments of God "understood"? It is not enough to know them; they have to be understood.

"I will meditate on thy precepts,
and fix my eyes on thy ways" (Ps 119:15)
"Open my eyes that I may behold" (Ps 119:18)
hide not thy commandments from me!" (Ps 119:19)
"Give me understanding, that I may keep thy law
and observe it with my whole heart." (Ps 119:34)

What does it mean to truly "know" the commandments? Three things: first, to know what they are; second to interiorize them; and third, to understand their intimate and indissoluble connection.

The first is the easiest. The majority of Christians—although not everyone, to the disgrace of the Christians and priests who ought to have taught them—have learned which are the ten commandments of the law of God, either in a catechism class or in their family. But to truly know the commandments well, one has to meditate upon them in his heart.

"With my lips I declare
all the ordinances of thy mouth.
In the way of thy testimonies
I delight as much as in all riches.
I will meditate on thy precepts,
and fix my eyes on thy ways.
I will delight in thy statutes;
I will not forget thy word." (Ps 119:13-16)

"Oh, how I love thy law!
It is my meditation all the day." (Ps 119:97)

The second meaning of knowing the commandments indicates understanding the value of each commandment. That is to say, all of its content. It has to be acknowledged that not everyone knows all that is implied by each commandment. For example, not everyone knows that each commandment includes a positive aspect (a good that should be obtained or defended) and a negative aspect (they prohibit acts that endanger the good). The commandments guard, that is, protect, defend, and promote, a person's fundamental goods, the goods without which he cannot mature, perfect himself, or be happy. For example:

The *first commandment* (You shall love the Lord your God above all things) covers all of our theological relationships with God, orders our acts of faith, hope and charity, and also puts us in the practice of the virtue of religion through acts of adoration, prayer, sacrifice, etc. It preserves us from all the religious perversions that threaten man, such as superstition, idolatry, irreligiosity, atheism, agnosticism.

The *second commandment* (Do not take the name of the Lord in vain) causes us to respect God and all that is sacred. It gives us an authentic sense of religion and prompts the praise of God to rise from our lips.

The *third commandment* (Keep holy the Lord's Day) makes us learn to dedicate our life to God and also teaches us to know how to rest and to cultivate our familial, cultural, social, and religious life.

The *fourth commandment* (Honor your father and mother) attains for us family and social virtues: respect between parents, children and siblings. It makes of each family a "domestic church" and humanizes and Christianizes all of society.

The *fifth commandment* (You shall not kill) teaches us to respect and value the gift of life and the dignity of every human being. It guarantees peace in society and in the world.

The *sixth commandment* (You shall not commit adultery) teaches the virtue of chastity and control over the emotions, thereby guaranteeing true human freedom, freeing us from the slavery of disordered passions. It makes chastity shine in all its forms: in consecrated virginity, in dating relationships, and in marriage. It guarantees fidelity between spouses.

The *seventh commandment* (You shall not steal) orders our relationship with material goods. It helps us to respect these goods and detach ourselves from them, to be generous with what we have, to be just in our life of labor and in our finances. It teaches us to love and help the poor.

The *eighth commandment* (You shall not give false testimony or lie) makes us love and live in the truth. It guarantees honesty and frankness among men. It is a pledge of true friendship.

The *ninth commandment* (You shall not covet your neighbor's wife) brings chastity and purity to the realm of thoughts and desires. It makes us pure of heart and truly free.

The *tenth commandment* (You shall not covet your neighbor's goods) orders our hearts regarding earthly goods and frees us from the tyranny of greed and avarice. It takes away the sadness that attachment produces.

Thus it can be understood how the book of the Acts of the Apostles calls the commandments *Words of life* (Acts 7:38).

To educate according to the commandments, from my point of view, means making the goods the commandments offer us understood, making them valued as goods; which is to say, presenting them as "loveable," and making it understood why it is necessary to love and practice them. It also means understanding that they *do not have to be followed just because God says so* but that *God commands them because our well-being and our happiness is in them.* Before showing his authority, God shows his infinite Goodness, thereby shedding light on our path towards happiness.

We must convince ourselves that we will never be happy if we do not live with these goods in our life. Not only because we cannot save ourselves if we do not follow the commandments, but also because we will be unhappy even during this earthly life. In other words, we will be nothing more than mediocre.

So, the commandments are not a barbed wire fence that limits and punishes us, forbidding us to cross to the happy field; on the contrary, they are a supernatural lighthouse that guides us on the safe way through the storms of life. They are luminous guides in our itinerary of perfection. Let us remember what the Psalm says:

> *"The law of the Lord is perfect,*
> *refreshing the soul.*
> *The decree of the Lord is trustworthy,*
> *giving wisdom to the simple.*
> *The precepts of the Lord are right,*
> *rejoicing the heart.*
> *The commandment of the Lord is pure,*
> *enlightening the eyes* [...]
> *The statutes of the Lord are true,*
> *all of them just.*
> *More desirable than gold,*
> *than a hoard of pure gold,*
> *Sweeter also that honey*
> *or drippings from the comb."* (Ps 19:8-9, 10b-11)

> *"Thy word is a lamp to my feet*
> *and a light to my path."* (Ps 119:105)

3. THE COMMANDMENTS AND OUR MATURITY

If you ever hear that a mature person does not let himself be guided by anything or anyone and, therefore, it is immature to "tie oneself" to any law or any commandment, don't go for it! I dare to tell you that reality is so different from this slogan that it is precisely the opposite. For this reason, if you have understood what we have said up to this point, you will understand that every authentic maturing process occurs by doing what the commandments direct. Affective psychological and spiritual immaturity is always rooted in ignorance of one or more of the commandments and, therefore, the lack of the goods which the commandments require us to maintain strong in our life. Ask any psychiatrist or psychologist what types of immaturity there are and they will respond that they correspond to people who are unable to carry out family life, or who are unable to live the chastity proper to their state, or those who are not dependable in their commitments, those who mix truth with lies, those who are dependent on superficial things, those who do not find any meaning in life, those who are unable to forgive insults, those who are angry, hopelessly superficial, etc. All of those people lack some good that could be gained if they respected the divine commandments.

What a good educational plan for parents, teachers, catechists, and priests it is to help make the Wisdom of the commandments of God understood!

I am not just referring to the fact that we should teach what the commandments are, but that we should teach how to live them. I am sometimes asked: what things should we keep in mind in forming our children or our students or those we direct on the path of maturity or perfection? It must begin by looking at what the commandments of God aim. Jesus

Christ started here. To the rich young man who approached him asking, *"Teacher, what good deed must I do, to have eternal life?' Jesus responded, 'If you would enter life, keep the commandments.' He said to him, 'Which?' And Jesus said, 'You shall not kill, you shall not commit adultery, you shall not steal, you shall not bear false witness, honor your father and mother, and, you shall love your neighbor as yourself'"* (Mt 19:16-19). By disposing us to the fundamental moral goods, the commandments become the conditions for attaining virtues. And only the virtuous man is human in an authentic, full, and mature sense.

However, I should insist upon a third element. It deals with the fact, often insufficiently understood, that the commandments should be observed *in their entirety*. This is to say, either *all of them* are observed or the building crumbles. No real estate agent would offer us a house saying: "I recommend this house: It is big. It has two levels, a terrace, a view of the sea, natural gas, and a telephone. It is true that it has a crack that has already separated the foundation and some of the beams... but it is still very comfortable." Every ruin starts with a crack!

What should we think, then, when someone tells us that he is good because he does not rob or kill? I feel like telling him, "Keep going, you're only missing eight more things!"

Pope John Paul II has said this very clearly making reference to current crimes against life: "It is thus the Law as a whole which fully protects human life. This explains why it is so hard to remain faithful to the commandment *'you shall not kill'* when the other *'words of life'* (cf. Acts 7:38) with which this commandment is bound up are not observed. Detached from this wider framework, the commandment is destined to become nothing more than an obligation imposed from without, and very soon we begin to look for its limits and try to find mitigating factors and exceptions."[235]

Many who end up in real moral disasters started by failing in some particular commandment. One sin leads to another.

If we do not follow *all* the commandments, we should not deceive ourselves by thinking that we are following the law of God. Therefore, we must strongly insist on this point: parents and educators cannot be content that children avoid the worst—that they do not use drugs or commit crimes—but they must teach them all human values. How many parents see their children become alcoholics or drug users after they have told them so many times not to do it! Yes, they gave them a lot of advice, but only in one area: regarding drugs and alcohol. But they did not care to teach them about chastity, modesty, self-control, supernatural prudence, humility, how to avoid pettiness, prayer. They cannot make a great man or a great woman with only a couple of virtues!

At the root of it all, we should understand and make understood that there is a great truth hidden in those words of Christ: *"Whoever has my commandments and observes them is the one who loves me [...] Whoever loves me will keep my word [...] Whoever does not love me does not keep my words"* (Jn 14: 21-24). I say "hidden truth" because many understand this phrase in a good, but incomplete way. They think that Jesus is saying that those who wish to love Him accept the condition of following his words or commands. But Jesus Christ is also saying that the same love that they have for Him will impel them to love what his words or commandments contain. For the man who truly loves, the commandments

---

[235] ST. JOHN PAUL II, *Evangelium Vitae*, no. 48.

are not conditions, or obligatory, but "attractive;" the commandments appear to them as *viae amoris*, paths of love.

For someone who loves God with a pure heart, chastity, respect, truth and all of the other moral goods contained in the commandments attract Him; they stir Him; He is in love with them. For the hardhearted, in contrast, living out all moral goods is only a hard task that must be carried out if they do not want to be condemned. This second view of the commandments was held by many men before the Incarnation of the Word. Those who belong to the New Testament in spirit have the former view, because the grace infused in our hearts inclines us, for the sake of love, to do just what the commandments demand. This is why Jesus says: *"My yoke is easy and my burden light"* (Mt 11:30).

For beginners and the hardhearted, the commandments are like going to the dentist: we go because we do not want our teeth to fall out, but still we would like to run away! For the loving heart what the commandments prescribe seems like telling a child he must eat ice cream every day. I don't think I would need to tell him twice!

Often, educators (I think of parents, teachers, professors, and catechists) fall into this error: teaching children and youth that they have to respect their neighbor, they mustn't steal or lie, must avoid bad conversations and impure acts, must go to mass every Sunday, and not to slander, etc., insisting only on the *obligation*, the *duty*, and the *punishment* those who don't obey deserve, is to point them in the wrong direction.

Now, I do not mean to say that this is not also necessary! We have to be realists. St. Thomas, commenting on the ancient philosopher, Aristotle, said: "persuasive words can challenge, and move to good, generous youths who are not slaves of vice and passion and who have excellent natural dispositions inasmuch as they are inclined to virtuous operations. [...] But many men cannot be induced to virtue because they are not subject to shame which fears disgrace, but rather are coerced by the dread of punishment. They do not refrain from evil because of disgracefulness but because of the punishments feared. In fact they live according to their passions and not according to reason; thus their own desires increase and they avoid pains opposed to the pleasures soughtpains inflicted on them by punishments. They do not know what is really good and pleasant, nor can they taste its delight."[236]

This is true. But reducing all education to this is an error. It must not be forgotten that parents themselves begin to educate their children before any passions begin to control them. They *can* begin to teach them to love the good and the moral goods commanded by God.

Therefore, the main emphasis that must be given in education is to make the virtues shine before the eyes of children and youth. Why? So that they fall in love with them. Love will then do the rest. Clearly this is much more demanding, because one cannot teach how to love what one does not himself love! Nor can one demand of others what he does not do in his own life. Example is the first lesson, but many are not motivated to give a good example. Many are overwhelmed by trying to make their children fall in love with moral goods and values like: faithfulness to God, obedience to the Church, love for the poor, modesty and chastity, disinterest in things, etc. . . . They are afraid that their children will ask, "But if this is so beautiful, why don't you live it?" This is why, for parents or catechists who do not want to be virtuous and who do not want to be holy, it is

---

[236] ST. THOMAS AQUINAS, *Commentary on the Nicomachean Ethics,* trans. C. I. Litzinger (Chicago: Henry Regnery Company, 1964), nos. 2140-2141.

more comfortable for them to teach the commandments as if they were traffic laws. "No U-turn," "Speed 60," "Speed checked by radar," "Stay right," "No passing on turns," etc. Seen only from this point of view, the road of life is made very difficult; and therefore, at the first religious and moral crisis, they step on the accelerator, although they know they could crash headlong into a truck.

Therefore, summarizing what I have wished to say here:

1. All educators should better prepare themselves in their understanding of Gods' moral law. They have to know what a law of virtues is and that the commandments aim at these virtues; and that the beauty of divine law is only understood when one carries out the whole thing. If you are studying to be a professor or to obtain a teaching certificate, keep this in mind.

2. They have to internalize the Law of God. They have to know it in an interior, meditative, thorough manner. Knowing not only what is commanded but why it is commanded—knowing the splendor proper to each virtue.

3. They must also know the great men and women who have made the virtues shine in their lives, such as Don Orione or Mother Teresa of Calcutta who show charity for the rejected, the innumerable martyrs who show fortitude; Father Miguel Pro who shows joy and humor in trials; St. Francis Xavier, missionary zeal; St. Maria Goretti, virginity even to martyrdom; St. Therese, fidelity in little things; etc.

4. They have to take up the work of speaking about the commandments and virtues with our children, students and friends, taking the time to teach them and making them fall in love with God. They have to prepare them for life and for difficulties. Father Lebbe, a missionary who arrived in China at the turn of the twentieth century when the Boxer Rebellion that gave many martyrs to the Church had just ended, wrote

in his letters about inspiring examples of parents preparing their children not to abandon the faith in the midst of torture. He told about how one father "knowing the risk he was running, met daily with his children exhorting them to remain courageous in the faith of Christ to death. This man asked his youngest son: 'If the pagans were to offer you pardon in exchange for renouncing Christ, what would you say?' And the child answered: 'I would say, I am Christian.' The father continues, 'And if they threaten you with death or if they cut off your little hands or want to pull your eyes out, what would you say?' The little boy repeated with a sweet voice, 'I would say, I am Christian.' This father," adds Father Lebbe, "suffered martyrdom and was admired even by the pagans for the peace and happiness reflected in his face."

These were parents who loved their children's virtue and eternal life more than their earthly life or wellbeing. The mother of the youngest canonized Chinese martyr, Andre Wang Tianquing, loved her nine-year-old son very much. The pagans wanted to save the child, but at the price of his faith; at this moment his mother said with a firm voice, "I am Christian, my son is Christian. You will have to kill us both." And Andre dies kneeling, looking at his mother with a smile. Today they are both saints.

Much more can be said about this topic. But what has been said is enough, I think, to show the importance of teaching the virtues, based on a deeper understanding of God's commandments.

I want to end with an old story. At the beginning of the 1600s, in a ceremony for Jewish boys during a ritual of Initiation into the life of the Synagogue, the following dialogue took place. The Rabbi, putting the point of the Scroll of the Law on the chest of the boy asked, "What do you feel?"

And the boy responded, "I feel a heart that beats."

Then the Rabbi replied, "It is the Heart of God! Listen to his Word! Fulfill his Law!"

The law of God is the living Heart of God. He who tries to take this law from you does not want to do anything but to kill your heart.

*   *   *

He who does not accept a natural law—or the divine commandments—because this implies restricting his liberty, should remember that liberty is a great value, but that it is also an analogous term that can be applied to many different things, even losing its true meaning. Not all that bears the name of liberty is true liberty, nor is all dependence slavery. If you are closed in a cage and you escape from it, the act of escaping deserves to be called liberation and your prize can be called freedom. If you are addicted to drugs or alcohol and you succeed in untying yourself from its knots, you can call this liberation and you really will be a free man. If you have been locked in an elevator, it is freedom to get out of it, and freedom is what you experience in returning to breathe pure air in the street. If you are weighed down by pain and sickness, you will be freed when you are cured, and you will be free when you regain your health. But if you slip on ice while climbing a mountain and are left hanging in the air held by only the security rope, you will not call cutting the knot liberation, nor will you consider it freedom to become a red mark on the white glacier waiting for you hundreds of feet below. If you pull out the oxygen tubes with which you are diving at a depth of 250 feet, you will not call such stupidity freedom, nor will you consider yourself free while floating drowned in the salty water. To take a weight off is not always freedom, as poor Marie Antoinette would have understood the day the guillotine unjustly relieved her of the weight of her head. Not every knot that ties us enslaves us, as a marionette will tell you, if he could talk—for him to be alive is to be hanging, because the puppeteer gives him life in the world of the puppet theater.

There are, then, liberties that are slavery, and servitude that is independence, as the Bible says in that pleasing and beautiful sentence: *to serve God is to reign.*

For Further Reading

- Aquinas, St. Thomas. *Summa Theologica* (Westminster, MD: Christian Classics, 1981), I-II, q. 94ff.
- Finnis, John. "The Natural Law, Objective Morality, and Vatican II." In William May, ed. *Principles of Catholic Moral Life*. Chicago: Franciscan Herald Press, 1981.
- May, William. "The Natural Law and Objective Morality: A Thomistic Perspective." In *Principles of Catholic Moral Life*. Chicago: Franciscan Herald Press, 1981.
- Messner, Johannes. *Social Ethics: Natural Law in the Modern World*. B. Herder Book, 1949.

Available in Other Languages

- Adeva, Ildefonso. "Ley Moral." *Gran Enciclopedia Rialp*. Madrid: Ediciones Rialp, 1991.
- Aubert, Jean-Marie. *Ley de Dios, Leyes de los Hombres*. Barcelona: Herder, 1979.
- Derisi, Octavio Nicolás. *Los Fundamentos Metafísicos del Orden Moral*. Madrid: C.S.I.C., Instituto "Luis Vives" de Filosofía, 1969.
- Lachance, Louis. *El Concepto de Derecho Según Aristóteles y Santo Tomás*. Buenos Aires: Taladríz, 1953.
- Mausbach, J. and G. Ermecke. Vol. 1 of *Teología Moral Católica*. Pamplona: EUNSA, 1971.
- Messner, Johannes. *Ética General y Aplicada*. Madrid: Rialp, 1969.
- Montejano, Bernardino. "Ley: Planteamiento General." *Gran Enciclopedia Rialp*. Madrid: Ediciones Rialp, 1991.
- Ramírez, Santiago. *Doctrina Política de Santo Tomás*. Madrid: Instituto Social León XIII, 1952.
- Soaje Ramos, Guido. "Sobre la Politicidad del Derecho." In *Boletín de Estudios Políticos*. Mendoza: Universidad Nacional de Cuyo, 1958.
- Soria, Carlos. "Introducción al Tratado de la Ley." In S. Tomás de Aquino [St. Thomas Aquinas]. Vol. VI. of *Suma Teológica*. Madrid: BAC, 1956.

8.

THE STOLEN
TRUTH ABOUT
YOUR SEXUALITY

The Truth that Chastity is Possible

One of the truths that most affects a person's life is the one that relates to his or her sexuality. Is it true that you should control your sexual impulses? Or, first we should ask: Are our impulses and desires controllable? Our society has not very clearly settled this point. Instead, it is one of the realms where you will find the most confusion. You will encounter friends (what friends!), professors (what educators!), and above all, those who control the media, who will try to fill your head with *sexualized* ideas about man and woman. This is all the more true if you are studying in any of the fields related to psychiatry and psychology, about which, Leonardo Castellani, a well-known Argentinean author, said, "There is no other science where it is so easy to sell a dog for a cat, and which so often attracts swindlers."[237] If you doubt this, you should read any reliable book about Sigmund Freud and his theories, not the myths that circulate about him.

It is not difficult to understand this phenomenon. Certainly the inclination towards sexual pleasure is one of the strongest in our nature (because nature uses precisely these means to guarantee the conservation of the species). It is easy for a person to degrade himself by reducing the entirety of man to sex and by identifying happiness with mere sexual pleasure. It is not difficult, then, to confuse the root of all ailments with some problem of sexual repression, nor, as a logical consequence, to reduce all therapy and healing to liberating this repressed sexual instinct. Combine all of this and you will have the substance of Freudian doctrine.

According to this vision, imagine what awaits the doctrine taught by our faith with its ideal of chaste lives, sincere

---

[237] LEONARDO CASTELLANI, "La Realidad del Alma: El Espíritu del Subterráneo," in *Psicología Humana*, 2nd ed., ed. Carlos Biestro (Mendoza: Ediciones Jauja, 1997), editorial translation.

engagements, and of faithful and monogamous matrimonies. If they don't label you as a prude, they will at least consider you demented.

Wherever you may be, (although, I principally direct myself to university students, these pages may as well reach a broader audience), I know that you will be subjected to terrible pressures on your sexual instinct. Not only are television shows, movies and magazines dedicated to sex, but at present sexual disorder (including blatant pornography) comes buried in amusement literature (novels and stories) and science-fiction, found in a collection of lecture halls. It will assault you through the key tool of modern media: the Internet (the business of sex is the third most important business driving the cyber-world. For this authentic *mafia of pornography*, you are a client to be won over!). And your vulnerability will grow exponentially[238] if you have any confused ideas about sex and chastity, and worse yet, if they are poisoned ideas. Unfortunately, our modern school system, among countless sectors, plays a corrupting role in this sense (one has to only think of what is taught under the guise of *sex education*).

This point can be clarified in two ways: first, by presenting what some of the principal thinkers (like Freud and many of his followers) teach on this subject and by making critiques pertinent to the case. This is something that has already been done in extensive studies, and so I would not be doing anything other than summarizing and repeating. The other way, which better suits my goal for this book, is to show you that chastity is necessary and possible. This is what I offer you here.

---

[238] "Exponential" means that the rate of growth always increases more quickly with time.

1. CHASTITY AND TEMPERANCE

Chastity, also called purity, is a virtue, part of the virtue of temperance, which inclines us to moderate the use of the sexual faculty according to reason (illuminated by faith, in the case of supernatural chastity).

Sexuality is an eminent good of a person. Christian thought, or at least its more illustrious thinkers, has always been very clear in this respect. We can note a few exceptions who have had a pessimistic view of sexuality, like those who thought and claimed that if Adam had not sinned there would not have been sexual propagation of the human species in the earthly Paradise.[239] In any case they name Tertullian (already a Montanist heretic) as the father of the pessimistic view of sexuality. For the authentic view of the great thinkers, like St. Thomas, one can read the pages Josef Pieper dedicated to him in his book, *The Four Cardinal Virtues*.[240]

Etymologically, the word chastity comes from the word, chasten (to correct by punishment).[241] This is not to be taken in a pathetic sense, invoking any imaginable pity, but understood only as an allusion to that by which reason, by

---

[239] These people thought that the transmission of the human genus would not have occurred by sexual union, but that God, "foreseeing" the fall of our first parents, disposed it in this manner from the beginning. Therefore, they were of the opinion that even if sexual relation was associated with the propagation of the human species from the first moment of human history, this was because of sin (since it was foreseen).

[240] Cf. JOSEF PIEPER, "Temperance," in *The Four Cardinal Virtues: Prudence, Justice, Fortitude, Temperance* (Notre Dame, Indiana: University of Notre Dame Press, 1966).

[241] *Editor's Note*: In Middle English, the word "chasten" came from the French word derived from the Latin words *castus* (pure) and *agire* (to drive). In Spanish, the word "castigo" (chastisement or punishment) came from these same Latin words.

means of this habit, subjects the concupiscible appetite to its own measure. It is the virtue that moderates the sexual and procreative, or generative, appetite. Its matter is properly reproductive activity, given that the secondary acts of sexuality (such as looking, touching, etc.) are the matter of the virtue of modesty;[242] although according to St. Thomas, this is not a virtue distinct from chastity but a circumstance of it.

The proximate end of chastity is the rational and moral control of the sexual instinct. The state of human nature requires a virtue that is a permanent and firm disposition of the soul toward such an object. The sexual appetite is very strong, and in man, it is not properly governed by the instinct, as it is in animals. A disordered imagination can take man's sexual life to numerous excesses of which animals are not capable. The norms of natural law that govern the human sexual life would be ineffective if reason limited itself to know them but lacked a virtue that inclines the will to fulfill the norms or give it the necessary strength to do so. Therefore, the virtue of chastity is indispensable for man's interior perfection and for harmony between body and soul.

Psychologically speaking, chastity is a moral habit by which the human person orders his reproductive instinct (the concupiscible appetite) making it look for the *authentic sensible good*,[243] in as much as it perfects the human person and controls him so that he does not turn towards concupiscible goods that are contrary to the integral good of the whole person. This habit, like all habits or moral virtues, acts in

---

[242] Cf. AQUINAS, *Summa Theologica*, II-II, Q. 151, Art. 4.

[243] Sensible good and concupiscible good are synonyms that indicate the pleasure or gratification produced in the senses; here we refer principally to sexual pleasure.

correlation with the virtue of prudence that dictates the right means (that is, the *true* concupiscible good) that should be searched for at every moment according to the specific state of life.

This habit is, properly speaking, an inclination (or attraction) imprinted on the concupiscible appetite (that is, in the affectivity)[244] towards the sensible moral good (that is, toward the legitimate and concupiscible good and ordered according to moral principles). In reality the inclination toward the good enjoyed by the senses is part of the sensible appetite; the habit of chastity adds "docility" or "consistency" (acquired by practice and discipline) of this inclination with the virtuous "measure" in which it is licit to look for or to enjoy these goods (according to one's proper state in life and situation). In order to acquire such docility, there are two more elements that form an integral part of chastity. The first is a *body of moral principles* (in this case, principles about sexuality) that pertain to different intellectual habits. It may be the habit of understanding the first moral principles (called synderesis), or elementary morals (often obtained through family traditions, religious formation—catechism—or even through common sense), or maybe a more scientific ethic, the fruit of personal study. These general principles are applied to each concrete situation by the habit of *prudence* that is always present in every virtuous act of the nature (there is no moral virtue without prudence, since it indicates the virtuous measure in which all habits should be practiced in given circumstances). The second element is the action of the

---

[244] The concupiscible appetite as the seat of our affection has as its object pleasurable sensible goods; it is a function of the sensible appetite. The other function is called the irascible appetite, and its object is the affections whose object is a sensible good that is difficult to attain.

will, perfected by justice and its associated virtues.[245] The will, ordered by love for the good, is what "governs" (with the so-called "dominion of exercise"),[246] controlling the sensible appetite and applying it to the search for sensible good according to the measure in which it perfects the subject (that is, in the measure it is lawful and virtuous). As a result of this continuous dominion of the will and its "application" to the sensible appetite, it ends up forming a "mold" or stable inclination (which is to always work in the same way), that is what we call a virtuous habit or simply "virtue."

2. WHAT THE BIBLE SAYS ABOUT SEXUALITY

If we try to look at the ideas of sexuality that Sacred Scripture presents to us, we must necessarily return to the story of the creation of man and woman in Genesis, not only because it was first, but also because it is "normative." We should not lose sight of the fact that Jesus Christ, when referring to matrimony in the argument against divorce with the Pharisees, said: "from the beginning it was not so" (Mt. 19:8). The "beginning" presents a norm, a norm of the divine will for matrimony and sexuality. Our Lord takes this up again in his moral preaching, which we should also do. In the story of Genesis 1:26-31, man is created male and female (v. 27); this shows the creation, as God desired, of two sexes, both made in the image of God. Then, it adds that God orders and blesses fertility, linking it to marriage (v. 28). In

---

[245] Justice is the virtue that perfects the will in the search for good. Associated virtues are those related to justice but, for one reason or another, are not strictly justice; such is the case of religion, gratitude, piety, veracity, prudent interpretation of the law, etc.

[246] Dominion of exercise or "active use" is the action by which the will "moves" the other potencies (in our case the sensible appetite or affections) to their proper operation (that is to say, "applies them," as said in ethics).

the complementary account (Genesis 2:18-24), the aspect of mutual support and companionship is especially highlighted (v. 18). Christ appeals precisely to this text when speaking of the indissoluble union, *in the beginning it was not this way*. There was no divorce (Mt 19:1-9) The worth and goodness of sex as it came from the hands of God is manifested in the purity of conscience of our first parents. They were naked and not ashamed (v. 25). There are also other elements of utmost importance that stand out in these first chapters. [247]

A view of sexuality in the Old Testament cannot leave out the wisdom books (especially the Song of Songs) and the prophetic books. In all of these books, conjugal love—even described with passionate qualities—is used as a symbol of the love between God and his people (and also the love of God for each individual soul). We emphasize the fact that human love serves to illustrate God's love towards men; it also implies the capacity of divine love to illuminate us (make us understand) human love up to a certain point. In the Old Testament, though perhaps without much development, the great gifts of love and sexuality are made evident: fidelity, loyalty, indissolubility, fruitfulness, etc.

Reading the New Testament, the most important and complete text is in 1 Corinthians chapters six and seven. In 1 Corinthians 6:12-20, St. Paul presents a clear and balanced view of pleasure and the flesh, speaking against both the laxity and the moral rigorousness that had already presented themselves as enemies of the Christian view of sexuality. The Apostle values the body in its religious dimension as a

---

[247] I have developed these in: MIGUEL FUENTES, "Al principio no fue así— El valor normativo del 'principio' en la moral conyugal [In the beginning it was not so—The normative value of the "beginning" in conjugal morality]," conference, Santiago de Chile, 2002, and the Second Family Encounter, Toronto, Ontario, Canada, 2003.

member of Christ (v. 15), destined for the resurrection (v. 13-14), and as a temple of the Holy Spirit (v. 19). Likewise, the text condemns fornication on two levels: the natural (it dishonors the body, v. 18) and the supernatural (sacrilege against the Holy Spirit). It adds that the body can and should glorify God (v. 20). The text in 1 Corinthians 7:1-10 has some noteworthy aspects: chastity and virginity are something good (v. 1), but marriage is also lawful (v. 2). It also points out the mutual obligation of "conjugal duty" (v. 3).[248] St. Paul speaks of the effect of marriage as a mutual possession on the part of the man and the woman (v. 4); and when he speaks of periodic abstinence from sexual union, he declares that in order for it to be lawful, it should take place with mutual consent and for an honest reason, like prayer (v. 5). Finally he recommends virginity (v. 8-9) and reminds them of the indissolubility of the marriage bond (v. 10-11). Other New Testament texts will appear throughout these pages.

---

[248] "Conjugal duty" refers to the obligation that a spouse has to give himself or herself to have relations when the other reasonably solicits them.

3. WHY THIS VIRTUE?

A human being is complex; he cannot be reduced to only one dimension without being at the same time deprived of his dignity; without, in some sense, destroying him. Reductions of man are dehumanizing. Materialism reduces him to his lowest dimension (which can include biological materialism, which is the basis of modern science; animal materialism or evolutionist materialism, etc.). False spiritualism reduces him to a pure disembodied spirit. Both of these visions are false. Man is a microcosm that summarizes the entire universe in his fragile being. He shares ("communicates" as the scholastics would have said) in the mineral universe, in the vegetative world, in the animal or sensitive world, and in the spiritual world. His whole being is a complex hierarchical world. The fruit of hierarchy is harmony. This is explained by saying that the lesser is subordinate to the greater, the inferior to the superior, serving it and permitting it to develop all its efficaciousness. This signifies that, while what is inferior (for example, the 'animal' part) remains itself subordinate and docile to what is superior (the soul, the intelligence, and the will); it is still permitted to develop all of its potentialities. This was the *original* condition of man in Paradise, if we rely on the Biblical narrative in Genesis. Man, in his beginnings, enjoyed a harmony based on a hierarchy of his potencies: the exterior world was under his control in the measure in which his body was subject to his passions, his passions were under the control of his will and intelligence, and his will and his intelligence served God. All this resulted from what the Catholic tradition has called *the preternatural gifts* (immortality, impassability, harmony, etc.), given by God to the human nature to freely guarantee this harmony (definitively to form the foundation of the friendship between man and God).

253

Original sin overthrew everything, breaking down the essential subordination of the soul with respect to God. As a consequence, all the other subordinations guaranteed by the preternatural gifts were reversed: the passions enslave the soul, the body weakens and walks toward death, man is often seized by unrestrained instinct and compulsiveness, and the external world forces sweat and tears from the man who tries to subject it.

This picture is important to interpreting the meaning of "the integral good of man" (a term that appears in some magisterial documents).[249] Something can be considered an "integral" (or "true and integral") good when it is a good for the entire human person (and also for all human persons) and not for one isolated potency (intelligence, will, sensibility) or for a particular aspect of his being. In order to be called an integral good, a reality cannot only be good in itself (*per se bona*) but must meet two more conditions: it must not enter into conflict with the other goods of the person, and, consequently, it must have a *measure* (*in medio virtus*). There are realities that are good in themselves (food, sexual pleasure, social interaction) but can enter into conflict with the entire good of the person. Either it directly contradicts (*per se*) other goods of the person himself (like sexual pleasure for someone who has made a vow of celibacy), or indirectly (*per accidens*), that is, when there is a contradiction in the manner, time, or disposition in which the said good is

---

[249] Cf. CCC 2294, 2361, 2375;

St. John Paul II, *Vitae Mysterium (The Mystery of Life)*, no. 3, Motu Proprio establishing the Pontifical Academy for Life (February 11, 1994) *www.ewtn.com/library/papaldoc/jp2vitae.htm* (accessed December 7, 2014);

VS, nos. 72, 79, 112.

procured (for example, excess of food—gluttony—or the immoderate search for sexual pleasure).

No reasonable person can deny the validity of this reflection.

The point is found perhaps in the argument about the "standard" of a person's integral good. Can a valid standard be established for all men and women, as much for our time as for the past or the future? We should respond, yes. That integral standard is based on natural law, which we spoke of in the previous chapter.

4. NATURAL LAW AND CHASTITY

This law lays the foundation for a norm of chastity; it also lays the foundation for all relations of the human person with himself, his neighbor and God.

In the concrete plan of chastity, concerning natural law (which is what our intelligence can grasp from the divine plan written in our nature)[250] we must say:

1. The first thing we can observe is the complementarity between man and woman (not only on the physical level, but also on the psychological level and, above all, on the genetic level). Therefore, all sexuality must be "heterosexual."

2. Second, we should point out the social end of sexuality. The act of sexuality (understood as heterosexuality) is necessary for the perpetuation of the human genus. This principle requires an addition, since the perpetuation of the

---

[250] This possibility to "read" or "interpret" a divine plan in nature itself and in creation in general is singularly apparent: it establishes the possibility of a natural dialogue between the creature and the Creator. It is the foundation of a natural "language" that the human being discovers in his nature and has from God.

human race is not obtained by simple mating between human individuals of different sexes. It requires a stable union, for the fragility and complexity of human beings require that the fruit of the sexual act (the child) be accompanied and educated over a long period of time.[251] Therefore, it can be deduced that *marriage (union between one man and one woman forever) is the only natural form in which the human sexual life can be adequately carried out.*

3. The third observation is that the attraction between a man and a woman (that is to say, between a male and a female of the human race) does not correspond exclusively nor primarily to the physical or hormonal sphere (as in other species) but rather, is born from a psychological and spiritual element: love. It is not a purely instinctual movement, but a free movement. This means that the movement that brings about the use of sexuality rises from an inclination to give of one's self to the loved one. This is what the term "unitive" signifies, that the end of love is union and self-giving. All self-giving has to be entire (psychologically, all self-giving that is not entire is not related to love, since love is total). Furthermore, this brings us to place the sexual act within the framework of marriage, since self-giving is only complete when sealed with a social contract and openness to life. In this case such giving is *total*, implying the giving of one's being, things, and procreative capacity without any intention of taking them back over the period of one's entire life.

4. The fourth observation is that man and woman possess physically the proper elements to express in body language these first three factors we have observed. The receptive

---

[251] If this accompaniment is not present, the child does not reach full maturity. In order to reach maturity, he needs a stable reference to his natural father and mother until he is well into his adolescence and youth.

capacity of individuals corresponds to their inclination and desire for self-giving, not only in its physical dimension but in its procreative capacity. This brings us to point out that through their physical dimension, man and woman have the keys to a language, each with his and her own (physical) words to express this mutual love and consummate it.

5. These elements we have expressed in a positive way can also be expressed in a negative way. Careful observation of the physical, psychological, and spiritual nature of man and woman permits us to distinguish uses for the genitalia which are contrary to the human being's integral good. Concretely: *egoistic* sex (masturbation, impure thoughts); *unfaithful* sex (the lack of fidelity to the legitimate spouse, in either an active way or in an interior way, unfaithful desires and thoughts); *unfruitful* sex (homosexuality, use of sexuality closed to life); *circumstantial* sex (the non-committed or non-permanent relationship, between unmarried people), etc. All of these sexual expressions, which are destructive to true love and the integral good of the person, are prohibited—precisely because they contradict this integral good—by the commandment that requires us "not to commit impure acts."

5. THE NECESSITY AND PURPOSE OF CHASTITY

The Magisterium of the Church has said with much insight: "The alternative is clear: either man governs his passions and finds peace, or he lets himself be dominated by them and becomes unhappy."[252]

This phrase is the explanation of another affirmation: : "Chastity includes an apprenticeship in self-mastery which is

---

[252] CCC 2339.

a training in human freedom."[253] The importance of this assertion is clear if we turn the concepts around: human liberty requires, like pedagogy, self-control on the part of the human being; and chastity is one of the areas where this control applies (maybe one of the most important areas). The lack or absence of chastity leads to man's lack of control over the most powerful forces that he experiences within himself; lack of dominion, or lack of control means slavery and slavery is synonymous with subjection, defeat and disgrace.

When the above quote from the Catechism notes that a sensual man (someone who does not have control over his passions, which is to say, lacks chastity) is unhappy, it is not making a childish observation nor resorting to the perceived threats of a sour-faced education, but it is indicating that we are before an objective truth of experimental psychology.[254]

The text from the Catechism explains its affirmation with a passage from *Gaudium et Spes*: "Hence man's dignity demands that he act according to a knowing and free choice that is personally motivated and prompted from within, not under blind internal impulse nor by mere external pressure. Man achieves such dignity when, emancipating himself from all captivity to passion, he pursues his goal in a spontaneous choice of what is good, and procures for himself through effective and skillful action, apt helps to that end."[255]

---

[253] Ibid.

[254] I completely agree with those who criticize a bad education in chastity based on false threats that are probably ineffective and inhibiting (for example, affirming, as one reads in some books, that some impure acts can cause blindness, physical problems, etc.). However, it must be added that most people who express these criticisms are not seeking to correct these excesses (some of which can be explained by faulty medical or psychological knowledge in past times) but rather are proposing a complete sexual liberation.

[255] *Gaudium et Spes*, 17.

Chastity aids a recovery (as far as it is possible) of original harmony, that is to say, of the intellect and will's control of the inferior, sensitive potencies (in other words: the "political" subjection of the sensitive plane to the rational plane[256]). St. Augustine teaches: "Indeed it is through chastity that we are gathered together and led back to the unity from which we were fragmented into multiplicity."[257] This is no longer achieved by a preternatural gift, but by the acquired human virtue of chastity, elevated to the supernatural order through grace, or rather, accompanied by the complementary infused virtue.[258]

The Catechism also teaches "chastity means the successful integration of sexuality within the person and thus the inner unity of man in his bodily and spiritual being."[259] This means that without chastity, sexuality may be part of a person's life (it could in fact be a large part of it), but it is not *integrated* into his person. Without this integration, it becomes a disintegrating element. Sexuality has to be "human;" what is proper to human sexuality is the capacity to be a bridge of "relationship" with other people and of "total gift" within the exclusive relationship of a man and a woman. This

---

[256] The term "political" means—in contraposition to "despotic"—that the said control is not complete but analogical to that which a society exercises over free men.

[257] ST. AUGUSTINE, *Confessions*, 10, 29, 40, quoted in CCC 2340.

[258] I am avoiding the argument about whether the Christian virtue of temperance is the same human virtue of temperance elevated by grace (doctrine of St. Bonaventure) or if the human virtue of temperance and the infused virtue of the same name co-exist in a man in the state of grace (doctrine of St. Thomas).

[259] CCC 2337. The text continues: "Sexuality, in which man's belonging to the bodily and biological world is expressed, becomes personal and truly human when it is integrated into the relationship of one person to another, in the complete and lifelong mutual gift of a man and a woman. The virtue of chastity therefore involves the integrity of the person and the integrality of the gift."

differentiates "human" sexuality from "animal" sexuality. Animal sexuality is instinctive, it is possessive, not free; it responds to purely biological stimuli (hormones, periodic sexual heat) and is by nature opposed to fidelity (although there are known cases of a certain fidelity and stability in some animal species; this is not, properly speaking, a response of love, but of the necessity of the species itself and in particular a necessity of the offspring). The human being cannot exercise his sexuality in a free, faithful, total, regulated way if he is not the master of his instincts.

Why does chastity produce this integrity? "The chaste person maintains the integrity of the powers of life and love placed in him. This integrity ensures the unity of the person; it is opposed to any behavior that would impair it. It tolerates neither a double life nor duplicity in speech."[260] The lack of chastity implies disintegration because lust is one of the corruptions of the human person. Chastity permits man to direct all his strength towards one purpose, the person loved. Lust wastes a person's strength on multiple objects (for lustful person there are no people who are loved but people who are objectified.)[261]

Chastity and purity are a "capacity;" that is to say, something positive, not something negative (it is wrong, or at least incomplete to define it as merely "absence of moral stain or sin"). It is an interior force that gives the possessor the power to do something. This capacity is the power to order the faculty of the concupiscible appetite with all of its force and vigor and direct all of its power towards a concupiscible object that *should* be loved with all the strength of the person,

---

[260] CCC 2338.

[261] On this point, see studies on sexual addictions (like those by Patrick Carnes).

including his sexual strength (in the case of spouses). Also, chastity includes the capacity to transform ("to elevate") this strength, integrating them into the spiritual life (in the search for truth, into merciful love toward our neighbor, into love for God, etc.).[262]

In understanding this aspect, what St. Paul says in his first letter to the Thessalonians is important: *"For this is the will of God, your sanctification: that you abstain from unchaste thoughts and acts; that each one of you know how to take a wife for himself in holiness and honor, not in the passion of lust like heathens who do not know God"* (1 Thess 4:3-5).[263] In this text the dimension of "moderation" that purity exercises over the passions can be seen (the capacity to contain the impulses of sensible desire is proper to the nature of purity or chastity; for this reason, this virtue is part of the virtue of temperance). But here another—positive—function and dimension is

---

[262] In this respect, it is interesting what St. John Paul II wrote: "Purity is a 'capacity,' that is, in the traditional language of anthropology and ethics, an aptitude. And in this sense it is a virtue. If this ability, that is, virtue, leads to abstaining 'from unchastity,' that happens because the man who possesses it 'knows how to control his own body in holiness and honor, not in the passion of lust.' It is a question here of a practical capacity which makes man capable of acting in a given way, and at the same time of not acting in the opposite way. For purity to be such a capacity or aptitude, it must obviously be rooted in the will, in the very foundation of man's willing and conscious acting. Thomas Aquinas, in his teaching on virtues, sees in an even more direct way the object of purity in the faculty of sensitive desire, which he calls *appetitus concupiscibilis*. Precisely this faculty must be particularly 'mastered,' subordinated and made capable of acting in a way that is in conformity with virtue, in order that 'purity' may be attributed to man. According to this concept, purity consists in the first place in containing the impulse of sensitive desire, which has as its object what is corporeal and sexual in man. Purity is a different form of the virtue of temperance." (ST. JOHN PAUL II, "St. Paul's Teaching on the Sanctity and Respect of the Human Body," General Audience, January 28, 1981, in *L'Osservatore Romano,* English ed., February 2, 1981, no. 2.)

[263] Cf. ST. JOHN PAUL II, "St. Paul's Teaching on the Sanctity and Respect of the Human Body."

highlighted: the capacity of preserving the sanctity and honor of the body. In reality, both functions ("abstinence from the lustful passion" and "care for the bodily order") are reciprocally dependent because one cannot "care for the body with holiness and honor" if abstinence "from unchastity" is lacking. At the same time, such maintenance of holiness and bodily honor gives sense and value to the struggle of abstaining from disordered passions.

6. CHASTITY FOR EVERYONE

Chastity is necessary for all human beings in all walks of life: married, single, or celibate, though in a different way for each one. On account of some articles in which I mention the topic of chastity, I have received questions and criticisms claiming that when the Magisterium of the Church addresses martial chastity, it would demand an impossible sexual abstinence from married people, but that is not what "conjugal chastity" means; it means something quite different. This proves that many Christians understand neither the meaning nor the practice of this virtue.

There are different ways of living out chastity, according to each person's state of life.[264]

There is chastity proper to those who have consecrated their life in celibacy or virginity. There is also another form of chastity proper to those who think they have a vocation to marriage, but they are single or preparing for marriage while engaged; this chastity is called "simple chastity" or more

---

[264] A classic and very valuable book on this topic is that by DIETRICH VON HILDEBRAND, *In Defense of Purity: An Analysis of the Catholic Ideals of Purity and Virginity* (Baltimore: Helicon Press, 1962). The author examines purity or chastity in itself, in marriage, and in consecrated virginity.

properly, "continence."[265] There is yet another form of chastity, analogous to the other two, to which are called those who, for one reason or another besides the desire to consecrate their life to God or to a higher ideal, are not (and may never be) in a condition to form a family. This could be either because they never found the right person to marry, or because they have an attraction toward those of the same sex (homosexual inclinations), or because they suffer a pathological fear to commit themselves in a life of emotional or sexual intimacy, or because they struggle with some other sexual deviation. In all of these cases, we have to consider, in fact, that the single chaste life has to be proposed to them as a model. Conversely, there is a way of living chastity proper to spouses, denominated for this reason, "conjugal chastity." There is also the chastity that is proper to the people who, though having had the vocation to marriage, for one reason or another, cannot live in that state any more (for example, widows and widowers, or married people who have separated).

The moral norms are different for each one.

Those who have voluntarily entered the state of consecrated virginity or celibacy (with vows or promises) are obligated to live purity in its most elevated form, renouncing any sexual or sensual act voluntarily sought, and also any sexual or sensual thoughts or desires. This chaste way of life requires the mortification of the external senses (sight, touch, etc.) and the internal senses (memory, imagination).

---

[265] "Those who are *engaged to marry* are called to live chastity in continence. They should see in this time of testing a discovery of mutual respect, an apprenticeship in fidelity, and the hope of receiving one another from God. They should reserve for marriage the expressions of affection that belong to married love. They will help each other grow in chastity." (CCC 2350.)

Those who are not yet married but are preparing for marriage (fiancées and single people who are not engaged) should live in perfect chastity for as long as this state lasts. Clearly, this does not exclude sexual activity once they are legitimately married, nor does it exclude a more affectionate behavior with the person they may hope to marry. The rule in this case is very delicate, but it can be summarized in what respected authors have indicated: (1) displays of affection accepted by custom that are signs of courtesy, politeness and good manners are licit; (2) on the other hand, modest expressions (embraces, kisses, looks, thoughts, desires) that are carried out with the expressed and deliberate intention of producing venereal or sexual pleasure, even without the intention of reaching sexual relations, are illicit; (3) with even more reason, lustful expressions or full sexual relations are illicit.

In the case of married persons who no longer live with their legitimate spouse due to separation (sometimes not due to any fault of one spouse) or because a spouse has died, it is not permissible for them to have sexual relations with someone to whom they are not legitimately married. However, for them, it is not sinful to think of or remember the acts carried out with their legitimate spouse, since all that is licit to do, is also licit to desire or remember (except in the case that it would be a proximate danger to consummate their desires with an illicit act).

Finally, married people have a special rule of chastity that consists in fulfilling the marriage act in a manner that is open to life. They may, in some cases, choose the woman's naturally infertile periods for their complete sexual act (periodic abstinence) when there are grave reasons that suggest it inconvenient to place all the conditions of a new conception (the complete sexual act). But this does not imply that incomplete sensual or sexual acts (that is to say, those that do not end in a full act or orgasm) are permissible during these periods or any other time. Chastity requires them to direct all of their desires and thoughts towards their legitimate spouse alone and prohibits viewing or imagining images that have another person as their object (even if this were only seen as a means to later carry out the sexual act with a legitimate spouse).

7. BUT, IS CHASTITY POSSIBLE?

Chastity or purity is possible. There are many people, even those who are consecrated, who think that perfect (total and permanent) chastity is impossible. There are those who think that there is no sense in even talking about the value of a life deprived of sex. There are also those who think that maybe they can aspire to be chaste most of the time, lifting themselves up after occasional falls. I have often received questions based on the idea that certain problems with purity (usually referring to masturbation) are "normal," and by "normal" they mean that everyone, without exception, falls into this vice, at least during adolescence ("When I was young," a person wrote to me: "I did *what everyone does*, I masturbated frequently." His question was about a problem with *sexual addiction*, which enslaved him even after he was married and had grey hair). The same idea, presented in another way, is part of a common thought that relates happiness with the exercise of sexuality. "Sex is happiness," announced a group of sexologists who over the past few years has offered their services in the front pages of Argentinean magazines. In reading similar advertisements, it reminded me of an observation of Fr. Benedict Groeschel, who in his book *The Courage to be Chaste*, emphasizes that the majority of people who we are likely to meet on a bus, in the subway, in the mall or even at Sunday mass have probably had some sort of sexual experience over the last few days. But happiness is not seen in most of their faces; if happiness depended on sex, the religious psychologist said, the world would shine like the sun, at least half of the time.[266] We should recognize that sex, while very important in the lives of many people, is not able, in and by itself, to give happiness. On the other hand, voluntary and perfect abstinence is not a synonym with frustration, sadness, or depression and it is even less true for the ordering of sexual activity within marriage according to the canons of natural and divine law.

Thus chastity is possible. If in our time it is harder, the reason is not intrinsic to the human being (outside of the disorder introduced by original sin, which I have already mentioned) but because of the insubstantial interior life of the majority of our generation.

"Continence is perfectly possible for one who is psychologically healthy. It is undeniable that just as there are kleptomaniacs and pyromaniacs there are also those whose accountability regarding sexuality is greatly diminished or even non-existent, but such cases are the exception [...] On the other hand, passionate temperaments conquer their appetites [...] Ordinarily, when the sexual instinct imposes itself as a necessity, it is because a person has permitted it to become a habit. Chastity is not a question of temperaments: it is a matter of education, of principles, of will."[267]

---

[266] Cf. BENEDICT GROESCHEL, *The Courage to be Chaste* (New York: Paulist Press, 1985), 18.

[267] ALBERTO HURTADO, "El Adolescente: Un Desconocido [Original title: La crisis de la pubertad y la educación de la castidad]," in vol. 2 of *Obras Completas* (Chile: Dolmen, 2001), 184, editorial translation.

Chastity is possible. The first thing necessary for this possibility to be a reality is—as the great educator, Fr. Hurtado, pointed out—a "sexual philosophy that represents the mastery of the spirit over the material."[268] That is to say, it requires a healthy and harmonious view of sexuality (a view which has God's plan for man and woman as a clear conception of human anthropology, the main ideas of which we have covered in previous pages). In effect, the same author remarks that "an extremely large part of human weakness in modern life does not come from an irresistible organic urge, but from a materialist conception of life, which, openly or covertly, has us imprisoned." And he adds, "When man comes to obtain this scientific certainty, which so many doctors attempt to dissipate, the sexual system will find the peace that it cannot find in the midst of today's stimulating formulas or in the midst of the uncertain disciplines of modern thought. The body readily obeys the spirit , which has come to be sure of itself."[269]

Thus, chastity is not possible for those who have a distorted anthropological view, that is, for those who reduce the human being to mere matter or give primacy to the instincts and place a mantle of uncertainty over the spiritual capacity of a human being to govern himself. Certain security about the aptitude of the spirit and about its supremacy over matter is indispensable (although this conviction presupposes the help of divine grace).

It cannot be denied that there are causes that notably influence the collapse of the ideal of purity. There are physical causes (certain hereditary inclinations, mental states, sicknesses, weather changes, etc.) and habits which are not

---

[268] HURTADO, "El Adolescente: Un Desconocido," 185, editorial translation.
[269] Ibid.

themselves vices but which make it difficult to observe chastity (lack of hygiene, a sedentary lifestyle, listlessness, etc.). But the principal causes are psychological: when the curiosity, imagination and memory are undisciplined, and especially when they are deprived of a healthy philosophical framework (that is, when they are in need of correct guiding principles) or are set within the framework of a system of distorted thought (materialism, hedonism, Freudianism, consumerism, liberalism, etc).

Evidently, forming the habit of chastity is not only a question of rational principles, but requires several other things; the first of which is the formation of the will through the habits of justice, fortitude, and temperance (applied to areas other than sex, like moderation in eating and drinking), vigilance, sports and physical work, etc. In addition to these, those who persist on the path of chastity should keep in mind what Fr. Groeschel rightly calls "hidden occasions of unchastity."[270] Among these he mentions four principal occasions.

The first is *self-pity*—the unjustly negative sentiment about oneself—which, in many cases, can present an authentic possibility of psychological regression to childish behavior. It is common that these people fall into a certain sexual tolerance, especially of masturbation. These destructive thoughts are at the root of all sexual addictions. It must be said that self-pity sometimes takes the form of a false humility. It is really a type of inferiority complex. Its contrary does not consist—as the modern therapy of new age self-help techniques might propose—in strengthening self-confidence or forming big ideas about oneself; this would bring us to egoism or sterile pride. The opposite of self-pity

---

[270] Cf. GROESCHEL, *The Courage to be Chaste*, 70-74.

is healthy realism, of a natural and supernatural balance. This is to say, being conscious of our value as person in the eyes of God and both the social and supernatural greatness of our vocation.

The second danger is wrought by *feelings of anger and rage*. Many people, even Christians, carry a great resentment toward the world, toward themselves, and—at its root— toward God. This anger is deeply buried in the heart and is exteriorly manifested as frustration and depression.[271] It may, consequently, also manifest itself as disordered sexual activity; in these cases, sexual behavior takes on the character of self-punishment.

The third danger is represented by *unexpected love*, which usually happens when two people, in similarly poor spiritual states, meet each other. It is not strange to meet people who, in a moment of psychological or spiritual weakness, resentment or abandonment of ideals, of spiritual failures, etc., find the "ideal" person that "understands" them like no-one else ever has before. Sometimes the game starts with something innocent, long conversations, confiding difficulties, advice, comfort, etc., and two people can end up (as often happens) falling in love illicitly (for example, when this happens to married people or religious).

The fourth danger is embodied by the *forces of evil* themselves; diabolic action can be greatly responsible for many abuses on the sexual plane. Sexual disorder degrades the human being, and the devil is the enemy of our nature. The devil must be very involved with the corruption of the sexual sphere, especially with relation to: sexual perversion

---

[271] With this I am not saying that all states of depression have a common cause of repression. Be careful not to misinterpret the extent of these claims.

and digression, and when tied to the destruction of life (abortion) or the denial of life (contraception).

But, returning to our theme of the education of chastity, one of the keys to its pedagogy and conservation is found in working on the sense of modesty or healthy reserve about one's intimate life.

8. MODESTY IS THE DEFENSE OF CHASTITY

It is not possible to defend or achieve chastity if one does not begin to educate oneself in modesty. Modesty denotes the tendency to hide something in order to defend one's own intimacy with respect to external intrusions. "It is a quality, in part instinctive and in part a fruit of deliberate education, that protects chastity. It is carried out in the sensible-instinctive sphere as in the conscious-intellectual, as a psychological brake to the rebellion of sexuality."[272] St. Thomas says that it is a healthy sentiment by which, after original sin, the passions related to sexuality produce in man a feeling of disgust, *of shame*, of uneasiness, to the point that he *instinctively* wants to hide everything related to the body, intimacy, and sexuality from indiscrete looks.[273]

Modesty and pudency. Modesty pertains as much to the instinctive sphere as to the conscious. In the former, modesty exists in the strict sense of the word; in the latter, what exists is a superior organization of the same thing, which enters into the category of virtue and is denoted as *pudency*.[274] The virtue

---

[272] ZALBA ERRO, "Pudor," in *Gran Enciclopedia Rialp* (Madrid: Ediciones Rialp, 1989), editorial translation.

[273] Cf. AQUINAS, *Summa Theologica*, II-II, Q. 151, Art. 4.

[274] C. SCARPELLINI, "Pudore e Pudicizia," in *Enciclopedia Cattolica* (Vatican City: Libro Cattolico, 1953).

of pudency or of modesty "is intimately related to chastity, given that it is an expression and defense of chastity itself. It is, therefore, the habit that forewarns of dangers to purity—the arousal of senses that can result in affection or sexual excitement and the threats against the right governing of the sexual instinct—both when these dangers come from the outside and when they come from the intimate personal life, which also calls for discretion or withdrawal from the eyes of others and caution before one's own senses. In this sense, modesty acts as the moderator of the sexual appetite and helps the person develop as a whole, without reducing him merely to the sexual realm. This is not to be confused with chastity because it does not have as its object the regulation of sexual acts according to reason, but the *protection of what is normally closely associated with those acts*. It becomes a providential defense of chastity by reason of the psychophysical makeup of the human genus, which is disturbed by original sin."[275]

On the purely instinctive plane, we can say that it consists of an unconscious resistance to all that would reveal the disordered concupiscence of the flesh in us. When this becomes conscious, it consists in the elevation of this healthy instinct through the practice of the virtue of prudence, given that it tends to eliminate circumstances and restrain thoughts in order to prevent any violation of the moral order that such activity would cause.

Modesty and education. In a way, since human education is the actualization of the human values that are in potency in every man and the affirmation that spiritual values surpass material values, it can very well be concluded that the quality of education is measured by the development and refinement given to the practice of pudency, which tends to

---

[275] ERRO, "Pudor," editorial translation.

fortify the spirit more than any other operative habit.[276] The education of chastity cannot exist without the development of the sense of modesty. The possibility and the capacity for resistance against the external causes that continually attack moral integrity and purity depend in a large part on the preservation of this natural faculty.[277]

Instinctive modesty and conventional modesty. *Instinctive modesty* exists linked to the psychological makeup of man, and is therefore universal. It is manifested as a sense of fear, or shame, which is in some way linked to sexual emotion. "Although some deny this natural characteristic of modesty, claiming that it only refers to a habit acquired as the fruit or effect of its education, it must be said, nevertheless, that anthropological studies reveal the existence of modesty in all peoples. It even exists in primitive peoples, and is only differentiated by what is called secondary individualization of modesty; that is to say, their sense of modesty is focused on different parts of the body. Modesty does not depend on conventionalism or custom; rather, it is essentially a rational process that conforms to the nature of man."[278]

But education and surrounding conditions notably influence the personal elaboration that each one makes of modesty, which though instinctive, does not exclude, but implies a certain flexibility common to all the instincts. "The concrete conditions to which modesty adapts its prudent action are diverse, for example, age, the difference of erotic

---

[276] Cf. SCARPELLINI, "Pudore e Pudicizia," col. 297.

[277] *Modesty* is not only a childhood phenomena; it is a force that more deeply manifests itself when the development of sex arises during puberty. Then it acquires a new aspect, which it did not possess during childhood, that is to say, the feeling of one's own dignity, respect towards one's own body, and the feeling of repugnance to all kinds of subjection to vulgarity or sensuality.

[278] ERRO, "Pudor," editorial translation.

attraction executed by different body parts, the psychological type of the individual, etc. These diverse factors explain the differences between the forms of modesty among the nations."[279] This is to say, they explain the existence of a *conventional modesty* that essentially depends on the time period, the education, the individual, the region, etc.

The multiple reactions towards modesty in a person are not all manifestations of instinctive modesty. Those linked to *absolute stimulants* (which are relatively few) are manifestations of *instinctive* modesty, while those linked to *conditional stimulants* are *conventional* manifestations of modesty. Conventional modesty deserves consideration, but it is not always sincere nor does it reveal any profound virtue. Some depraved people, though not ignorant of social conventions, surround themselves with superfluous precautions in order to hide their perverse instincts. But this is not true modesty.

False education of modesty: prudishness. Modesty must be cultivated with prudence. Too narrow of an education in this field would multiply difficulties and would not do anything but aggravate the restlessness and uneasiness of adolescents and youth. It is an undeniable fact that through too strict of an education, past centuries have carried modesty into terrain where it has no business going and thereby caused evil to be seen everywhere. Unfortunately this type of "bad education of modesty" does not cause anything but adverse reactions—it leads to immodesty.

---

[279] SCARPELLINI, "Pudore e Pudicizia," col. 296, editorial translation.

Cf. WILLIBALD DEMAL, *Psicologia Pastorale Pratica* (Roma: Paoline, 1955), 120.

So, the education of modesty means to cultivate it and at the same time to defend it from all petty deeds that are so easily confused with modesty.

The falsification of modesty has a name: "prudishness." It indicates an unbalanced modesty, generally caused by a false education. Prudishness does not make people chaste but only makes them imitators or caricatures of chastity. "Prudishness is the natural enemy of modesty, as affected piety is the enemy of true and conscious religion. The adolescent spirit rebels and is bothered by petty and low ideas."[280]

Authentic education of modesty. The education of modesty must be *indirect* because a direct education would necessarily imply directing attention to the very objects that modesty should make less attractive. Nonetheless, while indirect, it should be *positive*; that is to say, it should prepare a spiritual atmosphere that, in addition to stopping degradation in the area of animal sexuality, will make it easier to gradually reveal the necessary things at the opportune moment.

This education in modesty should be part of a moral education of emotions, of affectivity in general (what some call "educating the heart"). Educating the heart can be summarized as successfully making a person fall in love with virtue and correcting abnormal deviations of sensible love. It also implies educating the will. This requires, along with constant and daily exercise, the "spiritual gymnasium" that forms and shapes us so that we are capable of putting into act what we understand with ease and what we declare with

---

[280] ETTORE PAGANUZZI, *Purezza e Pubertà* (Brescia: La Scuola Editrice, 1953), 222, editorial translation.

Cf. ARNOLD STOCKER, *La Cura Morale dei Nervosi* (Milan: Vita e Pensiero, 1951), 155.

even more ease, but what we carry out with much more difficulty. We cannot forget that the virtue of chastity, as much as it is a moral virtue, has its seat in the will. But above all, the education of religiosity must rule: for a chaste life, religious education "is the first and most powerful effect, because other human effects have only temporary value, remaining only while their corresponding interests last in the child's spirit. Only religion possesses an efficiency that surpasses the limits of time, place, space, environment, and circumstances, provided that it is felt, conscious and active [...] Religion has always established a singular power for sexual education. Religion values purity and presents it to the young as one of the highest and most beautiful virtues; at the same time, it indicates the means for preserving and defending it with careful attention, reserve, interior discipline of the imagination and desires and the exterior discipline of the senses."[281]

* * *

Even when chastity is a challenge, do not ever give it up. Do not give up your happiness. Do not cease to forge a holy family. Do not give up a pure engagement or true romance. Do not exchange the flight of the seagull over the open sea for the limping of a bird of prey that spends his days picking through decomposing flesh near the filthy mouth of a stream.

---

[281] PAGANUZZI, *Purezza e Pubertà,* 249, editorial translation.

For Further Reading

- Fuentes, Miguel. *He Made Them Male and Female*. New York: IVE Press, 2007.
- Groeschel, Benedict. *The Courage to be Chaste*. New York: Paulist Press, 1985.
- Pieper, Josef. *The Four Cardinal Virtues: Prudence, Justice, Fortitude, Temperance*. Notre Dame, Indiana: University of Notre Dame Press, 1966.
- Von Hildebrand, Dietrich. *In Defense of Purity: An Analysis of the Catholic Ideals of Purity and Virginity*. Baltimore: Helicon Press, 1962.
- Wojtyla, Karol. *Love and Responsibility*. Boston: Pauline Books & Media, 2013.

Available in Other Languages

- Castellani, Leonardo. *Freud: Diccionario de Psicología*. Mendoza: Jauja, 1996.
- ―――. *Freud en Cifra*. Buenos Aires: Cruz y Fierro, 1966.
- Erro, Zalba. "Pudor." In *Gran Enciclopedia Rialp*. Madrid: Ediciones Rialp, 1989.
- Fuentes, Miguel. "La educación de la sexualidad, un desafío para padres y educadores." *Diálogo* 18 (1997): 45-66.
- ―――. "Pornografía y Sexualidad." *Diálogo* 12 (1995): 131-158.
- Hurtado, Alberto. "El Adolescente: Un Desconocido [Original title: La crisis de la pubertad y la educación de la castidad]." In vol. 2 of *Obras Completas*. Chile: Dolmen, 2001.
- Innocenti, Ennio. "Sigmund Freud." *Diálogo* 4 (1992): 73-104.
- ―――. "Las Características del Psicoanálisis." *Diálogo* 5 (1993): 45-63.
- ―――. "Freudismo y Ciencia [1ª parte]." *Diálogo* 7 (1993): 89-110.
- ―――. "Freudismo y Ciencia [2ª parte]." *Diálogo* 8 (1993): 109-121.
- ―――. "Freudismo Entre Filosofía y Antifilosofía." *Diálogo* 9 (1994): 95-117.
- ―――. "Freud y la Religión." *Diálogo* 11 (1995): 75-120.

9.

THE STOLEN TRUTH ABOUT CONSCIENCE

The Nobility of Your Conscience Depends on Docility to the Truth

Your conscience is something sacred. Some will try to steal it from you and replace it with something that superficially appears to be like it, but in reality it is no more than an image of your conscience. It could be that they will tell you that you should let your conscience guide you, or you may hear phrases like "my conscience doesn't bother me," "you have to let your conscience decide," or "let everyone follow his own conscience." There would be no objection to these phrases, if the concept of conscience behind them were correct; but if the conscience is understood as *deciding what one wants without any external interference, without anyone guiding us or simply without such a conscience having the obligation to "accommodate itself" to a higher rule*, then we are not properly speaking about the conscience but about a more crass subjectivism. Nero also followed his conscience, as did Hitler and Stalin and all of the tyrants of history. People who are insane also obey their conscience, as do thieves and murderers. But when they do what their conscience permits or suggests, they do not understand the conscience as the philosophy of old or as the great thinkers of Christianity have always understood it. What they call the conscience is very different.

If anything, listen to what Jean Jacques Rousseau, a character of doubtful orthodoxy, said in the beginning of a work entitled "Confessions." There, addressing himself without remorse to the Creator, he said: "Let the trumpet of the Day of Judgement sound when it will […] Gather round me the countless host of my fellow-men; let them hear my confessions […] let each of them in turn reveal, with the same frankness, the secrets of his heart at the foot of the Throne, and say, if he dare, 'I was better than that man!'"[282]

There you have a man with a clear conscience. Actually, Encyclopedia writer, Denis Diderot said that Rousseau was lucky because whatever he did, *his conscience always came down in his favor*, up to such a point that he considered himself to be without blemish. But if you take it upon yourself to read the life of this man with irreproachable conscience, you will see that such a conscience did not stop him from taking from his concubine the four little children that he had had with her in order to leave them at the home for "abandoned children," or from covering it up, when the fact was scandalously made public, by saying that it had been a "mistake" and not a dirty trick. Once again his conscience was cleared. As you see, conscience on the lips of Jean Jacques is a term that he borrows to justify any selfish ploy. This is an interesting idea of the conscience, so elastic that it can excuse the darkest moral downfalls. Jean Jacques' "conscience" is what they want to sell to us today. Be careful. It is not a conscience; it is a type of "intellectual immunodeficiency syndrome." He who accepts it catches whatever ethical infection passes by.

For this reason it is worthwhile for us to see what the true concept of the conscience is (that which authentically ennobles the man who follows it) and the necessity of educating it.

---

[282] JEAN-JACQUES ROUSSEAU, *The Confessions* (Hertfordshire: Wordsworth Editions Limited, 1996), 3.

1. WHAT IS THE CONSCIENCE?

The Second Vatican Council has referred beautifully to the conscience saying that it "is the most secret core and sanctuary of a man. There he is alone with God, Whose voice echoes in his depths."[283]

What we call "conscience" is nothing other than certain movements of our intelligence. Our intelligence knows what things are, why they are, what they are for, and—in some cases—why they should be, and in this we are specifically differentiated from the rest of the animals. When those "things" that man comes to know are our own acts, and our reason tells us what we are doing, or what we have done or what we are planning to do, and speaks to us about their goodness or malice, such an act of the intelligence is what we call the "conscience." There is the "psychological" conscience (which tells us "what" we do or have done, such as writing, walking, praying, or working) and the "moral" conscience (which advises us about the good or evil of that which we do, have done, or are going to do).

How does this happen? All of us carry imprinted within ourselves a law that indicates to us good and evil, which perfects us, and which is morally damaging to us; the knowledge of this law is natural. Man realizes, in a way that we can call "spontaneous," that certain things are good and certain things are evil. (It is not necessary to teach that loving our parents is something good or that betraying one's country is something abominable. Nobody is taught to protect his mother or his children; and if one was taught this, then when he does do it, it is not done because he was taught, but because he spontaneously recognizes that it is the only thing

---

[283] *Gaudium et Spes*, no. 16.

that should be done in that circumstance). This is why one author has said: "We carry our truth within ourselves, because our essence (our nature) is our truth."[284]

"*The same law* that was revealed by God through Moses and confirmed by Christ in the Gospel (cf. Mt 5:17-19)," John Paul II has said, "*was written in human nature by the Creator.* This is what we read in St. Paul's letter to the Romans: '*For when the Gentiles, who do not have the law, by nature observe the prescriptions of the law, they are a law for themselves, even though they do not have the law*' (Rom 2:14). Thus the moral principles shown by God to the Chosen People through Moses are the same that he inscribed in the nature of the human being. Therefore, by following what from the beginning is part of his nature, every individual knows that he must honor his father and mother and respect life; he is aware that he should not commit adultery, nor steal, nor give false witness; in a word, he knows that he should not do to others what he would not want done to himself."[285]

It is for this reason that every time we act, we realize that what we do is consistent and in harmony with this knowledge that we have written on our heart regarding good and evil, or that it simply does not correspond with it. This is the conscience. The conscience is the intelligence when "in the depths of his conscience, man detects a law which he does not impose upon himself, but which holds him to obedience. [...] the voice of conscience when necessary speaks to his heart."[286] The conscience in this manner fulfills a triple office within us:

---

[284] *L'Osservatore Romano,* October 15, 1993, 22, editorial translation.

[285] ST. JOHN PAUL II, "God's Commands Bring Life," Angelus Message, June 12, 1994, in *L'Osservatore Romano,* English ed., June 17, 1994, no. 3.

[286] *Gaudium et Spes,* no. 16.

1. It is the witness to what we are doing or have done, of the good or evil that we perform. In this sense St. Paul says in Romans 9:1: *"...my conscience testifies with me in the Holy Spirit."*

2. It is the judge of our acts: it approves of us when what we do is good, and condemns us (remorse of conscience) when we have done or are doing evil. St. Paul refers to this in 2 Corinthians 1:12: *"For our boast is this, the testimony of our conscience."*

3. It is our pedagogue or teacher, as Origen called it: uncovering and indicating to us the path of good action. Thus the Apostle can say in Romans 14:5: *"Let everyone be fully convinced in his own mind."*

This light in our intelligence by which we judge our actions was placed in us by God himself when he created us. It is nothing other than the capacity that we have to know the good and evil in things. And this light is a participation in his Light and his Eternal Truth. Therefore we can say with surety that it is the voice of God. Thus, St. Bonaventure said: "Conscience is like God's herald and messenger; it does not command things on its own authority, but commands them as coming from God's authority, like a herald when he proclaims the king's edict. This is why conscience has binding force."[287] John Paul II explains it by saying: "In his Letter to the Romans, St. Paul adds: *'They show that what the law requires is written on their hearts, their conscience bears witness of it'* (Rom 2:15). *Conscience is presented as a witness*, both by accusing man when he violates the law written in his heart, and by justifying him when he is faithful. Therefore, in accord with the Apostle's teaching, there is a law intimately linked to man's nature as an intelligent and free being, and this law is echoed

---

[287] ST. BONAVENTURE, quoted in VS, no. 58.

in his conscience: for man, to live at peace with his conscience means living at peace with the law of his own nature, and, vice versa, living in accord with this law means living in accord with his conscience; obviously, with a *true and upright conscience*, that is, with a conscience that correctly interprets the contents of the law written in human nature by the Creator."[288]

As we can see, we have here an idea of the conscience as the "mediator" between the objective truth of things (expressed in the nature of things and the revelation of God) and our acts. On the other hand, there is another idea of the conscience that we can define as a conscience that does not "comply" with the truth of things but "creates" its own truth. John Paul II has said in his encyclical, *Veritatis Splendor* that the cultural tendencies that oppose and separate liberty and law, falsely promoting the latter, have resulted in and "lead to a 'creative' understanding of moral conscience, which diverges from the teaching of the Church's tradition and her Magisterium."[289]

In our day, there are three currents of thought that highlight the *creative character of the moral conscience.*

1. The current of thought belonging to those who hold that *the personal intention* with which we act indicates the good or evil of our actions. What I do with a good intention ("for love," as some say) is good. What I do with an evil intention is evil. What I do or chose (called the "moral object of the act") is cast aside, for it does not matter what I do but the intention with which I do it. My conscience can leave me in peace if it shows that I may lie to defend an innocent person, sterilize a woman to prevent future risks to her health, or

---

[288] ST. JOHN PAUL II, "God's Commands Bring Life," no. 4.

[289] VS, no. 54.

carry out homosexual acts for love (this was taught by authors like B. Haring, D. Capone, M. Vidal).

2. A second current of thought minimizes the objective norms (laws) and only gives moral value to the result of the action. This means that when we are about to act, we make a judgment about the good or evil of our acts (one should not steal because it is bad, one always has to tell the truth), but this judgment is impersonal, theoretical, and pre-moral; and therefore, it does not count for much. At the same time we make another judgment, which these authors (for example, J. Fuchs) call the judgment *of operation*, which is concrete, subjective, the fruit of the personal conscience and, therefore, always good, even when it opposes the former judgment. For example, a woman who does not want children reasons that: "In general terms I know that contraception is something wrong and therefore in general I reject it; but here and now, keeping in mind my economic problems or that I already have three children, it seems to me that this is a lesser evil and is what requires more feasible sacrifices from me; therefore, in good conscience, I judge that for me it is licit." Here you have two judgments: the first Fuchs calls *pre-moral* (just as some call an embryo that is a few days or hours old a *pre-embryo*, and therefore feel authorized to kill it; this way this author also calls the judgments of our conscience pre-moral and therefore feels authorized to disregard them. The reasoning is useful, but not scientific). The second they call judgment *of conscience*; and they assume that the second is never wrong and the first is. The reason is that the first is universal and the second concrete. The day that you encounter a murderer, who tells you that he is going to kill you to rob your of a few coins, do not remind him that this is wrong, since he already knows that, but with his *pre-moral* judgments. The problem is that if he read Fuchs (which I

don't think he did since he's not so easy to understand), he will tell you that while he accepts on general terms that it is not good to kill or steal, in these concrete circumstances (the circumstance in which you are the owner of the money or the car that he wants) his conscience tells him that it is better to take your money and then to kill you so that nobody will find out. At the final judgment, you will be able to complain to Fuchs and his followers.

3. A third current of thought, which ends up asserting the same thing, identifies our conscience with the decisions we make (this was held, for example, by Peter Knauer and A. Molinario). They basically teach that what we decide is good because we have decided that it is. I come into contact with this type of reasoning fairly often. For example, when someone hears: *"Jane has become a nun, poor thing! Well, what is important is that she's doing what she likes."* Be careful, we are in this third current. If what Jane has done in entering the convent is good, it does not originate in that she has decided it or that she likes it, but in that it is good to enter a convent to consecrate oneself to God. We cannot say: *"John is a thief, but at least he's doing what he's always wanted to do since childhood."* If John has decided to be a thief, liar or traitor, it will always be wrong in spite of being what he has decided to do.

What all these positions have in common is that they all basically take into account what we can call the "creative character" of the conscience. Creative how? It is creative regarding the truth. These positions coincide in teaching that whatever the conscience decides, determines or resolves is good; and if it is good, it is the truth (at least for the person making the decision). We recall the words of Marxism: What is truth? It is whatever serves the party's cause!

This is the idea that underlies and drives many other expressions. For example, those who say that one must reach *self-fulfillment* (they do not mean that each person must *discover the truth*, which would be exactly right; but what they mean is that each one should *invent his own reality, his own world*). There are also those who want to live *autonomously* (that is, without any law that does not come from their own self).

With these currents of thought we are before what Ratzinger has called "the divinization of subjectivity, the infallible oracle of which is conscience, never to be doubted by anyone or anything."[290] This is why it is not strange that they claim, like Rousseau does in *Emilio*,[291] that the conscience is infallible; or as the more modern B. Schüller has said, "The conscience cannot deceive itself about good and evil; what it orders is always infallibly the moral good."[292] If I were to tell you that Schüller was the one who appeased Hitler's conscience, you might believe it; nevertheless, that was not the case since Schüller is a Catholic Moralist who wrote forty years after this Nazi leader. And yet, Hitler, Stalin or Nero himself would have kissed his feet for having justified their actions so well! This shows us that, despite our particular moment in time, they can teach us in the classrooms of today the very things that repulse us about the

---

[290] JOSEPH RATZINGER, "The Problem of Threats to Human Life," *L'Osservatore Romano,* English ed., April 8, 1991, §IV, no. 2.

[291] "Conscience! Conscience! Divine instinct, immortal voice from heaven; sure guide for a creature ignorant and finite indeed, yet intelligent and free; infallible judge of good and evil, making man like to God!" (JEAN-JACQUES ROUSSEAU, *Emile,* trans. Barbara Foxley (New York: E. P. Dutton and Co., 1911).)

[292] BRUNO SCHÜLLER, *La fondazione dei giudizi morali: Tipi di argomentazione etica nella teologia morale Cattolica* (Assisi: Cittadella Editrice, 1975), 72, editorial translation.

men of yesterday. Anyway, before rending your garments at the scandal caused by these brutal claims, check whether we do not say the same with respect to other ideas that are more compelling to us, like pre-marital relations, abortion, contraception and other points that might hit too close to home. If these theories should not justify the conscience of a person committing genocide, neither should we allow them to appease our consciences in the face of immoral behavior.

If the conscience neither creates nor invents the truth, what is its relationship with truth? It is a relationship that is at the same time humble and exalted: the conscience *depends on and manifests the truth*. It is dependent! Yes, it is dependent, but at the same time it receives its dignity from the truth. It is like iron in the fire. A wretched piece of iron put in fire glows from the fire's heat. You see it red and burning, and the iron transformed by the fire is capable of cauterizing, burning, and giving off heat and light. If you take it out of the fire, it will return to be a dark and rusty piece of iron. Our conscience depends on the truth, but the truth transforms our conscience and makes it *true, illuminating, ardent.*[293]

How do we know that this is so? First of all, that the conscience depends on the moral truth is a fact of experience. Our psychological experience shows us that within ourselves we have two kinds of judgments. On one hand, there are certain hypothetical or conditional judgments, that is to say, judgments by which each person feels obliged only insofar as he wants what such a requirement calls for. ("If I don't want

---

[293] Cf. CARLO CAFFARRA, "Conscience, Truth, and Magisterium in Conjugal Morality," in PONTIFICAL COUNCIL FOR THE FAMILY, *Marriage & Family: Experiencing the Church's Teaching in Married Life* (San Francisco: Ignatius Press, 1989), 21-36.

Cf. VICTORINO RODRÍGUEZ, "Función Mediadora de la Conciencia," *Mikael: Revista del Seminario de Paraná* 24 (1980): 111-124.

to get sick on this cold day, I should wear a coat;" I have to wear a coat, only if and insofar as I do not want to get sick.) But there also exists another category of judgments that is, in a certain sense, absolute. That is to say, that they impose themselves immediately without depending on any conditions and we cannot excuse ourselves from them. (For example, "I have to respect my parents." Here no condition exists that makes this requirement necessary; it imposes itself for its own sake.) We properly call such judgments 'judgments of the conscience.' The fact that man instinctively perceives that he cannot excuse himself from the obligations his own conscience imposes, shows that through these judgments the person knows a pre-existent truth that is independent of his conscience. This reality that prevails over our conscience is not real because our conscience knows it; on the contrary, it prevails over our conscience because this truth is real and exists independently and autonomously apart from us. In other words, the truth does not depend on our conscience, but instead the conscience depends on the truth.

Furthermore, it is also a biblical fact: *For when Gentiles who do not have the Law do instinctively the things of the Law, these, not having the Law, are a law to themselves, in that they show the work of the Law written in their hearts, their conscience bearing witness and their thoughts alternately accusing or else defending them* (Rom 2:14-15). According to the words of St. Paul, in a certain sense the conscience puts man before the law, the conscience itself being *man's "witness."* It testifies to his fidelity or infidelity to the law, or to his essential righteousness or moral evil. The conscience is the only witness. What happens in the interior of a person is hidden from the view of others looking on from the outside. The conscience gives its testimony only to the person himself. At the same time, only the person knows his own response to the voice of his conscience.

Finally, we can deduce the conscience's dependence on truth if we take into account the nature of our judgments. The judgments of our conscience (*I should take this medicine, I have to go to the doctor, I shouldn't pay attention to this fool, etc.*), says St. Thomas, are products of an application (*applicatio*),[294] or he also uses an equivalent expression, a fitting accommodation,[295] of the universal truth to the particular or concrete case. Or as some translate, it is a happy adaptation of the universal truth to the concrete case.[296] In other words, the judgment of conscience is the conclusion of a process of practical reasoning that starts with the most universal principles and goes on to state that this or that particular case fulfills or rejects a universal requirement (law). For example, the consciences reasons thus: (1) First principal of natural reason: *Evil must be avoided*; (2) Principle of moral science: *Stealing is an evil*; (3) Conclusion of moral science: *Stealing must be avoided*; (4) Impersonal conclusion: *This action is stealing and therefore must be avoided*; (5) Judgment of conscience: *I should avoid this action*. It is of little importance to the case whether this process is more or less complicated, whether or not it follows these steps, whether it arises from universal moral knowledge (called synderesis) or from a concrete point of the science of morality or from a principle

---

[294] Cf. AQUINAS, *Commentary on the Nicomachean Ethics*, book VI, lecture 7, no. 1198.

Cf. LIVIO MELINA, *La Conoscenza Morale* (Rome: Città Nuova Ed., 1987), 187-188.

[295] Cf. AQUINAS, *Commentary on the Nicomachean Ethics*, book V, lecture 15, no. 1075.

[296] This term "application" (*applicatio*) is also used by the Supreme Sacred Congregation of the Holy Office, quoted in VS, no. 59.

received from the Magisterium. It is always discovering a relation between the universal order and a particular case.

As we can see, the function of the conscience is to be the interpreter and mediator between the universal objective truth and our concrete actions. This is why Paul VI said: "The conscience of itself is not the arbiter of the moral value of the actions that it suggests. The conscience is the interpreter of an interior and superior norm which it does not create by itself. It is enlightened by the intuition of certain normative principles connatural in human reason. The conscience is not the source of good and evil. It is the warning; it is to listen to a voice, which is called precisely the voice of conscience."[297] And Thomas Aquinas expresses this function of the conscience saying that man's reason (and in this case, the conscience) is a "kind of rule which is itself regulated" (*regla regulata*).[298] Like our common rules (of measurement): What is your height? Five foot four or six or eight? How can you be sure this is your height? Because you have measured with a ruler. And how do you know that "the ruler is not lying"? Because it respects the *standard* from which all take measurements. (This is how the meter became defined a long time ago as the international standard of measurement as the distance between two ends marked in a metal alloy of platinum and iridium that is conserved in Paris.) When you buy a pound of sugar, how do you know the shopkeeper isn't

---

[297] PAUL VI, General Audience, February 12, 1969, *www.vatican.va/holy_father/paul_vi/audiences/1969/documents/hf_p-vi_aud_19690212_it.html* (accessed October 19, 2014), editorial translation. The Second Vatican Council has said: "In the depths of his conscience, man detects a law which he does not impose upon himself, but which holds him to obedience […] For man has in his heart a law written by God; to obey it is the very dignity of man; according to it he will be judged." (*Gaudium et Spes*, no. 16.)

[298] ST. THOMAS AQUINAS, vol. 2 of *Truth (De Veritate)*, trans. James McGlynn (Indianapolis: Hackett Publishing Company, Inc., 1994), Q. 17, Art. 2, ad. 7.

lying to you, selling you "15 ounces" instead of the 16 that make up a full pound? Because if your shopkeeper is honest, he will have calibrated his scale with the universal standard of measurement for pounds and ounces. Your conscience is like this. It tells you that it is good to do this or that, but how do you know that it does not lie or deceive you? Only if it regulates itself to a standard (a fixed norm) that does not lie and cannot be wrong; and this is precisely the natural law which expresses the wisdom of God, and our reason can discover that law in our own nature.

2. THE FALLIBILITY OF THE CONSCIENCE

So, the conscience is not an infallible judge. Its judgments will always be acts of our created, finite, fallible, wounded and easily influenced intelligence.

The judgments of our conscience are very complex because they are not abstract or purely speculative affirmations (like when we say "the sun rises in the East," "two plus two equals four"), but rather affirmations that end up being involved in our way of acting (they are "practical judgments"). For example, knowing the difference between an equilateral triangle and an isosceles triangle does not in any way change the way of life one had while still ignorant of this truth. However, perceiving that a determined habitual behavior in my private life, in my business affairs, or in my married life, contradicts natural law, that it is intrinsically evil, means I cannot remain indifferent or continue in that behavior as I did before I knew. On the contrary, it requires me to change my life. Likewise, recognizing that it falls to me in an immediate and unavoidable way to carry out this duty imposes the obligation of fulfilling it in spite of the sacrifices it requires. Therefore, our judgments of conscience are always threatened by the interference of our defects, habits, comforts or inclinations, which will fight so that I do not interiorly recognize what I do not desire to do or to give up.

We must insist one more time that the conscience maintains its dignity and imposes upon man the requirement of always following his conscience whenever it is shown the truth, or if it were to be mistaken, it errs involuntarily and without fault. For this reason Sacred Scripture constantly insists that we search for the truth and make judgments in accordance with the truth: "Certainly, in order to have a *'good conscience'* (1 Tim 1:5) man must seek the truth and must make judgments in accordance with that same truth. As the Apostle Paul says, the conscience must *be confirmed by the Holy Spirit* (cf. Rom 9:1); it must be *'clear'* (2 Tim 1:3); it must not 'practice cunning and tamper with God's word,' but 'openly state the truth' (cf. 2 Cor 4:2). On the other hand, the Apostle also warns Christians: *'Do not be conformed to this world but be transformed by the renewal of your mind, that you may prove what is the will of God, what is good and acceptable and perfect'* (Rom 12:2)."[299]

When one falsifies or disowns the truth through negligence or little love of truth or virtue, or through failing to make the effort of forming the conscience or clarifying things with a more knowledgeable person, he cannot excuse himself from sin by simply saying: "I am following my conscience." "A human being must always obey the certain judgment of his conscience. If he were deliberately to act against it, he would condemn himself. Yet it can happen that the moral conscience remains in ignorance and makes erroneous judgments about acts to be performed or already committed. This ignorance can often be imputed to personal

---

[299] VS, no. 62.

responsibility. This is the case when a man 'takes little trouble to find out what is true and good, or when conscience is by degrees almost blinded through the habit of committing sin.' In such cases, the person is culpable for the evil he commits."[300]

That is why John Paul II said: "It is not sufficient, therefore, to say to man: 'always follow your conscience.' It is necessary to add immediately and always: 'ask yourself if your conscience is telling you the truth or something false, and seek untiringly to know the truth.' If we were not to make this necessary clarification, man would risk to find in his conscience *a force which is destructive of his true humanity*, rather than that holy place where God reveals to him his true good."[301]

3. A WORD ABOUT THE FUNCTION OF THE MAGISTERIUM AND THE CONSCIENCE

Permit me to say a word about the function of the Magisterium of the Church in educating our conscience. As we have said already, correspondence with objective truth is an essential element of the upright conscience. But even though we have the principles necessary to derive moral truth, it is not always within reason's power to itself reach the truth from which all else must follow. The universal principles are there, but in their universal condition. Discovering the close relationship between our concrete actions and such principles can be clear or sometimes not so

---

[300] CCC 1790-1791.

[301] ST. JOHN PAUL II, "Moral Conscience is the place of dialogue of God with man," General Audience, August 17, 1983, in *L'Osservatore Romano*, August 22, 1983, no. 3.

clear, and this due to several reasons. On one hand, our reason is wounded and weakened by original sin. On the other hand, some of the truths that guide our concrete actions are the product of deductions of which not everyone is capable. At the same time, pressures of an atheistic and hedonistic society and culture interfere to a certain extent, creating a consequent manner of thinking in accord with their maxims. Finally, the practical judgment of reason preserves a strong dependence on our moral habits. When our moral habits include deeply rooted vices, they interfere, notably influencing one's mode of judgment. That is where the necessity of the Magisterium comes in.

The relationship between the Magisterium and the conscience is analogous to light and our eyes. If there is no light, our eyes do not see: "Thus to speak of a conflict between conscience and Magisterium is the same as speaking of a conflict between the eye and the light."[302]

A new confirmation of the harmony between the Magisterium and the conscience can be reached, beginning with the action of the Holy Spirit over the Magisterium and over the conscience of the faithful. The New Law, instituted by Christ, is a fundamentally interior law; it is the action of the Holy Spirit operating through grace in hearts. But at the same time it supposes external elements that are also the work of the Holy Spirit, such as the written text of Revelation, the sacraments, and also the Magisterium of the Church.[303] The Holy Spirit acts in these two: in the conscience with grace and in the Magisterium with his assistance. "The spirit of God, while He assists the Magisterium in proposing

---

[302] CAFFARRA, "Conscience, Truth, and Magisterium in Conjugal Morality," 29.

[303] Cf. AQUINAS, *Summa Theologica*, I-II, Q. 116, Art. 1, especially ad. 1.

doctrine, illumines internally the hearts of the faithful inviting them to give their assent."[304] One cannot claim that the judgment of his conscience, when it is in opposition to the Magisterium, is a fruit of his conscience's docility to the same Holy Spirit which guides the Magisterium.

All this deems necessary the intervention of a teaching body that, on one side, guards the principles keeping them safe, and on the other side, enlightens daily action in light of these same principles. For this reason, Ratzinger, after analyzing Newman's famous expression, , "if I am obliged to bring religion into after-dinner toasts, [...] I shall drink,—to the Pope, if you please,—still, to Conscience first, and to the Pope afterwards."[305] understands that the conscience, or better, the conscience's necessity of being guided, enlightened, and preserved from error, explains why there is a papacy. Ratzinger writes, "One can comprehend the primacy of the pope and its correlation to Christian conscience only in this connection. The true sense of the teaching authority of the pope consists in his being the advocate of the Christian memory.[306] The pope does not impose from without. Rather, he elucidates the Christian memory and defends it. For this reason the toast to conscience indeed must precede the toast to the pope, because without conscience there would not be a papacy. All power that the papacy has is power of conscience. It is service

---

[304] PAUL VI, *Humanae Vitae (Of Human Life)* (Boston: St. Paul Books & Media, 1968), no. 29.

[305] JOHN HENRY NEWMAN, *A Letter Addressed to His Grace the Duke of Norfolk* (New York: The Catholic Publication Society, 1875), 86.

[306] Here Ratzinger understands memory as *anamnesis*—what the theological tradition calls "synderesis": the habit of understanding the first moral principles. The equivalency between memory and synderesis could be debated, but for what we want to say, it expresses the meaning correctly.

to the double memory on which the faith is based—and which again and again must be purified, expanded, and defended against the destruction of memory that is threatened by a subjectivity forgetful of its own foundation, as well as by the pressures of social and cultural conformity."[307]

That is why John Paul II said compellingly in the speech he gave to the participants at the Second International Moral Theology Congress in 1988, that "the Magisterium of the Church was created by Christ the Lord to enlighten conscience."[308] This is why "to appeal to that conscience precisely to contest the truth of what is taught by the Magisterium implies rejection of the Catholic concept both of the Magisterium and moral conscience."[309] The Magisterium of the Church has been prepared by Christ's redeeming love so that the conscience will be preserved from error and ever more deeply and accurately grasp the truth that gives it dignity. Therefore, comparing the teachings of the Magisterium to any other source of knowledge trivializes the Magisterium and renders the redeeming sacrifice of Christ ineffective.

4. FORMING THE CONSCIENCE

This brings us to a final point: we must form or educate our conscience so that our judgments are always right. "Conscience must be informed and moral judgment

---

[307] JOSEPH RATZINGER, "Conscience and Truth," in *On Conscience* (San Francisco: Ignatius Press, 2007), 36.

[308] ST. JOHN PAUL II, Address to the Second International Congress on Moral Theology, November 12, 1988, in *L'Osservatore Romano,* English ed., December 19-26, 1988, no. 4.

[309] Ibid.

enlightened. A well-formed conscience is upright and truthful. It formulates its judgments according to reason, in conformity with the true good willed by the wisdom of the Creator. The education of conscience is indispensable for human beings who are subjected to negative influences and tempted by sin to prefer their own judgment and to reject authoritative teachings. The education of the conscience is a lifelong task. From the earliest years, it awakens the child to the knowledge and practice of the interior law recognized by conscience. Prudent education teaches virtue; it prevents or cures fear, selfishness and pride, resentment arising from guilt, and feelings of complacency, born of human weakness and faults. The education of the conscience guarantees freedom and engenders peace of heart."[310]

To educate our conscience we must do two things:

First of all, we must enlighten and illumine our conscience about goodness and truth. And this is done through the Faith, the Word of God and the clear teaching of the Church. In other words, we should be faithful to the truth. The exhortation of the Pope to the Bishops of France is meaningful for all Christians: "Pastors should form consciences, calling what is good, good and what is evil, evil."[311]

One can be sure of working with a right and honest conscience when he has put in place all the means for it to be upright. This has particular value for delicate issues in our moral and spiritual life, especially those about which we have doubts.

---

[310] CCC 1783-1784.

[311] St. JOHN PAUL II, *L'Osservatore Romano,* March 15, 1987, 9, no. 5, editorial translation.

Finally, one sees the reason why there can be no divergence between the teaching of the Church and the Christian's conscience. It is because the Magisterium is not just one more opinion; it is one of the sources from which we must enlighten the conscience. The Pope has said, "[…] The Magisterium of the Church was created by Christ the Lord to enlighten conscience."[312] And in *Veritatis Splendor*, "It follows that the authority of the Church, when she pronounces on moral questions, in no way undermines the freedom of conscience of Christians. This is so not only because freedom of conscience is never freedom 'from' the truth but always and only freedom 'in' the truth, but also because the Magisterium does not bring to the Christian conscience truths which are extraneous to it; rather it brings to light the truths which it ought already to possess, developing them from the starting point of the primordial act of faith. The Church puts herself always and only at the service of conscience, helping it to avoid being tossed to and fro by every wind of doctrine proposed by human deceit (cf. Eph 4:14), and helping it not to swerve from the truth about the good of man, but rather, especially in more difficult questions, to attain the truth with certainty and to abide in it."[313]

In second place (although not secondary in importance) we must live virtuously, searching for truth and building our virtues. Only virtue can guarantee that our conscience will not want to "justify" our imperfect behavior or our sins. The encyclical *Veritatis splendor* says, "Indeed in order to 'prove what is the will of God, what is good and acceptable and

---

[312] St. JOHN PAUL II, Address to the Second International Congress on Moral Theology, no. 4.

[313] VS, no. 64.

perfect' (Rom 12:2), knowledge of God's law in general is certainly necessary, but it is not sufficient: what is essential is a sort of *'connaturality' between man and the true good*.[314] Such a connaturality is rooted in and develops through the virtuous attitudes of the individual himself: prudence and the other cardinal virtues, and even before these the theological virtues of faith, hope and charity."[315] Virtue is essential in order that passions and vices do not alter the objectivity of our judgments. Just as someone who has burned his tongue cannot judge tastes as accurately as someone with a healthy tongue, similarly, on a moral level, only the virtuous can judge what is immoral. For example, the drunkard or the lustful person loses his sensibility before his sins (and this does not excuse them because such moral dullness has come about through his fault), and only the chaste and the sober discern clearly.

It is for this reason that when there is no virtue the passions can make even a good man cast aside his right judgments. We can say this along with these verses by the famous Roman poet, Trilussa, titled precisely "Coscenza," that is, "Conscience":

C'era un bel pollo sopra la credenza.
Er Cane, che lo vidde, disse ar Micio:
—Io nu' lo tocco: faccio un sacrificio,
ma armeno sto tranquillo de coscenza.
—Per te, va bè: ma io che ce guadagno?
–je chiese er Micio che fissava er piatto–
Co' 'sta fame arretrata? Fossi matto!

There was a beautiful roast chicken on the counter.
The Dog, sighing, said to the Cat,
"I will not touch it: I will make the sacrifice, and have peace of conscience."
"That's good for you, but what do I gain?" said the Cat looking at the tray, "To fast while I'm

---

[314] Aquinas, *Summa Theologica*, II-II, Q. 45.
[315] VS, no. 64.

Preferisco er rimorso e me lo magno.[316]   this hungry? No way! I would
prefer the remorse and eat it!"

[316] TRILUSSA, "Coscenza," in *Campionario Delle Favole* (Rome: Colombo Editore, 1943), 78.

For Further Reading

- Caffarra, Carlo. "Conscience, Truth, and Magisterium in Conjugal Morality." In Pontifical Council for the Family. *Marriage & Family: Experiencing the Church's Teaching in Married Life*. San Francisco: Ignatius Press, 1989.
- St. John Paul II. Address to the Second International Congress on Moral Theology. November 12, 1988. In *L'Osservatore Romano*, English ed. December 19-26, 1988.
- Ratzinger, Joseph. *On Conscience*. San Francisco: Ignatius Press, 2007.

Available in Other Languages

- Fuentes, Miguel. "La Conciencia y el Magisterio." *Gladius* 34 (1995): 37-50.
- ———. "Psicología y Teología de la Conversión." *Diálogo* 25 (1999): 93-120.
- ———. "Sentido del Pecado y Remordimiento." *Diálogo* 24 (1999): 141-156.
- García de Haro, Ramón. *La Conciencia Moral*. Madrid: Rialp, 1978.
- Melina, Livio. *La Conoscenza Morale*. Rome: Città Nuova, 1987.
- Bl. Paul VI. General Audience. February 12, 1969. www.vatican.va/holy_father/paul_vi/audiences/1969/documents/hf_p-vi_aud_19690212_it.html (accessed January 18, 2015).
- Rodríguez, Victorino. "Función Mediadora de la Conciencia." *Mikael: Revista del Seminario de Paraná* 24 (1980): 111-124.
- Roldán, Alejandro. *La Conciencia Moral*. Madrid: Razón y Fe, 1966.
- Supreme Sacred Congregation of the Holy Office. Instruction on "Situation Ethics." *Contra Doctrinam* (February 2, 1956): *AAS* 48 (1956), 144-145.

10.

THE STOLEN

TRUTH ABOUT

HISTORY

The Importance of Respecting Historic Truth

Many years ago I read a book entitled, *The Lies of the Modern World*. There, in written evidence, one can see—at least in certain matters—how our society's great means of communication constantly distort the facts we use. One of the greatest falsifications of our times relates to historical facts. If your career brings you along the paths of history, sociology, teaching, etc. it is very probable that you will run into many claims that are not true. This means a great damage for your formation and for your future students.

1. MANIPULATING HISTORY

Distorting history: why and what for? Above all for ideological motives. Sometimes facts have been modified to create public opinion. For example, the legends against Spanish works in the Americas (which became the *black legend* par excellence) were created, in great part, by the enemies of the Spanish crown—principally English enemies and especially Free Masonry—to develop international opinion against Spain. With time these black legends have come to have an important place in the programs of study in our schools, including our Catholic ones.

In many cases, these *black legends* have formed part of the degrading campaign against the Catholic Church and against those civil and political institutions that have defended the Church at some moment in its history. This is the case of Sixteenth Century Catholic Spain.

Manipulation has also been motivated by political interests. It is often said that history is written by the conquerors. This has some truth to it, although it is not all true, because sometimes history is written while fighting is taking place and is written precisely as one of the most useful weapons to gain a victory (at least a political and military victory but never a moral victory which can only be obtained with the truth). But how many politicians, sociologists or ideologists would care about *moral* victory? This happened with our own history,[317] which was why Juan Bautista Alberdi himself accused the liberal Argentineans of having disfigured history. And some of them confess to it, like Mitre when he writes to Vicente Lopez, "We have almost the same predilection for great men and the same repulsion for the barbarian troublemakers [...] whom we have buried historically."[318] And Sarmiento wrote to General Paz offering him his book *Facundo*: "I have written with the object of favoring the revolution and building spirit. Improvised work is by necessity full of inaccuracies, sometimes by design [*on purpose*], to help destroy one government and to prepare the way for a new one."[319] This is a confession. No more proof is necessary.

The "inaccuracy by design" and the "historical burials" of the great exemplars of humanity... it is sad knowing that our history is plagued by lies and falsifications.

What benefits follow from the adulteration of the past? Many. The most important is the domination of the present and the future. "The history of what we were explains what we are,"[320] wrote Hilaire Belloc. If I change history, then I will conceal who you really are; and if you do not know who you are, then *you will be who I want you to be*. If I change your past (at least in your mind), I can make you fight against your father and mother, making you believe that they are your enemies. I can make you hate your benefactors and I can get you to kiss my hands full of gratitude even though I am the thief that has brainwashed your mind.

---

[317] *Editor's Note:* "Our own history" refers to the history of Argentina.

[318] BARTOLOMÉ MITRE, quoted in E. BRADFORD BURNS, et al., *Elite, Masses, and Modernization in Latin America, 1850-1930* (Austin: University of Texas Press, 1979), 40.

[319] Cf. ANÍBAL ROTTJER, "Desde La Instalación Oficial Hasta El Fin Del Siglo," in *La Masonería en la Argentina y en el Mundo* (Buenos Aires: Nuevo Orden, 1972), 296-297, editorial translation.

[320] HILAIRE BELLOC, quoted in VICTOR FESKE, *From Belloc to Churchill: Private Scholars, Public Culture, and the Crisis of British Liberalism, 1900-1939* (Chapel Hill: University of North Carolina Press, 1996), 22.

It is not strange that the manipulative management of history has become one of the most powerful weapons in the brainwashing of generations—because with history I can make you love what in reality is hateful and make you hate what is lovable. With the domination of history (written and oral) I can paint for you a diabolical Jesus Christ and a devil doing good for humanity, as the New Age does in our times. I can present you with an idyllic paganism persecuted by a tyrannical Church. I can make you believe that those who brought you the faith only wanted your blood and your gold. I can make the missionaries into pirates and make tyrants into angels. Marxism understood the destructive power of cultural manipulation very well, especially beginning with a man who was as intelligent as he was intellectually perverted, Antonio Gramsci, the ideologist of the Cultural Revolution. In any case, it was not his discovery, as you can see if you take into account the black legends of antiquity.

A great deal has been said about the Inquisition, the witch hunts, the genocides of America, the persecutions against paganism, the Spanish gold rush, and the idyllic situations of the indigenous Americans. This view does not jump out at us from the documents, nor from the contemporary eyewitness accounts of the events, and in many cases not even from the testimonies of the "victims" themselves.

Therefore, you should always look at who is saying things; you must observe the motives they may have in saying them and what advantage they get from their assertions. And never listen to only one source. Research and study.

Let us say, in passing, that those who defend themselves against these black legends by unduly exalting what others malign are also not doing a great service. Their pain and the motivation that can bring them to vindicate what others have falsified and indecently trampled on is understandable. But they do not give authentic service to the truth if they do not expose the whole truth. There are some cases without a doubt in which injurious, fictitious stories without any basis in truth have been woven around a historical situation, institution or characters. Let us simply think of the accusations against Jesus, which are repeated throughout history against many saints and heroes. But in many cases we do not find such integrity of doctrine or life. The Lord himself predicted that in his fields we would find weeds mixed among the wheat. If we confront those who are trying to make us believe that everything has been weeds by saying that it has all been wheat, or that the weeds have been almost nonexistent, we will serve well neither history nor our credibility.

There have been many mistakes, as is expected from a cloth woven by beings of flesh and blood, with uncontrolled and often shameful passions (and I speak not only of lust but also injustice, envy and greed). There have been abuses on the part of those who have been basically good and just but at the same time neither completely good nor just. Let us keep in mind that the saints have been many, but saints have never been the majority in any generation.

There are cases in which the things that are criticized have actually been involuntary errors or instances where unknowingly mistaken people made wrong decisions. Therefore, we must judge them justly: it is involuntary (so we would not lay the blame on them as the material author) but *it is an error*. In many other cases, the things that scandalize us nowadays were not understood in their times or they did not offend the sensitivities of their century as sometimes occurs in ours. The greatest men have been *children of their times*; we cannot judge them with the criteria that has cost us sweat and tears to reach over decades and centuries. We must not judge a fifth or thirteenth or sixteenth century man with the mentality of a twentieth century man, *regarding those things that depend greatly on temporal or cultural circumstances*, as could be the case regarding many of the ideas of our ancestors about phenomena like slavery, the right to war, freedom of opinion, and other experiences in this vein. In any case, we should not believe ourselves to be *sensitive* in an age where we put down the slavery of the past while at the same time accepting modern slavery *that is graver and more extensive than that of the past*, like prostitution or drugs or economic oppressions that drown whole classes in injustice and misery. We condemn the killings and the wars of old, *closing our eyes to daily genocides like abortion, ethnic "cleansing" and religious exterminations, etc.*! But we neither wish to justify any past perversion because it happens today, nor any present degeneration because "things like this always happen." The truth will always be true; lies will always be lies; injustice will never be justified.

Thus we all must be conscious that with reason one can reach many truths that pertain to the natural law—at least secondarily. Therefore, we can assume a certain culpability in many erroneous judgments from the past. We cannot excuse them, but neither can we accuse them as we would our contemporaries.

I would like to mention a few writings that have had a particular impact on me regarding the way of carrying out a seriously historic work. The first of these works centers around the debates about Friar Bartolemé de Las Casas. As is known, the anti-Spanish black legends owe a lot to him. The enemies of Spain and the Church put Las Casas on a pedestal. His detractors accuse him of being paranoid, inventing calumnies and infamies (some of them—not all—prove his intention to be good, saying that he believed the things he invented and that a sincere love for indigenous Americans brought him to make up such stories). For me, one very enlightening document was a letter written from Taxcala in 1555 by a person of unquestionable honesty to Emperor Charles V. I am referring to a contemporary of De Las Casas, Friar Toribio de Benavente, known in the Americas as Friar Toribio Motolinía,[321] a man beloved by the Mexican indigenous. (They named him, Motolinía, which means *Poor* in their language, and he adopted it as his proper name from then on.) His letter has great value, since a few years earlier (1541), he had dedicated a marvelous work entitled *History of the Indians of New Spain* to the same person; there he had no difficulty denouncing—as many times as was necessary—abuses on the part of Spaniards and non-Spaniards and putting things in their place (one of his chapters is entitled

---

[321] See: Real Academia de la Historia. Col. de Muñoz. Indias. 1554-55. T. 87. f.ª 213-32.

precisely: *"Of some Spaniards who have ill-treated the Indians, and the end to which they came."*[322] In this letter to the Emperor, he again denounces abuses. Not everything is praises and defenses, but he is setting the record straight. It is not, therefore, someone with a personal interest in favor of the conquistadors. Then, in this letter, Motolinía writes to Charles V because of the campaigns discrediting the conquistadors, which De Las Casas was carrying out in Spain. He warns the Emperor saying that "This Las Casas is wrong in what he says, writes, prints and urges"[323] and he accuses him: "quia mercenarius est et non pastor [because he is a mercenary and not a pastor]."[324] for having abandoned his sheep to dedicate himself to defaming others. And later on he says about this friar, who was a disturber of the peace: "Many times he gives the conquerors, encomenderos and merchants the names of tyrants, robbers, violators, ravishers and thieves. He says that always and every day they are oppressing the Indians [...] Surely, for the bit of canon law that Las Casas studied, he dares too much; his confusion appears great, his humility small. He thinks that all err and he alone is right, because he also makes this statement, which follows word for word: 'All the conquerors have been robbers and ravishers, the most qualified in evil and cruelty that there ever have been, as is manifest to the whole world.' All of the conquerors, he says, without making a single exception [...] I am amazed that your majesty and those of your councils have been able to bear for so long with a man so vexatious, unquiet, importunate, argumentative and litigious, in a friar's habit, so restless, so poorly bred, insulting, prejudicial and troublemaking. For fifteen years I have known Las Casas [...] always writing indictments of other people, seeking out the crimes and bad things that the Spaniards had committed

---

[322] TORIBIO MOTOLINÍA, *Motolinía's History of the Indians of New Spain*, trans. Elizabeth Andros Foster (Westport, Connecticut: Greenwood Press, 1973), ch. X.

[323] TORIBIO MOTOLINÍA, quoted in *Letters and Peoples of the Spanish Indies, Sixteenth Century*, trans. and ed. James Lockhart and Enrique Otte (Cambridge: Cambridge University Press, 1999), 222.

[324] MOTOLINÍA, quoted in *Letters and Peoples of the Spanish Indies*, 229.

through this whole land, to exaggerate and make worse the evils and sins that have occurred. In this he seemed to do the work of our adversary, though he thought himself more zealous and more just than the other Christians, including the friars; but he had hardly anything to do with religion here."[325] When Motolinía compares Marqués del Valle, that is to say, Hernán Cortés, with his detractors (De Las Casas among them) he claims: "I believe that before God their deeds are not as acceptable as those of the Marqués. Although as a human he was a sinner, he had the faith and works of a good Christian, and a great desire to employ his life and property in widening 'and augmenting the faith of Jesus Christ, and dying for the conversion of these gentiles. He spoke of this with much spirit, as one to whom God had given this gift and desire."[326] With good reason, Motolinía criticized De Las Casas, saying: "He never sought to know the good, only the bad."[327] Closer to reality Friar Toribio makes up for his judgments claiming that "As to the overseers, tribute-collectors and miners, he calls them executioners, soulless, inhuman and cruel. And granted that some have been greedy and of ill repute, certainly there are many others who are good Christians, pious and charitable, many of them married and of good life."[328]

This balance in his writings, criticizing what needs to be criticized, praising what is praiseworthy and going into detail where detail is needed, shows us clearly that judgments of temporal realities can never be true if a landscape is painted only in black and white. Life has a lot of shades; ignoring them will bring us to do history an injustice.

The second work that I do not want to fail to mention is the monumental text by Marcelino Menéndez y Pelayo, *History of the Spanish Heterodoxy* (Historia de los herterodoxes españoles), with its

---

[325] MOTOLINÍA, quoted in *Letters and Peoples of the Spanish Indies*, 224-225.

[326] MOTOLINÍA, quoted in *Letters and Peoples of the Spanish Indies*, 244.

[327] MOTOLINÍA, quoted in *Letters and Peoples of the Spanish Indies*, 228.

[328] MOTOLINÍA, quoted in *Letters and Peoples of the Spanish Indies*, 229-230.

eight admirable volumes. One which must be read is the volume that refers to the problems of the *Illuminati* and in particular the investigation that the Spanish Inquisition made of Friar Bartolomé Carranza who was nothing less than the archbishop of Toledo. Marcelino begins his work by writing: "If we had to narrate at length the results of the dry and extremely irritating study of Carranza's trial, the work of this chapter would be a difficult and immense task, *rudis indigestaque moles*[329], as it consists of no less than twenty-two volumes in folio and close to twenty thousand sheets of paper, not counting the documents from Rome, the archbishop's works themselves and what Salazar de Mendoza, Llorente, Sáinz de Baranda, D. Adolfo de Castro and D. Fermín Caballero (1731) and (1732) wrote about him. The reader can without difficulty see that I have come to hate such a tiresome yet important affair, and I await the hour when his story could be told in the least amount of words as possible, because I am afraid of losing my head and the little bit of literary liking that God gave me if I remain entangled any longer in the abominable and curial reading of the tomes that the writer, Sebastian de Landeta copied and put together. On the other hand, since I did not write a monograph on Carranza, but an extensive history with many different characters and events, it allows me to only take the important parts, leaving the rest for the archbishop's future biographers. I begin this work without any like or dislike towards Carranza or his judges, and I will formulate my judgment only after scrupulously narrating the results of the documents."[330] It can be gathered from this work that Menéndez y Pelayo did not write upon hearing about it, but after having read, analyzed, and studied each step of the trial—after reading thousands of pages! In spite of

---

[329] *Editor's Note:* The Latin phrase *rudis indigestaque moles* means "a rough unordered mass."

[330] MARCELINO MENÉNDEZ Y PELAYO, "Historia de los Heterodoxos Españoles," book 4, ch. VIII, *Biblioteca Virtual Miguel de Cervantes, www.cervantesvirtual.com/obra-visor/historia-de-los-heterodoxos-espanoles/html/fee78e52-82b1-11df-acc7-002185ce6064_77.html* (accessed December 7, 2014), editorial translation.

this, he never allows his historic judgments to stray from his good sense and the facts in front of him, stopping himself when his sentences could constitute an insult. Therefore, we should not find it strange that at the end of his study he asks: "What should we think of Carranza?"[331] and he responds with an extraordinary prudence and impartiality: "That Carranza *wrote, taught and dogmatized* propositions with Lutheran leanings was clearly and simply affirmed."[332] But immediately after, remarking that Carranza made a declaration on his death bed that he never held, taught or professed a heresy, this same author adds this memorable paragraph: "Frankly, if we did not have the profession of faith made by Carranza on his death bed in front of Jesus in the Blessed Sacrament, in which he claimed he had never fallen into any voluntary error, there would not be any human means to save him. It is fitting to keep a respectful silence faced with this declaration. Of the hidden thoughts only God can judge. I do not believe that Carranza would knowingly lie on his death bed. And, in summary, excusing the intention, I judge him as his sentence judged: *Strongly suspect of heresy, nursed on the perverse doctrine of Luther, Melanchton and Oecolampadius.*"[333] This is how a historian should write: knowing to stop on the threshold of someone else's conscience and leaving the last judgments to God. What would Don Marcelino think of our writers of magazine stories, booklets and Internet pages, who write about things they are ignorant of, cutting and pasting some texts without any criteria, and then making judgments that seem infallible? This is not making history; nor do they become historians; nor do they obtain the right to judge the history of those who have gone before with such superficiality as can be seen nowadays. All this occurs even though they have degrees and extraordinary credentials (which can also be falsified).

---

[331] Ibid.

[332] Ibid.

[333] Ibid. All this can be read in the eighth book of his work that has fortunately been published online [in Spanish] by the University of Alicante (*www.cervantesvirtual.com*); though without the author's notes.

It is necessary, therefore, that we form our minds with a great critical sense. I have often received questions about topics that many of the Church's adversaries use as battle cries without in reality having the smallest idea about the topic. They only repeat pre-fabricated slogans that some borrow from others and then they mutually cite each other in an attempt to establish credibility. Jack invents a rumor and makes it public, maybe embellishing it with some "it could be," "maybe," or "it may not be," etc. Another takes his turn passing it on, based on what he has read (precisely on what Jack spread to the four corners of the earth), then a third promotes it, now applying the plural, "they say that". Finally the chain becomes unending and of course is "solidly established" since "the whole world says that;" but no one has taken up the work of verifying the facts or challenging any document. This is similar to the story about the "unfounded rumor" that ended up appearing true because of the effects it produced. (The story is found in authors as different as Chesterton and García Márquez.) The legend is about a mother who sends her son to buy bread—one loaf, like always—but today, since the afternoon is overcast and dreary, she says, "Buy two, just in case something happens." The child says to the baker, "Two loaves of bread just in case something happens." A neighbor overhears and at the market also requests double her normal rations "in case something happens." Others upon hearing it do the same repeating the same phrase. By nightfall the cupboards are full "in case something happens." Husbands arriving home hear their wives' worried explanations. One of them decides to escape, since they think they will not be able to handle it if something should happen. They go out with their wagon laden with everything they can carry. Their neighbors hear, come out, and share the same thought that they should abandon the town "in case something happens." Now everyone is in the streets grieving over leaving these houses where they alone have lived, and they have no qualms about burning them so as to not abandon them to the fate of intruders. Already far off in the sad caravan of confused people with a cloud of dust rising from the road, in the middle of the fire lit night the mother looks sadly at the flames of the town and says to her son, "I told you, something was going to happen."[334]

In this way they create completely false but firmly believed "parallel histories." We are infinitely far away from the reliability of the great historians like the eminent Ludwig von Pastor. I mention this German historian (1854-1928) since he is the author of one of the most monumental works of historical criticism, his *History of the Popes ("Geschichte der Papste seit dem Ausgang de Mittlelalters. 1305-1799")*, a work translated into the principal Western languages and published in various volumes (according to the editions they range from sixteen to forty volumes), and praised by Catholic and non-Catholic authors alike. Von Pastor studied history at the Universities of Louvain, Bonn, Berlin, Vienna, and Graz. He was a professor at Innsbruck and directed the Austrian Historic Institute in Rome. He was Protestant and ended up converting to Catholicism. His work combined a love for the Catholic Church with the most meticulous knowledge and academics. He was privileged to have access to the Vatican's secret archives; and, based largely on previously unconsidered documents, his history surpasses all previous histories about the Popes. (From 1921, Pastor paid his dues as the Austrian minister to the Vatican.) According to the Columbia Encyclopedia, Pastor's fundamental idea is that the defects of the papacy have reflected the weaknesses of every era. *El Grande Dizionario Enciclopedico UTET* says that Pastor's work "represents a great quantity of noteworthy study; the author's Catholic thesis does not impede him from freely explaining and criticizing the actions of some Renaissance Popes, while the richness of the documentation allows him to correct many of the more common prejudices, above all those on part of the Protestants."[335] In order to write his work, "for

---

[334] I read this story years ago in an interesting letter from a reader directed to an Argentinean newspaper; unfortunately I do not have the author's references except that authors like Chesterton and García Márquez had used it.

[335] Vol. XV of *Grande Dizionario Enciclopedico* (Turin: Unione Tipografico-Editrice Torinese, 1989), 557, editorial translation.

the space of fifty years [this author] researched the archives of two hundred and thirty European cities [...] This demonstrates a perfect mastery of the documentation."[336]

I have recommended reading this work to many who have asked about the apparent scandals of some Popes or about less than edifying situations in the Church. At least to read the passages regarding the topics they have questions about, because they are important questions—their adherence to Catholicism is at stake in some cases—and they cannot be resolved with summary answers. Unfortunately, in many cases I have confirmed that my inquiring interlocutors are not interested in any deep, serious, documented or thoughtful study, but only in short and quick—*and completely preliminary!*—answers ("fast food" mentality) a bad sign for intellectual health. Truth will always demand the use of our intelligence to the maximum.

2. CONFRONTING THE TRUTH

On this question I think that the Church has given us an extraordinary example of scientific examination. We had the opportunity to observe this very closely in the year before the great Jubilee Year 2000, when John Paul II wanted to carry out the significant act of asking pardon, in the name of the whole Church, for the wrongs committed by her children throughout the last two thousand years of history that we have lived. But before proceeding to ask for pardon, they completed many historic studies (including international symposiums) in which they studied the documents to determine exactly what these faults were (in particular accusations relating to the Crusades, the Inquisition, and anti-Semitism). On the occasion of the publication of the Acts of the International Symposium on the Inquisition, the Pope wrote: "it is appropriate that [...] the Church should become more fully conscious of the sinfulness of her children, recalling all those times in history when

---

[336] I. GOÑI GAZTAMBIDE, "Pastor, Ludwig Von," in vol. XVIII of *Gran Enciclopedia Rialp* (Madrid: Ediciones Rialp, 1974), 35, editorial translation.

they departed from the spirit of Christ and his Gospel and, instead of offering to the world the witness of a life inspired by the values of faith, indulged in ways of thinking and acting which were truly forms of counter-witness and scandal."[337] And in reference to the concrete case of the Inquisition, he added "In public opinion, the image of the Inquisition is as it were the symbol of such counter-witness and scandal. How faithful to reality is this image? Before asking for forgiveness, it is necessary to have exact knowledge of the facts and to put shortcomings with regard to what the Gospel requires in the context *where they are effectively found* [...] The *sensus fidei* must be asked to exercise the criteria of a level judgment of the life of the Church in the past."[338]

Cardinal Georges Cottier, O.P. explained, "Obviously, a request for forgiveness can only affect *real and objectively recognized events.* Forgiveness is not asked for images spread by public opinion, which *are part of a myth and do not correspond to reality.*"[339] And the historian, Agostino Borromeo, professor at the Roman University *La Sapienza*, added "Historians can no longer use the topic of the Inquisition as an instrument to defend or attack the Church [...] The debate has moved to the historical level, with serious statistics."[340] And the same professor confirmed, "the propagandistic catholic apologetic was in opposition to the black

---

[337] ST. JOHN PAUL II, *Tertio Millennio Adveniente* (Boston: Daughters of St. Paul, 1994), no. 33.

[338] ST. JOHN PAUL II, "Letter to Cardinal Roger Etchegaray on the Occasion of the Presentation of the Volume 'L'Inquisizione,'" June 15, 2004, nos. 1-2, *www.vatican.va/holy_father/john_paul_ii/letters/2004/documents/hf_jp-ii_let_20040615_simposio-inquisizione_en.html* (accessed December 7, 2014).

[339] "Papal Household Theologian at Presentation on Inquisition Symposium," *ZENIT,* June 15, 2004, *www.zenit.org/en/articles/papal-household-theologian-at-presentation-on-inquisition-symposium* (accessed December 14, 2014).

[340] AGOSTINO BORROMEO, quoted in MICHAEL THOMSETT, *The Inquisition: A History* (Jefferson, North Carolina: McFarland, 2010), 261.

legend, which was created against the Inquisition in protestant countries; neither case helped to achieve an objective vision"[341]

Therefore we should say that strictly historical investigation and research will never be a bad thing, and there should be no need to fear it—on the contrary, there is a need to trust it. Truth is evident in itself; it does not need our poetry, rhetoric, or our sophisticated arguments. As John Paul II has said, "The Church is certainly not afraid of the truth that emerges from history and is ready to acknowledge mistakes wherever they have been identified, especially when they involve the respect that is owed to individuals and communities. She is inclined to mistrust generalizations that excuse or condemn various historical periods. She entrusts the investigation of the past to patient, honest, scholarly reconstruction, free from confessional or ideological prejudices, regarding both the accusations brought against her and the wrongs she has suffered."[342]

3. BLACK LEGENDS AND ROSE-COLORED LEGENDS

In general the black legends and deceptions of history are very numerous. It is very difficult for us not to have heard something appalling about the case of Galileo Galilei, about the Inquisition, about the expulsion of the Jews from Spain, about the Crusades, about the conquest of America, about the riches of the Church, about Pope Pius XII and Nazism, about anti-Semitism in the Church, etc. To complement these we must also add those legends of events seen through *rose-colored* glasses—myths just as false as the previous—we think of the celestial halos that surround certain

---

[341] "Balanced History of the Inquisition is Possible, Says Expert," *ZENIT,* June 16, 2004, *www.zenit.org/en/articles/balanced-history-of-the-inquisition-is-possible-says-expert* (accessed December 14, 2014).

[342] ST. JOHN PAUL II, General Audience, September 1, 1999, *www.vatican.va/holy_father/john_paul_ii/audiences/documents/hf_jp-ii_aud_01091999_en.html* (accessed December 14, 2014), no. 3.

past acts like the almost idyllic state in which the indigenous were found pre-Columbus, which the European conquistadors destroyed with their military presence. (They close their eyes to centuries of violence and extermination that reigned between the different American tribes, the Demonic rituals, the practice of cannibalism, ritual human sacrifices, deportations of entire towns, the slavery common between tribes, the famous "Floral Wars" carried out in order to obtain human victims for idolatrous sacrifices, etc.) The same can be said about the idyllic state they ascribe to pre-Christian paganism (a theme very much in style in New Age movements). Or, more relevant for us, the sympathetic presentations of bloody and inhuman events like the French Revolution, the liberal plots of some American Revolutions, British imperialism, etc. The black and rose-colored legends that affect the history of every country, in particular those with Catholic roots, must be added to all this. Among us there has been no lack of the idealization of individuals who have not been models of goodness, justice, patriotism, or culture, in spite of undeniable greatness in other areas. In spite of this, they name the majority of Argentinean plazas, towns, streets and monuments after them. I'm thinking of Sarmiento, Mitre, Rivadavia, Moreno, Lavalles, Pelligrini, Roca, Justo José de Urquiza, Adolfo Saldias, Juan Andrés Gelly y Obes, Santiago Derquie, and many others whom Argentinean history—many times written by those men themselves—placed on a pedestal in hymns, poems, compositions, and childish schoolbook fables. And this while in many cases they had to do with the causes of the loss of our culture, the de-Christianization of our customs, the impoverishment of our country and also the spilling of innocent blood, and futile, unjust wars between brothers. But in the literature we extol them as "great," "illustrious," "glorious," and all those epitaphs our ordinary textbooks enumerate. At the same time the true heroes of our history, those who forged our homeland and built its culture are often unknown and their true marks of greatness are hidden from us (in many cases their Catholicism.) Just observe that in schoolbooks they never recognize or recount the labor of the great missionaries, many of whom are martyrs who have planted the seeds of faith, culture, and civilization in our lands. Fortunately, in our country we have great historians we can trust who have done an authentic job of *revisionism,* aiming to discern the truth within a history woven with subtle ideological inventions. We should have in mind the great works of Vicente Sierra, Federico Ibarguren, Rómulo Cárbia, Enrique Díaz Araujo, Guillermo Furlong, Cayetano Bruno, etc. Unfortunately many of these studies have yet to come before the majority of the public. They remain stagnant in the libraries of the most educated, while they continue drinking the turbid springs of falsified history in the schools, high schools, and universities.

It is not the intention of these pages—nor the expertise of the author—to refute any of these referenced anti-historical legends. Although we have mentioned a few of them, it would not be fruitful to even try to superficially present the principal falsifications. It is enough for me to caution your innocent mind about this danger and advise you to forge within yourself a true critical spirit. A critical spirit does not mean a nitpicky mind, but an intelligence capable of discerning a cat from a dog. How will you achieve that? Through serious study, not contenting yourself with the "official" versions. Study the serious authors, especially those whose credibility and intellectual honesty you can judge. Study well-documented books and examine their sources. If you can, read the books written by those who lived during the events. And above all do not "form" your intelligence with pamphlets, magazines, mass market books or any old textbook. And be careful of ideologies!

4. MODERN ENEMIES OF THE TRUTH

Today the dangers of false formation have grown formidably because the enemies of truth have discovered some sources to be veritable "gold mines" of distortion. I want to mention three: cheap literature, films and Internet.

Literature that "sells" to a superficial public (for some reason the main qualifier used today is "best seller!") has channeled its ideological forces through the genre of "historical novel." In the majority of cases, it is not in reality historical, since the qualifier "historic" only means that the situations described have been set in the past; but historic does not have the significance of "truth," although it pretends to! On the contrary, monstrous lies, falsities, distortions of reality, calumnies about institutions, facts, and individuals underlie this genre. We mean "historical fiction" novels. Take as a very recent example, some of these writings that claim to be "historical investigations," such as: Margaret Starbird's books: *The Woman with the Alabaster Jar: Mary Magdalene and the Holy Grail*,[343] *The Goddess in the Gospels: Reclaiming the Sacred Feminine*; those by Picknett and Prince: *The Templar Revelation, Turin Shroud*; the well known one by Michael Baigent, Richard Leigh, and Henry Lincoln, *The Holy Blood and the Holy Grail*; and the currently famous one by Dan Brown, *The Da Vinci Code*. In a note at the beginning of that book, the author shamelessly declares that "all descriptions of artwork, architecture, documents, and secret rituals in this novel are accurate."[344] However those who have

---

[343] The publisher's description of this work says: "In this work, *researched with the greatest seriousness,* Starbird demonstrates to us that Jesus did not die on the cross, that Mary Magdalene was his wife, and that it was her to whom Jesus entrusted his teachings. To restore the place that corresponds to Mary Magdalene in the Christian religion, Starbird recovers a part of the roots of Christianity that had been ignored until now." (This description was done by *Editorial Planeta* until November, 2004: MARGARET STARBIRD, *María Magdalena y el Santo Grial: La Mujer con el Frasco de Alabastro* (Barcelona: Editorial Planeta, 2004), *www.editorial.planeta.es,* editorial translation.)

[344] DAN BROWN, *The Da Vinci Code* (New York: Double Day, 2003), 1.

taken up the work of critically reading *The Da Vinci Code* have published entire pages listing the errors, inventions, deceptions, and simply fictitious accounts that abound in the entire book with marked evil intention. Examining the bibliography that Brown has used is enough to realize that serious books about history or art are not part of his personal library or even his intellectual storehouse. On the contrary, his sources of information are pseudo-sciences, esoteric books, and pseudo-historical conspiracies, etc.[345] In order to see up to what point there is a "conspiracy" against the truth, just read the literary criticism from some magazines which, in spite of the book's lies have categorized it as a "historical" work, "several doctorates' worth of fascinating history and learned speculation,"[346] or simply "impeccable research."[347] All these books call their efforts *a return to the historical truth*, re-asserting the "Gnostic" image of Jesus Christ (the theme of the Gnostic gospels is a common tune today) as the "original truth" about Jesus Christ and that in the first centuries the Catholic Church altered and erased the true figure of Jesus, creating an anti-feminist Jesus, who was the founder of a religious movement, celibate, long-suffering and divine. But this is nothing more than projecting into the past a strictly modern phenomenon, "brainwashing the masses." Pretending that the "ecclesiastical leaders" together with the political power of the fourth century were able to completely erase the real image of Christ and impose the divinized image that has

---

[345] Cf. the meticulous and complete study of CARL OLSON and SANDRA MIESEL, *The Da Vinci Hoax: Exposing the Errors in The Da Vinci Code* (San Francisco: Ignatius Press, 2004).

There are other books of criticism like: JOSÉ ANTONIO ULLATE FABO, *La Verdad Sobre el Código Da Vinci* (Madrid: Libros Libres, 2004);

AMY WELBORN, *De-Coding Da Vinci* (Huntington: Our Sunday Visitor, 2004).

[346] *Chicago Tribune,* quoted in "The Da Vinci Code: Book Reviews," *The Official Website of Dan Brown, www.danbrown.com/novels/davinci_code/reviews.html* (accessed May 3, 2009).

[347] *The New York Daily News,* quoted in *The Official Website of Dan Brown, www.danbrown.com* (accessed May 3, 2009).

prevailed up to our days; they suppose that there was a capacity for lying (and a capacity for deceit) in the ancient world that we have only known (with real intensity) in the last century. It is our time that has come across and put into motion the greatest brainwashing apparatus by the means of communication driven by spurious interests.[348] But the very fact that after half a century of work its objective has still not been achieved while *counting on such a large apparatus*, shows that it was not possible in the past. The Church in those first periods could not have succeeded in imposing the legendary image of Christ due to the simple fact that with an almost infinitely superior power of communication and techniques of persuasion (press, television, Internet, movies, publishing, etc.) the means of mass media have not succeeded in imposing a contrary image.

Not even the credulity of the ancients could explain it. It is true that in the first centuries of our Christian era, a great number of people existed who were foolish and gullible (this is a human phenomenon that started when Eve believed the first reporter of all creation, the serpent who preached in paradise his own version of divine actions). However, men of our times who enthusiastically accept everything sold to them daily without any criticism are even more gullible, in spite of being—also almost daily—shown the fact of the adulteration of fundamental information.

The reality of what has happened, on the other hand, is the contrary of this theory that imposes a falsified image of Christ. What happened was that the attempt to defraud the truth about Christ failed. Gnostic writings (which are not as many as Dan

---

[348] It is the methods of the press in our times (allied with television, movies, and literature for the illiterate) that bring about the most relentless disinformation of the masses that has been known in history. It is the world of modern journalism (with some major exceptions) which, in recent decades, sells and pushes (to those willing to swallow it) a false self-image of seriousness, wisdom, and omniscience that leads to so-called "research journalism" and "research" journalists. (These are labeled as such by their own colleagues who throw flowers and incense to one another giving themselves authority that they do not have, cannot have, and cannot even know in what it would consist.)

Brown pretends there are) were the first attempt to introduce a "denaturalized" Christ. The attempt utterly failed, not due to political maneuvering but because the truth about Jesus Christ is indicated in the blood of the martyrs, who did not give their lives— nor would it have occurred to them to do so—for the "sentimental companion" of Magdalene (the Jesus of feminists), nor for Kazanzaki's tormented Jesus, nor the lewd Jesus Christ *superstar*. If the current defenders of the *mythicized* Christ theory think that the first century Christians put their necks under the lions' paws for a Christ such as this, then they suppose that the martyrs were as empty-headed as they are. But, just as those from back then were not foolish, these modern writers are not Christian martyrs.

In many cases, cinema is the second phase through which these modern fictitious stories pass. To mention a few of the movies that claim to contain historical elements: *Jesus Christ Superstar* (Norman Jewison, 1973), *The Last Temptation of Christ* (Martin Scorsese, 1988), *Priest* (Antonia Bird, 1995), *Godspell* (David Greene, 1973), *The Body* (2001 — which is about the supposed discovery of the body of Christ and is therefore against His Resurrection), *Stigmata* (1999 — which features the discovery of the apocryphal gospel of Thomas, which, if older than the Gospels integrated into the canon of the Christian Bible, could put the Catholic Church in danger of collapse), *Amen* (Costa-Gavras, 2002 — which is against Pope Pius XII and his supposed participation in the Nazi persecution of the Jews), etc.[349] The same process of announcing that the facts therein described are "strictly true and historical" or allowing advertisement or propaganda to let it be left as understood that it

---

[349] Other well-known films that also distort Catholic doctrine out of ill-will are: *The Order* (2003), a horror story about a renegade priest who discovers within the Church a sect dedicated to hiding monstrous crimes; *The Magdalene Sisters* (2002), which shows a "reformatory" equal to a Nazi concentration camp; *Sister Mary Explains It All* (2001), which tells the story of a macabre killing nun; *Dogma* (1999), a parody about the last descendant of Joseph and Mary who works in an abortion clinic and is driven to save two fallen angels under the command of god (who is a woman); *Priest* (1994), which depicts a homosexual priest who denounces corruption in his parish; *Agnes of God* (1985), which depicts a religious who killed his newborn son.

is such also occurs in these cases. "Calumny, calumny, something of it always sticks," said Voltaire, a specialist in this tactic. And he had reason, since at least doubt always remains ("If they said it, there could be something to it"). Regarding cinema's campaign against Catholicism it may be useful to see the 1996 documentary study titled, "Hollywood vs. Catholicism."[350]

The Internet has also become one of the tools of the distortion of history. This resource in particular offers anonymity, the capacity to publish an enormous mass of information without any documented proof, and above all, anonymity in its huge potential to "capture" a large number of men and women who search for information without any requirement of scientific rigor. In this case it doesn't only deserve the name "net," but can also be compared with a spider web that catches the "fly-men" (those who, superficial in their demands and weak in their intellectual principles, fly around impertinently inspecting where they shouldn't). They are those who pursue facts without caring about their level of certainty, or their scientific or hypothetical value, or their simple gossiping character. Many of these people look for information but not *formation*. Internet is the realm of "cut and paste," of "it's all done," and of triviality. Often in my work I have tried to trace some fact and received the disagreeable surprise of finding that, among the abundant places a topic is treated, in reality it is all copied, textually, without adding anything, from one or another; and none of them have any serious backing whatsoever. However, we don't want to unduly exaggerate the case against the Internet. A great deal of serious information can be found by means of the Internet, including studies, articles, and books of high investigatory value that are almost impossible to find any other way. The problem lies in them being lost in the great confusion of falsifications that makes it difficult for anyone without a good dose of discernment to prevent himself from falling into the nets of the "myth manufacturer." My work in particular has brought me into

---

[350] LEONARDO DEFILIPPIS and MITCH PACWA, *Hollywood vs. Catholicism,* VHS (Dallas, Texas: Chatham Hill Foundation, 1996).

contact with good but naive people who have been the victims of enormous confusion. This occurs because they put themselves within the reach of crazy, fanatical, sectarian, and even perverted people, while navigating whatever webpage; they look for *prefabricated* information in order to avoid the work of reading serious things, that are large or difficult to digest. They ask the magical world of the Internet—as Aladdin asked the genie hidden in his lamp—to obtain ready-made information needed for their job, study, or profession, eluding the work of doing it themselves. How many times I have received questions and requests for help in mending the holes these corruptors have left in their faith, in their confidence in the truth, the Church, their cultural conviction!

I will only cite one personal example since Fr. Juan Carlos Sack, a great friend of ours took up the work of refuting it. He has degrees in Biblical exegesis and is the director of one of the most important Catholic apologetic web pages that I know of. His work dealt with the "black legend" of the *Taxa Camarae*. The *Taxa Camarae* (the full name is *Taxa Camarae seu Cancellariae Apostolicae*) is the Latin name for a supposed pontifical document attributed to Pope Leo X (1513–1521) where he drew up a detailed list of grave sins at the same time stipulating a determined *price* necessary to be able to receive absolution for each one of the sins. This deals with the simple *sale of sacramental absolutions*, that is to say, the sin of simony organized by the pope himself. According to this document, the established price varied according to the sin and should be paid to the Pontifical treasury. The document—made public in our times by the Spanish journalist, Pepe Rodríguez who is known for his constant campaigns against the Church, against the Gospels, and against the Catholic faith in general—contains thirty five items (some three pages). The supposed document has been categorized as the "culminating point of human corruption." And to tell the truth, it would be… *if it were authentic*. In reality, what Mr. Pepe Rodríguez published on his website is nothing more than a pack of absurdities. Many of them have the unmistakable flavor of someone making a great song and dance over proclaiming lies; for example, that the *Taxa Camarae* is secured in a hidden place in the Vatican Secret Archives and guarded by six strict security checkpoints, three of them with Swiss guards armed with tommy guns, which would be why it is inaccessible, etc. Just that suffices for a person with common sense to realize the hoax. Nevertheless, the majority of the people that fall into the trap of this type of web page do not have sufficient common sense to get around Rodríguez's inventions. (In passing, among the documents that Pepe Rodríguez cites in his favor, he speaks of a book on the *Taxa Camarae*, but this book takes its information precisely from the works of Pepe Rodríguez! It is as if he said "this is true not only because I say so, but also other authors say so"; and where did they get it from? "Well, they read it in my books!?") Fr. Sack took up the task of not only asking Mr. Rodríguez to show the documents on which he had based such serious accusations (without any result, as was expected), but also trying to examine the confusion of authors that supported the authenticity of the document. He ended up concluding that "of all the documents we have reviewed, we have not found any of the documentary evidence claimed by Rodríguez."[351] This is how they run these sorts of campaigns. What interests do the people involved in these degenerate campaigns pursue? Are they anticlerical fanatics, responding to a particular or worldly interest? The devil only knows, since only he will benefit. I just want to underline here that we should take care; particularly the student who sees the Internet as a source of documentation. Internet serves for research, but we should see this massive amount of data as a giant library where some things are good and useful, surrounded by many others (outnumbering them and more attractive) that really corrupt not only morals, but also the intelligence (and as a friend of ours says: it is a library with a librarian who *wants* you to see the bad things he offers). I have given only one example because I am familiar with it and I can

---

[351] MANUEL PEREZ, trans., "Taxa Camarae seu Cancellariae Apostolicae: Frequently Asked Questions over the document's authenticity based on the investigations done," *Apologetica.org*, *apologetica.org/site/index.php?option=com_content&task=view&id=487&Itemid=5* (accessed February 22, 2014).

offer true sources of documentation;[352] but the examples could multiply themselves into infinity.

5. OBSERVATIONS

Going back to the distortions of history, Cardinal Giacomo Biffi, when he was still Archbishop of Bologna, wrote the Preface to a very interesting book by Vittorio Messori (*Leyendas Negras de la Iglesia [Black Legends of the Church]*). In which, Biffi, the learned theologian, began by stating a painful truth, "When a boy with a Christian upbringing, educated by his family and parish community, hears the demonstrative assertions of some professor or some text, *he begins to feel ashamed of the history of his Church, and he objectively finds himself in grave danger of losing his faith*. It is a regretful but indisputable observation."[353] He continues by adding some observations of great value. I would like to made good use of a few of them in some final reflections.

First, what is in danger in our time is not only faith, but reason itself. The modern world, with its numerous attacks against vital institutions does not look only to demolish the faith and de-Christianize our society (which they have in part accomplished), but to bring us to the loss of reason and to resign ourselves to the absurd (which they have more thoroughly accomplished). The deception of history is part of this double campaign—not only against the faith (false legends about the Church), but against our bi-millennial culture. That is, against our reason and common sense.

Second, all the legends make an impression upon the mind by reproach or advice, principally upon those who do not have the "eyes of faith" with which to look at the Church. For the one with faith knows, as St. Ambrose said, that the Church is *ex maculatis*

---

[352] The argumentation and documentation can be seen on the website directed by Fr. Juan Carlos Sack: *apologetica.org*.

[353] GIACOMO BIFFI, Preface in VITTORIO MESSORI, *Leyendas Negras de la Iglesia,* 11th ed. (Barcelona: Editorial Planeta, 2004), editorial translation.

immaculata, an intrinsically holy reality, but made up of men who are all sinners in different qualities and measures. We do not need them to present a Church made up wholly of saints for us to believe in her. We know that all are sinners among her children; our hope is that they are repentant sinners. Therefore we are not scandalized when they speak to us about sins committed by men of the past, nor do we need to create golden legends to be able to support our faith. The truth is enough for us. I said already that it does truth little service to oppose a denigrating falsehood with another more idealized falsehood (which may be much closer to the truth, but is still partly false). We read the writings and letters of the first missionaries to America like José de Acosta, Jerónimo Mendieata, Toribio Motolinía, Antonio Ruíz de Montoyo, and we see that it isn't necessary to paint the conquistadors in an idealized manner in order to demonstrate the greatness of this unique and epic era. It was a great era *in spite of the miseries we find*.

The last thing that stands out in Biffi is that in all black legends there is something fundamental that provides us an *indirect service* certainly unforeseen by their authors. (I'm referring to those black legends whose object is making the Church responsible for the crimes of the past.) This indirect service deals with the fact that they are confessing the Church to be the only reality that remains the same over the course of the centuries in speaking of the "historic crimes of the Church." This is the reason it ends up being the only one called upon to answer for everyone's errors. Biffi said: "Did it occur to anyone to ask, for example, in the time of Galileo, what positions the universities and other socially relevant organisms had with respect to the Copernican hypothesis? Who asks today's judges for an account of the seventeenth century judges' common ideas and conduct? Or, to be even more paradoxical, does it occur to anyone to reproach the Milan political authorities (the mayor, the president of the region) for crimes committed by Visconti or Sforzas? It is important to observe that accusing the living Church today of events, decisions, and actions of past epochs is in itself an implicit but evident recognition of the effective stability of the Spouse of Christ in her intangible identity of being *almost-person*, and therefore only the Church is perpetually subject to responsibility and never to be swept away by history—in contrast to all other groups. It is a state of mind that very nearly reveals an *initium fidei* (beginning of faith) in the ecclesial mystery—revealed precisely through vengeful attitudes and the undying rancor against it—which possibly provokes the angels in heaven to laughter."[354]

*   *   *

This chapter, as you can see, has not displayed much order. In these pages I have laid out some disorganized reflections about serious research and the acceptance of what many professors teach us. In spite of their disorder, I believe that they can be very useful to you. I am satisfied if you at least clearly understand that not all that you receive is pure; that you should have an inquisitive and capable mind discerning what is put in front of you; that you should not—as it is often said—swallow whatever is put in front of you; and that you understand that the truth is won at the cost of being well-grounded and strong. Do not be a puppet in the hands of the manipulators of your past who look for nothing else but to seize your present and to use your beautiful future for their own interests.

---

[354] Ibid.

For Further Reading

- Belloc, Hilaire. *Europe and the Faith.* (1st printed in 1920.)
- ————. *How the Reformation Happened.* (1st printed in 1928.)
- ————. *The Crisis of Our Civilization.* (1st printed in 1937.)
- ————. *The Servile State.* (1st printed in 1912.)
- Jedin, Hubert. *Handbook of Church History.* 10 vols. New York: Herder, 1965-1981.

Available in Other Languages

- Bruno, Cayetano. *Historia de la Iglesia en Argentina.* 12 vols. Buenos Aires: Editorial Don Bosco, 1981.
- Calderón Bouchet, Rubén. *Apogeo de la Ciudad Cristiana.* Buenos Aires: Dictio, 1978.
- ————. *Decadencia de la Ciudad Cristiana.* Buenos Aires: Dictio, 1979.
- ————. *Esperanza, Historia y Utopía,* Buenos Aires: Dictio, 1980.
- ————. *Formación de la Ciudad Cristiana.* Buenos Aires: Dictio, 1978.
- ————. *La Ruptura del Sistema Religioso en el Siglo XVI.* Buenos Aires: Dictio, 1980.
- Caturelli, Alberto. *El Nuevo Mundo.* Mexico: Edamax, 1991.
- Llorca, Bernardino, Ricardo Garcia Villoslada, and Juan María Laboa. *Historia de la Iglesia Católica.* 4 vols. Madrid: BAC, 1980.
- Sierra, Vicente. *El Sentido Misional de la Conquista de América.* Buenos Aires: Dictio, 1980.
- Suárez Fernández, Luis, and Luis García Moreno, et al. *Historia Universal.* 13 vols. Pamplona: EUNSA, 1979-1985.

CONCLUSION

The Conjurer

The painting you observe on the previous page is an oil painting on wood found in the Municipal Museum of Saint-Germain-en-Laye. This is a faithful copy of the original (now lost), titled *The Conjurer*, which was painted between 1475 and 1480 by Jeroen van Aken, known as Hieronymus Bosch.

The scene is very suggestive in its simplicity and refers to the "conjurer's trick," a common episode in the author's times (times very similar to ours!). In order for it to serve as the final reflection, permit me to help you observe the scene.

The scene is very sober. In the background there is the ruins of a wall. As evidence of abandonment and desertion, plants and flowers have already grown over top of it, as you can also see in any modern uncultivated wasteland. In the center of the scene, there is a table with some elements used by the *conjurer* for his tricks. On our left, there is a group of ten people: six men, three women, and a child. On the other side of the table, the *conjurer* is represented with some objects proper to his office: there is a ball in his hands that he shows the public in order to get their attention; there is a basket with an owl, which he probably pulled out of it, as magicians do respectively with doves and rabbits; there is a top hat, useful for pulling out all sorts of objects from it, by the art of magic. Finally, note the prominent nose that gives the character the air of being a man in whom we should have little confidence.

The conjurer is doing a trick for an old man; it consists in pulling a frog out of his mouth. The others look on, astonished and entertained. A child comes close to see the "phenomenon," while the majority of the people split their gaze between the conjurer's hand and the old man's face. Only two people escape the general enchantment. One is the conjurer's accomplice, wearing glasses, acting distracted and dumb (the painter portrays him looking up) behind the old man who has lent himself to the trick; he removes the moneybag from the old man's pocket. The other is a youth who attends the spectacle with a young woman, over whose shoulder one of his hands rests. This individual observes the thief's handiwork but limits himself to pointing it out to his friend, whispering in her ear what is happening. This is a close representation of our civilization and what can happen to you in it.

In our scene, the backdrop of a society in ruins, which provides for men's deception, is like the wavering wall in the background (with the ruins of many affairs covered by the roots of the old weeds of sin, errors, and lies). In our times the conjurers (or, those with *quick to the draw*, meaning one who always having a quick response) disguise themselves in many different ways, directing our attention to the accidental realities of life (like the one in the painting who attracts the public's attention with an ordinary ball held in his hand); offering us astonishing feats (that are not much more serious than pulling frogs out of our mouths). While all this is going on, his accomplices steal our treasures. We cannot count on the public that surrounds us. It can be divided between foolish people who, like ourselves, have been dumbfounded by the *conjurer's* ability and those who realize what is happening, like the young man in the picture, but will not move a finger to defend us (especially if defending us requires him to remove his hand from resting delicately on the shoulders of pleasure.)

They sell you, sell us, sophisms instead of science, pulling toads out of our intelligence, robbing us of the common sense and intellectual rigor of which we are capable, and with these they steal our supernatural faith, because grace supposes nature and faith supposes a clear intelligence capable of allowing itself to be transcended by mystery but not degraded by sophisms. If we stop reasoning, we will first come to have *fideism* in place of faith, from which we will move on to *skepticism* and then on to an *intellectual void*.

As we reach the end of these pages that we have traversed together, the only thing left for me is to counsel you to form your conscience, your mind, and your will, in order to truly become a man or woman of knowledge with a full certainty that true knowledge will never obstruct your faith.

GLOSSARY

I have put here just some of the principal words that I used in this book that might be difficult to understand for someone not familiar with philosophical themes.

Agnosticism/Agnostic: (even though the word comes from the Greek "a = to deprive"; "guignósco = to know"; meaning therefore "not to know"; the term was coined in 1869 by Huxley) is the philosophical attitude (or falsely philosophical) that declares that human understanding can't know anything related to the divine or anything that transcends experience.

Allegory: is a fiction by which something represents or means another different thing; also the symbolic representation of abstract ideas by means of figures or groups of these or attributes.

Analogous/Analogy: means something that is in part the same and in part different to another thing, also something that can be said about different things in a true and proper sense but not exactly the same in all cases (i.e. "healthy" is an analogous term since you can apply it to a healthy man-meaning that he has health- a healthy food-meaning that is something not harmful- a healthy medicine- that can bring health back-, etc.)

Animism: is the belief that grants animate life and powers to objects in nature or else belief in the existence of spirits that animate everything.

Anthropology: is the part of philosophy that studies man.

Anthropomorphism: is the way of speaking that attributes to the divinity the figure or qualities of man (*e.g.* when it says in Genesis that God *walked through the garden in the fresh afternoon*, or when it says that God *fashioned Adam with the mud of the dirt*, etc).

Areligious: which should properly be called *irreligious*; means the person, or group or doctrine that does not accept or does not practice religion.

Atheist: is one who denies the existence of God.

Break in continuity: signifies "interruption;" thus "without breaking the continuity" means without interruption or cut.

Cause: is that which is considered the foundation or origin of something. The efficient cause is the first productive principle of the effect, or the one that does something or for whom something is done; the final cause is the purpose of doing something or why something is done; the formal cause is what makes something to be what it is formally.

Cloning: is the act by which a *clone* is produced, that is to say, a being genetically identical or almost identical to that from which it is formed (genetically identical means that it has a practically identical genetic patrimony; however, it has diverse individuality, as can be seen in siblings that are twins from the same zygote).

Consensus: is the agreement produced by the consent among all the members of a group or between various groups .

Cosmogony: signifies "story about the origin of the cosmos."

Cosmology: is the part of philosophy that studies the general laws that rule the physical world.

Determinism / determinist: is the theory that supposes that the evolution of natural phenomena is completely determined by the initial conditions; it is also said about the philosophical system that subordinates the determinations of the human will to the divine will.

Deus ex machina (pronounced: Dé-oos eks máh-key-na): is an expression of Latin antiquity taken from theater; it was a character that represented the divinity who descended to the stage by means of a mechanism and intervened in the plot, resolving very complicated or tragic situations. That is why some people say that they want a solution to fall from above.

Dogma: designates truths of faith. At the beginning the word signified the same as "opinion" (in Greek *doxein*= to think, to give an opinion); the first Fathers of the Church (see below) used it to indicate, rather, a moral principle of doctrine; since the 4th century it started to prevail in the sense of dogma as a truth of faith.

Effect: is that which follows by virtue of a cause.

Epigenesis: is the doctrine according to which the characteristic features of a living being are formed during the development, and are not pre-formed in the fertilized egg.

Epithelium is the animal tissue formed by cells in close contact and covers the surface, cavities and conduit of the organism.

Essence: is that which constitutes the nature of things, what is permanent and invariable in them; also usually used to designate the most important end characteristic of a thing.

Ethnologist/ethnology: ethnology is the science that studies causes, reasons, and origins of customs and traditions of peoples.

Exponential: is said about a growth that increases faster each time.

Father(s) of the Church: are those ecclesiastic authors who, according to the definition of Mabillon, contained four qualities: doctrine, sanctity of life, antiquity, explicit or tacit recognition of the Church. There are some other authors from Christian antiquity that have not been recognized as saints, or else their doctrine has been eminent in some points but not in others; these are designated not as Fathers of the Church but as *ecclesiastic authors*.

Fideism: is the doctrine that accepts everything by faith without rational argumentation, sometimes even explicitly despising reason.

Genome: is the group of all the genes of an individual or of a species, contained in a haploid set of chromosomes.

Hominid: is used, above all in evolutionist theories, to designate the individual pertaining to the order of superior primates; the survivor of this species is the human.

Immanent: etymologically signifies "to remain inside of" (remain in).

Immanentism: designates the philosophical/religious system that in its most rigid form reduces all reality to the subject; source, beginning and end of all its creative activity; also all the doctrines that deny that there is something superior to nature (that is to say something supernatural).

Implantation (signifies "to plant in"): we use it here to designate the act by which the embryo is fixed on the mucus of the mother's womb.

Innate (from the Latin past participle of *innātus, innasci*): signifies connatural and born with the person.

Laxism: is the moral doctrine that accepts every loose law.

Magic: designates the hidden knowledge with which one intends to produce results contrary to natural law, using certain acts or words or with the intervention of imaginary beings.

Magisterium: signifies "teaching" or "act of teaching;" we normally use it to indicate the official and authorized doctrine of the Catholic Church (the doctrine of its Popes and Councils).

Metaphoric/metaphor: the metaphor is the using of words in such a way that translates the straight sense of the voices to a figurative one, in virtue of an unspoken comparison. This is how in the metaphoric sense we speak about the "roaring of the wind," or of the "spring of life."

Monogenism: is a theory according to which all men come from a single human couple (Adam and Eve). It is opposed to polygenism (see definition).

Mystery: from Latin (and also from the Greek *mysterium*); is said about an arcane or recondite thing; it cannot be understood or explained. It is also used to indicate the arcane or secret in any religion. In the Christian religion, it is a thing inaccessible to reason, which should be an object of faith.

Myth: is a wonderful narration, situated outside a historical time and played by a protagonist of divine or heroic character. Frequently, the myth interprets the origin of the world or great events of humanity. It is also said of a fictitious story or literary or artistic character that typifies a human reality with a universal meaning.

Nature: is the essence and characteristic property of each being. The word is also used to refer to the unity, order and disposition of everything that composes the universe (nature). The term is also used in other meanings, such as to refer to the universal principle of all natural operations that are independent from all art or skill; also, the term is used to refer to a virtue, quality or property of things; finally, it refers to the instinct, propensity or inclination of things with which they seek their conservation and growth.

Orthodoxy: means "right doctrine;" it is also used to designate the "orthodox" Church, which is a schismatic Church, that is to say, separated from the Catholic Church; here we use it always in the sense of right doctrine or conformity to the Magisterium of the Catholic Church.

Paleontologist/paleontology: paleontology is the science that deals with extinct organic beings from their fossil remains. *"Paleo"* comes from the Greek and signifies in general 'ancient' or 'primitive.' Frequently refers to geological eras previous to the current. Other words are derived words from this, such as paleochristian (ancient Christianity), paleolithic.

Polygenism: is the theory according to which all current human beings come from several human couples.

Relativism: is the doctrine that there is not a universal truth that everyone can accept as valid, but everyone has his own truth. *Relative* also means that it has a relation to somebody or something.

Rigorism: is the moral doctrine characterized by the excess of severity in law. It is the doctrine opposite to laxism (see above).

Skeptic (the one who professes skepticism): is one who says or appears not to believe, or who affirms that the truth (even truth about God) does not exist, or if it exists, it cannot be known; *atheist* is one who affirms that God does not exist.

Sociology: a science that is part of philosophy and studies society and its behaviors.

Sophism/sophist: sophism can be applied to an apparent argument which wants to defend or persuade what in reality is false.

Subjectivism: it is the doctrine that makes everything depend (judgments, impressions etc.) on the subject (that is to say, each of us); it is in opposition to what is *objective*.

Syngamy: it is the term that designates the union of the two gametes (sperm and ovum).

Totem/totemism: the totem is an object of nature, generally an animal, which in the mythology of some societies is taken as a protective emblem for the tribe or the individual, and sometimes as ancestors or parents. From this the name derives the carved or painted emblem that represents the totem.

Venereal: the term comes from the Latin *venereus* that indicates something related to Venus (goddess of pleasure) and makes reference to sexual pleasure or things related to sex (for example, diseases of "venereal transmission," that is to say, by sexual conduct.